Of Bondage

Of Bondage

Debt, Property, and Personhood in Early Modern England

Amanda Bailey

PENN

UNIVERSITY OF PENNSYLVANIA PRESS

PHILADELPHIA

Published by
University of Pennsylvania Press
Philadelphia, Pennsylvania 19104-4112
www.upenn.edu/pennpress

Printed in the United States of America on acid-free paper
10 9 8 7 6 5 4 3 2 1

Library of Congress Cataloging-in-Publication Data

Bailey, Amanda
Of bondage : debt, property, and personhood in early modern England / Amanda Bailey. — 1st ed.
p. cm.
Includes bibliographical references and index.
ISBN 978-0-8122-4516-5 (hardcover : alk. paper)
1. Debt in literature. 2. Economics and literature—Great Britain—History. 3. Debt—Great Britain—History. 4. Property—Great Britain—History. 5. English drama—Early modern and Elizabethan, 1500–1600—History and criticism. I. Title.
PR3021.B35 2013
820.9'3553—dc23 2012046480

For my family

The debt immense of endless gratitude . . . still paying, still to owe.
Milton, Paradise Lost

Contents

Preface

"Poor Land in Jail as Companies Add Huge Fees for Probation" reads a front-page *New York Times* headline on July 3, 2012. The article tells of the "mushrooming of fines and fees levied by money-starved towns across the country and the for-profit businesses that administer the system," otherwise known as debt collectors. The result is that increasing numbers of "poor people . . . are ending up jailed and in debt for minor infractions." For instance, the unemployed Gina Ray, after receiving a $179 speeding fine, was imprisoned for defaulting on $1,500 in fees and interest from the original fine. On top of that, she was charged an additional amount for each day she spent incarcerated (forty in total). "More than a third of U.S. states allow the police to haul people in who don't pay all manner of debts, from bills for health care services to credit card and auto loans," writes Alain Sherter of *CBS Moneywatch*.[1] Medical debt put breast cancer survivor Lisa Lindsay behind bars when this Illinois teaching assistant received a $280 bill, which, according to the Associated Press, was turned over to a collection agency. Eventually, "state troopers showed up at her home and took her to jail in handcuffs."[2]

The amount of the debt is hardly the issue. A 2010 report by the American Civil Liberties Union focusing on Georgia, Louisiana, Michigan, Ohio, and Washington found that people were being jailed at "increasingly alarming rates" over what started out as a minor fee. According to the ACLU, "the sad truth is that debtors' prisons are flourishing today, more than two decades after the Supreme Court prohibited imprisoning those who are too poor to pay their legal debts. In this era of shrinking budgets, state and local governments have turned aggressively to using the threat and reality of imprisonment to squeeze revenue out of the poorest defendants who appear in their courts."[3]

This book comes out at a moment that may—or may not—mark the end of the most dramatic economic recession in the United States since the 1930s, matched by a catastrophic insolvency for several major European nations. In the fall of 2008 we witnessed a financial crisis that brought the world to a halt. After having been led to believe that oversight of markets had been rendered impossible by high-tech securitizations and sophisticated fiscal innovations, it turned out that the events leading up to this meltdown in the United States were fairly straightforward and entirely avoidable: families had been sold mortgages on which they would inevitably default, which in turn resulted in the failing of major lenders like Lehman Brothers, and huge losses by Goldman Sachs and Citibank. Even as phrases such as "commodity derivatives," "collateralized mortgages," and "hybrid securities" dominated the national conversation, some attempted to reorient the public discourse and initiate a meaningful conversation about debt in the United States and the role of federal and state governments in determining the fate of the individual defaulter. The solution to this crisis, it turned out, was that the same government that bailed out financial institutions put the full force of law behind prosecuting insufficient citizens. To many, this turn of events seemed both shocking (it was) and unprecedented (perhaps not).

What endures across time and space is the flexibility of debt as a concept that underwrites morally murky ideologies and ethically ambiguous practices. David Graeber in *Debt: The First 5,000 Years* has provocatively suggested that "the real origins of money are to be found in crime and recompense, war and slavery, honor, debt, and redemption."[4] Graeber is my interlocutor throughout this book, as I seek to set his bold claims in historical context and test their validity in light of the ways that early moderns understood debt bondage, ways that fashioned the framework for thinking about forfeiture for the next four hundred years. The question that drives me is: What can the historical imagination of debt tell us about our present imaginary? My innovation, however, is to begin not with this question but rather with what I understand to be the answer: Institutions are able to protect creditors because the state assists them in penalizing debtors. Who could have ever imagined such a phenomenon?

Introduction: Bound Bodies and the Theater of Debt

> Perhaps debt exists because we imagine it. It is the forms this imagining has taken—and their impact on lived reality—that I would like to explore.
>
> —Margaret Atwood, *Payback* (2008)

The 1998 film *Shakespeare in Love* begins with the debtor in duress. Philip Henslowe, "a businessman with a cash flow problem," is tied to a chair, while his creditors dangle his feet over burning coals. Unable to furnish the "twelve pounds, one shilling, and four pence" he borrowed, Henslowe obtains temporary release so that he may run to the garrett of Will Shakespeare. There, Henslowe begs Shakespeare for the long overdue playscript for which he provided him an advance. The profit the script will generate is Henslowe's only hope of repaying his creditors and avoiding prison.[1] On first blush this is a broad sketch of a theatrical enterprise, not unlike present-day Hollywood, shaped by the vicissitudes of a credit economy. Upon closer inspection, however, this scene has much to tell us about the ways a particular monetary instrument, the early modern debt bond, realized the domain of money as a regime of power. Unable to collect their coins, Henslowe's creditors claim his body. While Henslowe, himself a creditor, relies on bonds to connect to wider commercial and social networks, his failure to honor his own will result in the breaking of all ties. A future of freedom or fetters hangs in the balance.

For twenty-first-century viewers, the slide from remuneration to retribution renders the inviolability of the person a tenuous prospect. How, though, would Henslowe's contemporaries have made sense of the debt bond's inexorable provision for payback? A borrower who made use of a sealed bond gave his creditor a formidable collection mechanism. If the obligation was not paid, the unsatisfied creditor could, without filing suit, proceed directly to execution of its terms, seizing his debtor's goods or lands, and in the case of insufficiency, his person. In early modern England, money was considered a form of property, which entailed tangible matter (*res*) and the intangible rights one had in respect to *res*. This meant that the exigencies of the bond inaugurated a legal relation—not only between creditor and debtor but also between the body of the debtor and the coins he borrowed—that at once confirmed and vitiated the Lockean assertion that "Every man has a *property* in his own *person*."[2] This proposition may seem anachronistic when applied to a period in which bodies were seen as porous entities with permeable physiological and psychological boundaries. Yet at a historical moment at which debt litigation was not merely an aspect of society but "engulfed it completely," borrowers' strenuous objections to the bond's proprietary logic suggest an alternative notion of the body as proper to oneself. Because both money and bodies were conceived of as kinds of property, they impinged upon one another at the moment of default.[3]

Studies illuminating the social life of money have emphasized that lending and borrowing consolidated the link between persons and property through networks of trust that sustained mutual obligations. However, the formal debt bond produced a very different "culture of credit" than the neighborly networks traced by Craig Muldrew.[4] When we turn our attention to the popularity of written bonds and the staggering rise in debt suits, we are confronted with a more complex set of issues involving the quality of these obligations, as well as questions of what they consisted and how they affected people. A debt bond was a promise that could be quantified and enforced. More particularly, its terms instantiated an "econometric logic of justice," whereby restitution relied on the state's ability to convert the debtor's body from a form of collateral, a surety, into a forfeit, the equivalent of the unpaid loan.[5] Thus a study of debt bondage moves us beyond the arena of trust and places us in the realm of equity, introducing us to the political life of money.

Entailing more than the fiduciary functions of nations, the political life of money encompasses the contractual nature of civil obligation, the shifting terms of collective identification, and contested definitions of human rights. These were *political* concerns insofar as the state attempted to mediate them through the adjudication of forfeiture. Thus the central claim of this book is that in a period marked by a "massive increase" in debt litigation, lenders and borrowers who used bonds became embroiled in a series of ethical conundrums about owing and owning, conundrums more likely to engage political philosophers and legal theorists than merchants and economic writers.[6] Insofar as freedom granted one the privilege of owing others, through the right to make commitments with one's equals (the English word "free" is derived from the German root of the word "friend"), freedom was distinct from liberty, the privilege to own oneself, through the assertion of absolute control over one's person.[7] Debt bondage animated the inherent tension of property as a means of belonging and the foundation of autonomy, raising a host of practical questions about the extent to which a creditor had rights in the money he lent, whether a borrower could possess his loan through use, and, most importantly, what it meant that the body of the debtor could stand in for the original loan. An examination of the provisional responses to these questions suggests that self-possession was a highly valued but precarious entitlement dependent upon the goodwill of others.

While the claim that every man has property in his own person proved central to C. B. Macpherson's investigation of "the nature of ownership" as intrinsic to the "nature of the individual," the quotidian existence of the late sixteenth-century debtor remains underexamined in the historiography of English liberalism.[8] This is surprising since Locke's theories of political autonomy developed directly out of his explorations of property law and monetary exchange.[9] The practices of acquisition shaped early Enlightenment ideas about civil status, but the circumstances of dispossession elucidate earlier debates about what counted as property and who counted as a person. As one historian reminds us, from the late fourteenth century onward, "at least as many Londoners were locked up for debt as for crime" and these debtors "spent longer behind bars than the most serious offenders."[10] *Of Bondage* is then a book about the early modern theater, which because of its own embeddedness within a credit economy was preoccupied with debt bondage. This study shows that because debt was a bodily event at the center of complex political and philosophical issues raised by contract law, the theater was uniquely positioned to stage the emerging story of the possessive individual. This is also, though, a book about dramatic literature's heretofore unacknowledged contribution to another developing narrative, that of the possessed person.

The Shadow Side of Credit

How early modern men and women understood and used money was determined by complex webs of meaning. Given the incomplete development of late sixteenth-century markets, which were hindered by unstable currency, commercial activity depended upon an economy of trust. Credit, as Craig Muldrew explains, was "a public means of social communication"; friends and neighbors extended loans to those they believed would honor their obligations.[11] Yet, in this period, London's central courts witnessed an unprecedented rise in the number of debt cases, indicating that credit relations were as likely to sever as to solidify communal ties.[12] The anonymous author of a 1647 petition to Parliament advocates for the 10,000 Englishmen and women languishing in prison for debt, while another pamphlet laments the "millions of men and women in this Land [that] are oppressed, inslaved, ruined, yea destroyed in their Estates, Rights, Liberties, and Lives."[13] The steep increase from the end of the sixteenth to the mid-seventeenth century in incarceration for debt inspired an outpouring of literary, social, and political writings decrying a legal process that recognized the borrower's body as collateral. This book explores the early modern imagination of forfeiture in light of a commercial theater deeply invested in debt bonds on both artistic and fiscal levels. Through its preoccupation with what it meant to be economically, socially, and emotionally bound, the drama of Shakespeare, Middleton, and Massinger invigorates and interrogates developing concepts of ownership and self-ownership fundamental to an evolving English ideal of civic personhood.

The provisions of early modern debt law, records of playhouse practices, and stage plays are not typically seen as relevant to the history of the autonomous subject. But, as *Of Bondage* demonstrates, early modern writers and players had exceptional insight into money as an equivocal instrument of justice. The theater was an enterprise shaped by the exigencies of credit, but, more particularly, the business of playing revolved around managers' and players' reliance on the penal debt bond.[14] Bonds enabled the building and leasing of playhouses. Playscripts, costumes, and properties were obtained on bonds. And it was through the Articles of Agreement, known as the player's bond, that theatrical managers secured their labor. Moreover, players such as Nathan Field, Henry Chettle, Robert Daborne, John Duke, and William Haughton, as well as writers such as Ben Jonson, George Chapman, John Marston, John Lyly, Cyril Tourneur, Thomas Middleton, Thomas Dekker, and Philip Massinger, rotated in and out of debtor's prison.[15] The impressive number of personal loans issued to players by company heads, the exorbitant bonds that held players to their contracts, and the 1615 Articles of Oppression charging Philip Henslowe with, among other things, controlling his players by keeping them perpetually in debt, only gestures at the extent to which the fates of those whose livelihoods depended on the theater were shaped by the jagged course of chronic indebtedness.

Late sixteenth- and early seventeenth-century legal manuals, debt manumission petitions, and political tracts, as well as canonical and lesser-known dramatic texts, reveal widespread concern about the authority and scope of the penal debt bond even among those who did not work in the theater. By the late sixteenth century, the bond had become the standard form for contractual agreements in England and throughout Europe. Englishmen and women of all classes and occupations utilized bonds to ensure the performance of various actions, but they were most commonly used for monetary loans. The sealed debt bond, also referred to as a "recognizance," an "obligation" or "written obligatory," a "promissory note," a "deed," or a "bill," was composed on parchment in either Latin or English and was often, but not always, drawn up by a scrivener. While the bond was a formal document, its language was formulaic only insofar as it expressly bound the debtor to his creditor by identifying him as *se teneri*, or bound under seal. The early sixteenth-century debt bond devised between J.N. and R.B. is typical in its brevity and use of the phrase "*teneri et firmiter obligari*":

> Noverint universi per praesentes me R.B. teneri et firmiter obligari J.N. in centum libros sterlingorum solvenda eidem J.N. aut suo certo attornato seu executoris suis in festo nativitatis sancti Johannis Baptisti proximo futuro post datum presentium ad quam quidem solutionem bene et fideliter faciendam obligo me heredes exceutores meas et omnia bona mea per praesentes sigillo meo signatas datas anno regni . . .
>
> Let all know by these present that J.N. is bound and firmly bound to me, R.B., for 100 pounds sterling, to be released by the same J.N. or his authorized attorney or that of his executor on the feast of the birth of the holy John the Baptist the next one after this present date, on which a certain payment is to be made well and faithfully. I bind my hereditary executors and my present goods with my seal on these assigned dates in the year of the king . . .[16]

In legal terms, the bond was both evidentiary and dispositive; it simultaneously functioned as proof that the debtor was bound and served as the instrument of that binding. This meant that the binding of the debtor to his creditor was never simply figurative. The very language of the bond invoked the physical act of bondage. *Teneri*, the passive infinitive of *teneo*, meant to hold onto or to grasp something in one's hand and was the word used in documents that effected the binding of one party to another. The literal meaning of *obligari*, the passive infinitive of *obligo*, was to tie up or bind a person, as the word "obligation" stemmed from the Latin *ligare*, to bind or tie. The etymology of these words was amplified by popular understandings of what it meant to become bound.

In the early modern period, the English word "bond" referred to a specific monetary instrument, the debt bond, yet it more generally connoted any duty predicated on the negligible boundary between obligation and coercion.[17] "To be bound" implied that one had been put in bonds. "Bond" was also the word for the shackle, chain, or fetter used to physically restrain the body and, for this reason, a slave was called a "bondsman" (*OED*). The valence of the word "bond" hints at the historical relationship between the legal remedy for forfeiture and captivity. As legal scholar Allan Farnsworth reminds us, the ancient instance of credit arose out of blood feud. In Anglo-Saxon culture, a murderer could buy off the vengeance of his victim's kinsmen by a paying a larger "wergild" than he could afford. If he provided security, he could pay in installments. In most cases the security took the form of another person, a hostage who was held by the victim's family until the debt was settled. Over time, the debtor was allowed to serve as his own surety.[18] In late sixteenth-century England, when a borrower had no other asset at his disposal, he became a pledge or "an animated gage."[19]

The increased use of conditional bonds in the last decade of the sixteenth century suggests that creditors turned to this form of lending to accommodate, and arguably even capitalize on, an epidemic of default, since lenders stood to profit only when their borrowers were unable to repay their loans. Loans on sealed bonds were devised for fictitious sums that included both principal and an additional sum called the penal sum, which, significantly, was not construed as interest.[20] The penal sum, usually twice the amount of the loan, was "defeasible," meaning if the debt was paid by the agreed-upon date, then the borrower owed only the principal. Rather than illegitimately charging for the *use* of his money, as did the usurer, the creditor who loaned on bond legitimately built into the contract compensation for the loss he stood to suffer by the debtor's failure to repay on time.[21] However, if the condition of the bond was not met and the debtor was insolvent, then the creditor, unable to collect either the penal sum or principal, could lay claim to his debtor's person.

The bond was a new species of money whose conditional structure anticipated the speculative logic of the insurance claim, as well as other monetary arrangements that based their worth on projected value. The debtor's body initially served as a surety against future loss. At the moment of forfeiture, however, what was once a deposit became an investment, a transferrable form of property that could be held in reserve indefinitely. The bond's innovation lay in its ability to construe human flesh not as something to be used or exchanged but as a vehicle of promise. Thus even as the bond's penalty initiated the attachment of the debtor's physical person, in doing so, it rendered the body an abstraction. It became a redeemable form of property, the worth of which was determined by the creditor's interest and affirmed by the law's mandates.

As with any deed that included a penal clause, the bond's efficacy rested on the threat of physical harm. Because the bond allowed the creditor to possess his debtor's person, it was considered a contract that operated, in the words of Lord Dunedin, "*in terrorem* of the offending party."[22] Usually the prospect of indefinite incarceration was enough to convince the fraudulent debtor to reveal any hidden assets or pressure friends, family, neighbors, and employers to come forward. If the insolvent languished in prison over time, where he like all other prisoners paid for his room and board, a creditor could always hope that the escalating miseries of prison would break those who withheld funds, or that a chartable entity or eventual inheritance would satisfy the outstanding debt. In the meantime, the incarcerated debtor proved profitable to various prison administrators that depended on a steady influx of fees and bribes. Even in the absence of monetary repayment, the bond, unlike the usurious agreement, ensured the lender at the very least the satisfaction of justice served. Most significantly, the bond's penal condition buttressed the credit economy by ensuring that the insolvent would be penalized.

If the advent of the written bond ushered in the age of equitable contract for lenders, it also signaled an era of dispossession for borrowers, as explained by one early seventeenth-century commentator who notes that creditors have shown that "*bona corporis* are better than *bona fortuna*, a man's body is of more value than his estate."[23] As Muldrew stresses, by the beginning of the seventeenth century, most actions were taken against the debtor's person.[24] While this was partially because the feudal principles of land tenure did not permit estates to be regarded as assets for debt, the rise in imprisonment for debt speaks to the state's increasing interest in safeguarding local credit arrangements. Bonds were judicially processed with minimal jury involvement allowing the common law courts to quickly process an impressive number of debt cases, and through enactment of a series of fifteenth-century statutes, the purview for recoverable action had been expanded from king to manor lord to merchant. By the middle of the sixteenth century, any creditor could initiate the apprehension of his debtor without having first obtained judgment against him.[25] The writ of *capias ad satisfaciendum*, which was established within the reign of Henry III, allowed the sheriff to seize a debtor on the charge of breaching of the king's peace, otherwise known as *contra pacem* and *vi et armis*, casting default in the ambit of criminal offense. However, unlike the criminal, the debtor would not suffer loss of life and limb. Even though the judiciary rationalized that detaining the debtor prevented him from seeking sanctuary within the liberties of the city or in his own home, lawyers, such as Bacon and Coke, pointed out that *capias* in the case of default strained the bounds of law. If the logic of this procedure was difficult to justify on legal grounds, contemporary legal scholars have shown that the interpretation of forfeiture as trespass signaled a movement away from covenant, or breach of contract, toward what we would come to call tort or a wrongdoing for which an action for damages may be brought.[26] *Vi et armis* thus presumed that in failing to perform his bond, the debtor caused injury not merely to his creditor but to the Crown. This phrase legitimated the state's prerogative to exercise its authority in the adjudication of monetary agreements between private parties. Here late sixteenth-century common law parted ways with its medieval precedents, since up until the late fourteenth century, the law favored the borrower over the lender. As Richard Bowers explains, in the medieval period, "not only had debts been easily repudiated, but there had also been no satisfactory legal remedy by which a creditor could compel a debtor to pay a delinquent obligation."[27]

By the end of the sixteenth century, the law put teeth into the recovery of debt. Yet, despite insurmountable evidence that the legal remedy for forfeiture did not in any way relieve the creditor of an intolerable situation and caused the debtor to suffer, revisionists paint a rosy portrait of early modern credit relations. Richard Grassby, for instance, argues that indebtedness "far from creating a subordinate relationship reinforced connections and confidence," and Margaret Hunt understands economic obligation in the period as grounded in a moral economy.[28] There is much merit to historical work that has overturned the standard narrative that the rise of capitalism, exemplified by the vague, impersonal entity of "the market," resulted in the traditional networks of mutual aid becoming replaced by a social world marked by cold calculation. Yet despite their merits, these studies presume that people were for the most part willing and able to repay their loans. As such, they lose sight of the ways that an economy built on trust relied on external mechanisms to safeguard that trust. As David Graeber emphasizes: "The story of the origins of capitalism, then, is not the story of the gradual destruction of traditional communities by the impersonal power of the market. It is, rather, the story of how an economy of credit was converted into an economy of interest; of the gradual transformation of moral networks by the intrusion of the impersonal—and often vindictive—power of the state."[29] In lieu of institutional resources like banks, people could avail themselves of a range of credit options, most of which were small in scale and local, and thus, subject to personal vagaries. In this context, a culture of credit required not only trusting other people but also the bond's ability to serve as a secure instrument. Historical accounts that emphasize the importance of maintaining amicable relations among exchange agents have ignored the role of the state, which mobilized its right to punish as means of fortifying people's faith in the system itself. While it seems obvious that a creditor could not resolve his financial predicament by imprisoning an insolvent debtor, overlaying this particular strand was a web of various factions and interests that understood debtor relief as compromising the ability of property to function as a prerequisite of civil enfranchisement.

Off the stage, the imprisoned debtor was alive in body but dead in law. By losing his proprietary rights, he was subject to civil death, a "change of state of person which is considered in the law as equivalent to death."[30] In such instances, the debtor endures a loss of status so extreme that he is unable to exercise the rights normally attributed to members of society. Like one who has become excommunicated, the incarcerated debtor was wrenched from familial, social, and economic affiliations, and in this respect assumed the denigrated status of the slave.[31] On the stage, owing someone money could lead to the reinforcement of social inequity, the justification of physical abuse, and the subordination of one person to another. Dramatists depicted the portent of civil death, a fate suffered by legal persons, as the threat of actual death leveraged at human bodies. For instance, the insolvent Timon in *Timon of Athens* experiences his "broken bonds" as weapons that will "cleave [him] to the girdle" and "cut his heart in sums."[32] *Michaelmas Term*'s Easy is observed signing onto a series of bonds for an irredeemable amount of money and likened to a condemned man enslaving himself to his executioner.[33] Perhaps no other play than *The Merchant of Venice*, in which the state unequivocally validates Shylock's claim to "the pound of flesh" that he has "dearly bought," showcases the bond's power to make and unmake persons.[34] These plays' depictions of debt bondage as a corporal event need not, however, be read only as a reminder of the primitive blood fee subtending civilized debt law. Such representations also gesture toward the ways forfeiture inaugurated a decorporalizing logic of equivalence. By acknowledging Shylock's bond as well within his legal right, for instance, Shakespeare suggests that Antonio's person offers an imagined compensation that potentially exceeds any tangible, immediate monetary payment. As *The Merchant of Venice* reveals, those who lent on bond had property in their borrower, which in this play is made demonstrable by the creditor's contractual investment in his debtor.

By examining drama's awareness of the complex social, political, and philosophical underpinnings of debt bondage, what fades from view is a theater invested in representing the vengeful usurer. What comes into sharp focus, instead, is an artistic medium that posits the play as an active response to the idea of money as an instrument of freedom. The staying power of usury has prevented us from fully exploring literary insights into this form of money; it has also narrowed the broader historical implications of debt bondage. The general problem of usury was certainly a major concern of sixteenth-century moral debates, as demonstrated by the numerous treatises and sermons published on the topic. English legal literature, however, seems to be less influenced by debates over the prohibition of usury. Rather, the dubious ethics of debt bondage appear as a consistent preoccupation of lawyers writing about equity in exchange and the various procedures for the possession of property. Unlike the usurious transaction, the bond could instigate various conditions of usage, ranging from *usus*, the use of the thing, to *usufructus*, the collective enjoyment of the thing, to *abusus*, the proprietary privilege to destroy or waste the thing, also known as *jus abutendi*.

Fast becoming "by far the most important form of indebtedness after sales and service credit,—certainly much more important than moneylending," the bond was increasingly popular because it offered an alternative to usury.[35] If it provided borrowers with no ready-cash access to an interest-free loan, it allowed creditors to lend without the taint of usury and to avail themselves of secure agreements. The 1545 Act Against Usury, for instance, singles out the bond as a lawful obligation: "This Acte nor any thinge therein conteyned shall not in any wise extend to any laufull obligacion endorsed with a condicion, . . . so that the said obligacion, statute or recognizaunce be made for a true just and perfytt debte."[36] The author of the household manual *A Godlie Treatice Concerning the Lawfull use of Ritches* (1578) also underscores the legitimacy of the debt bond, and he emphasizes its efficacy. He explains "lendying

[on] contracte" enables "one manne [to] giveth his right of a *thyng* to another, without any price at all, but uppon condition that the same *thyng* in kinde be repaid."[37] Bonds were equitable instruments because the same rules of contract applied to the exchange of coins as to land, goods, and animals (among which common law made no distinction). The presumption of usury as the paramount form of moneylending in the period has effaced the historical primacy of debt bondage and muted crucial conversations traversing economic, philosophical, and theological arenas, conversations that persisted even as legal discourse asserted itself as the primary authority on credit relations.[38]

The conflation of debt and usurious transactions has also masked how chronic insolvency was in the period. Forfeiting on one's bonds was an all too common problem exacerbated by population growth, demand-driven inflation, and a social climate that encouraged lavish levels of consumption. At the end of the sixteenth century, the predicament of the borrower was, arguably, more dire than ever as the supply of coins could not keep up with the demand for cash. Bonds stood to play a central role in early modern payment systems as long as they were perceived as established payment media. Historians have estimated that during the second half of the sixteenth century the demand for coins grew by approximately 500 percent while the supply expanded only by 63 percent. Further contributing to the problem was the poor quality of coins. Unsophisticated minting techniques, as well as practices such as clipping and hammering, led to circumstances in which "high quality coins were often taken out of circulation to be kept as store of value to be used in international exchange."[39] In situations where people did not have anything to use as payment, they did not manage exchange through barter but rather relied on credit. Even as precious metals came to be established as the recognized tokens of value, bonds persisted as negotiable instruments. The lack of adequate coinage at the end of the sixteenth century limited the number of reckonings, and the increasing number of unpaid debts had a domino effect, negatively impacting more and more households. The number of debt cases that moved into advanced litigation in the common law Courts of Queen's Bench and Common Pleas escalated from 5,000 a year in 1560 to over 20,000 cases annually by 1606.[40]

When we abandon our preoccupation with usury, what comes into view is the impressive amount of energy commentators in the period devoted to exploring the ethical implications of defaulting on a bond rather than the moral failings of lenders and borrowers. The seventeenth-century engraving, "A Debtor Thumscru'd and Iron Pothooks about his neck," depicts a debtor bound to a fireplace by pot-hooks used as neck-irons. His body hangs in suspension, with his back to a roaring fire, while each of his thumbs is gripped in the vice of a thumbscrew. Off to the side, two men nonchalantly look on. The focus of this engraving is neither the rapacious usurer nor the victimized debtor. Rather the debtor is stoic: his pained upward gaze is juxtaposed with that of his creditors who politely avoid his glance. His creditors are well-dressed gentlemen, who are depicted as respectable and even vaguely sympathetic figures. They register neither menace nor alarm. One, with his arm slightly raised, communicates the futility of the situation and quiet dismay at the unfortunate outcome of forfeiture.

An attitude of vague sympathy colored by shadings of futility is echoed within the period's seriocomic prose pamphlets, broadsides, sermons, and household manuals. This attitude, however, coexisted alongside of passionate attempts by politicians and lawyers to reform England's method of legislating forfeiture. Debt manumission petitions, popular tracts, and legal manuals agitate against what they regard as a society overtaken by the expediencies of an expanding credit economy. In 1622 a group of King's Bench prisoners, for instance, petitioned James I and Parliament to curtail the growing popularity of "Contracts and Bonds," which they understood as producing a generation of creditors encouraged to bring their penalties to a new "high degree."[41] The petition castigates the state for summarily awarding "every Creditor his full damage" in the case of default, which, the authors argue, leads only to "the losse of [the debtor's] estate, credit, liberty, and many times of [his] life too" (C4r). The main objections to bonds expressed in this document are rehearsed within a host of contemporaneous materials aiming to show that despite the mandates of the common law, the creditor's authority is constrained by the terms of a more ancient contract, the Magna Carta. Section 29 establishes that "no man, on whatsoever account, can be arrested or imprisoned and deprived of his free-tenement, his liberties, or his free-customs . . . unless by the legal judgment of his peers or by the law of the land."[42]

By situating debt bondage in the broader context of evolving common law theories of contract, *Of Bondage* expands the parameters of the "new economic criticism." In the following chapters, I work with late sixteenth- and early seventeenth-century lawyers' manuals, debt manumission petitions, and case briefs, as well as canonical and lesser-known dramatic texts, to show how legal and aesthetic representations of debt anticipated Enlightenment ideas about the fundamental role of bonds—affective, social, economic, and legal—in social and political obligation at home and abroad. While civil law debates about

"A Debtor Thumscru'd and Iron Pothooks about his neck,"
c. 1660–1730. Engraving. © The Trustees of the British Museum.

intention and canon law considerations of consent factor into my discussion, my focus remains on the common law and how its practitioners grappled with a monetary form that was itself the product of a historical crisis around the shifting meaning of property as a form of value. The bond did not provide a blueprint for subsequent property relations but rather served as the terrain on which such relations were forged. Traces of this struggle may be excavated in dramatic depictions of debt bondage that exploit the conceptual imbroglio around the place of the body in the lending and borrowing of money, a problem that was more than an abstraction for those who wrote and performed these plays. Through its exhibition of persons whose own property status was obscured by their indebtedness to managers who financed them, writers who scripted their roles, and audiences that withheld or granted them creditability, drama proved itself to be an art defined by the body's ability to dispossess itself and even function as yet another stage prop. The very word "perform" bears the historical weight of both the institution of the law and dramatic practice, as in a court of law the performance of an economic contract referred to the fulfillment of its terms and on the stage performance held out the promise that a player would satisfy his audience. Players, however, did not always please insofar as plays about debt were marked, or as some have argued marred, by formal rupture. Writers of the period understood literary genre as a kind of contract, a set of shared assumptions between playwright and audience, and in upsetting viewers' expectations, debt plays repeatedly violated their bond, enacting the very problem they thematized.

Debt and Dramatic Form

Recent studies of the ways changing economic attitudes and practices have influenced dramatic literature have reinvigorated the claim advanced thirty years ago by Jean-Christophe Agnew: "The English stage developed formal, narrative, and thematic conventions that effectively reproduced the representational strategies and difficulties of the marketplace [and] the stage then furnished its urban audience with a laboratory and an idiom within which these difficulties and contradictions could be acted out."[43] Agnew's successors have gone on to productively explore the ways that financial and imaginative writing share, historically and theoretically, an engagement with the problem of representation.[44] More particularly, by attending to the intersection of political ideology, capital logic, and aesthetic form, scholars have investigated the influence of particular modes of exchange on specific dramatic genres.[45] I, too, am interested in how the tropic economy of particular plays is shaped by the logic of debt, but my primary objective is to investigate what *use* drama of the early modern period made of the bond. If theatrical representations of the bond exploited the contingencies of legal theory and practices around forfeiture for dramatic effect, they also opened up a space of intensified literariness. Just as the affective trajectory of debt required new kinds of narrative techniques, stagings of the ambivalent ethics of forfeiture created new conceptual conditions for what could be imagined as an economic problem. The dialogic relationship between bonds and playscripts comes to light, I argue, only after we distinguish between writings *about* money and writings that functioned *as* money.

The invisibility of money as a form of writing and the enfolding of monetary forms of writing into writings about money is all but axiomatic. So long as we turn to the economic tract as the authority on materials such as goldsmiths' receipts, bills of exchange, and debt bonds, we will continue to view such artifacts as epiphenomenal rather than dynamic entities. To ameliorate this tendency, I illuminate the bond as an instrument that called on the conventions of various genres of writings to advance its notion of value at a moment at which several kinds of monies competed with and contradicted one another. As Mary Poovey argues, "The very fact that we no longer notice that money consists of various kinds or that its function depends on writing means that money has been *naturalized* . . . money has become so familiar that its writing has seemed to disappear and it has seemed to lose its history as (various forms of) writing."[46] In the interest of plotting the bond as a form of writing on a continuum with other sorts of writing, which in turn mediated various kinds of value (moral and aesthetic), I have not privileged mercantile writing, early economic manuals, and other primary sources familiar to scholars working the this area.[47] The exclusion of economic writings may strike some as surprising, perhaps remiss, but reliance on such a narrow range of sources has stymied the compositional complexity of the bond.

On the most obvious level, a history of debt is a history of money. What unfolds in these pages, however, is an untold strand of an uneven and complex history. In general terms, my unorthodox approach orients me toward new sources and paradigms for thinking through what came to constitute the "economic" in early seventeenth-century England, and in this respect, I aim to further the findings of those seeking to understand what money was—or could be—before the epistemological break that defined it as an autonomous object of an autonomous discipline.[48] The analyses that follow shift the focus away from coinage, inflation, bullion, and trade, topics that are typically the purview of economically inflected studies. Instead, I stress that in this period, the relation between what counted as money and the legal apparatus that legitimated monetary instruments was contoured by an intellectual contest between the law and other kinds of discourses. For this reason, I am less interested in reading debt bonds at face value as I am in exploring how extralegal and extra-economic discourses contributed to creating the impression that bonds could—and should—serve as transparent tokens of exchange and accountability. The nature of my concerns has thus encouraged a critical practice guided by the tenets of historical formalism and energized by a deconstructive impulse.[49] More particularly, I begin with the scripted features of the bond, which reveal that the diverse conventions the bond mobilized in order to appear natural always threatened to denaturalize it.

As a study of the early modern political imaginary of credit, I emphasize throughout the instability of money, by which I mean not only fluctuations in value but also the uncertainty of money as object of ideology, or what we have come to call political economy. The bond was first and foremost an imperfect formal response to money's divided function between a medium of exchange and a measure of value. An understanding of this dual function and the confusion it wrought leads us to wonder, in a functionally unstable economy in which money was what money could do, what did bonds *do* in early modern English culture? This question enables me to think about this form of monetary writing as a kind of practice through which it, like any given text, establishes its utility via its relation to other forms (textual and social). Thus I aim to elucidate throughout this book how the bond functions as both the enabling condition and the product of its interpretative communities.[50]

This question of the bond's use brings us to the crux of substance and inscription within the monetary sphere. Face value and substantial value had long been at odds since the worth of coins was consistently compromised by discrepancies in their metallic purity and weight. Coins, in this period, were things that launched and ended relationships between exchange agents, and as such could function as commodities, as well as implied IOUs.[51] The bond, however, appeared to offer a viable solution to the potential crisis in monetary value that coins instigated. It was a handwritten document that evoked a particularly efficacious promise, not only in terms of its formal nature but also in regard to the intellectual tradition of the common law. Borrowers invested in the power of bonds to conjure something out of nothing; indeed at the signing of a bond, capital magically materialized. While metal coins attempted to represent value, the primary function of the bond was to incarnate it. Nevertheless, despite a grounding in the written culture of the law, the bond maintained an uncertain relationship to the value it embodied.

In the event of forfeiture, the body of the debtor stepped in to satisfy the unpaid creditor, begging the question of what value is the body of the debtor to his creditor? Here I defer to Shylock, who in refusing to explain why he would rather "have a weight of carrion flesh than [ ] receive three thousand ducats" (4.1.41), demurs to the juridical encoding of value by which the state presumptively yokes the seemingly separate spheres of commerce and finance and human traffic and the death penalty. Indeed, Shylock is alone in his recognition that the stakes of the trial transcend his personal relationship with Antonio. The logic subtending Shylock's elliptical reply remains submerged until we have a clear sense of the bond as a particular historical form of an ongoing crisis around owing and ownership that determined the influence of emerging market economies on the discourse of human rights. The bond as a genre of credit, in the sense that Poovey suggests, had agency insofar as it produced a new relation between money and the law.[52] It realized money as a medium of justice, which through the extraction of penalties and the granting of compensation enabled the "monetarizing anatomization of the body."[53]

What this pivotal scene in *The Merchant of Venice* demonstrates is not that the amassment of money leads to the accumulation of wealth but, rather, that money in the form of the bond has the power to create, destroy, and rearrange human beings. The task at hand is managing the tension between that which is regarded as alienable (property) and that which is regarded as inalienable (life). The bond allows a moral dilemma to be interpreted as a legal problem: the trial's resolution does not call for the murder or banishment of the debtor, or even for making him a slave, but transforms his body into a forfeit that is the product of a shared imaginary produced by the terms of contract. This juridical alchemy substitutes abstraction for violence, and in doing so, spares the debtor ritual sacrifice and acknowledges the creditor's right to his debtor as a form of property. At the same time, this solution affirms that the presumed liberty of all English bodies remains conditional on one's ability to meet one's obligations. Most important, the trial signals the triumphant extension of finance capital into the domain of the human by treating the debtor not as an object to be exchanged or used but as the bearer of "an abstract, theoretical, but entirely real quantum of value," akin to a "promissory note" whose worth is tied to redeemability.[54]

The written bond could, however, never be regarded as the same thing as the coins the lender had exchanged in the first place. Concomitantly, it could not in *actuality* stand in for the person of the debtor. The homology between legal and commodity form rested on a quantifying logic, whereby the incommensurability of property and persons was resolved by the bond's recourse to the logic of the universal equivalent. Here the bond advanced what Karl Polanyi describes as a "commodity fiction," whereby something that is "obviously *not* [a] commodit[y]" is transformed into one, as two entities assume an equivalency by means of convention but never in an absolute sense.[55] At such moments, what had initially backed the bond had shifted such that the substance of the original loan was transformed from the metal of coins to the flesh of the debtor. This transmutation was achieved through the elasticity of the category property. Always at once a material thing and immaterial concept, property was also a set of legal norms and as such, invented its own context by determining who is negotiating with whom, over access to and use and exchange of what.[56]

Yet even as the validity of the bond derived from the "commodity fiction," underwritten by a legal fiction, these fictions, in turn, relied on the integrity of the bond as a physical object. Any alteration rendered a bond void. How then would bonds, like subsequent kinds of paper monies such as bank notes, escape scrutiny for signs of textual adulteration—marks that would offer loopholes to its constitutive claims and penal condition? In order to perform its function, the bond had to transcend its own materiality. Yet plays insistently placed bonds at their dramatic crux and showcased them as stage properties that served multiple functions. On stage, the bond's written terms were performed variously as they were revealed to be real entities whose meanings were discursively and socially constructed.

While my analyses of plays about debt elucidate the interpenetration of economic practice and philosophical thought, my readings also reveal the ways in which formal encounters between bonds and playtexts generated a series of local pitfalls and possibilities for both dramatic and monetary forms of writing. The plays I discuss are driven by the problem of the overdue bond and, perhaps not surprisingly, showcase the themes of revenge and redemption. But what becomes clear is that these themes are not determined by any particular generic dictate, but rather emerge from the dynamics of debt bondage, which itself illuminates the torturous nexus of money and justice. In this respect, the plays I examine take the bond at its word, insofar as the ethos of payback has been historically integral to credit. Yet dramatic explorations of forfeiture are also anticipatory of problems that fall under the rubric of political theology—for instance, the sanctity of human life and the metaphysical implications of belonging—problems that may be discerned in a given play's aesthetic disturbance. Early modern viewers and contemporary critics have noted that the character, plotline, and thematic structure of each of these plays are inexplicably, and in some instances maddeningly, inconsistent. What warrants further investigation is how such formal problems stem from a play's sensitivity to the bond as comprised of several contested legal and economic forms. In exposing the fissures among these forms, writers posited a dialogic relation between real and fictive contracts. In some instances, a comedy is barely able to repress the intrusion of retributive violence in its staging of debt bondage as the means by which to achieve redemption and satisfaction. In other instances, a tragedy obfuscates the dangers of default and forecloses the possibility of catharsis by showing debt to be generative and a source of pleasure. Rather than interpret such suspensions or deferrals of formal expectations as indicative of a given play's structural weakness, I demonstrate that at those moments at which drama becomes charged by the economic scene of which it is a part, we witness its encounter with the complex discourse of debt, a discourse whose own horizon of meaning remained unfixed. The encounter between bonds and plays produced an array of unexpected problems and unintended solutions, such that the collision between the two could at any moment transform the political potential of each by opening up new social and cultural forms for imagining the relation among fiction, law, and money.

This book examines six very different plays that, nonetheless, revolve around the common problem of owing money. Each play considers how its protagonist got into debt and what he did and said upon discovering that he could not pay his bonds. Not surprisingly, these plays call on a shared repertoire. For instance, each builds to the moment at which, according to the stage directions, the creditor confronts his debtor with actual physical bonds. At some point in each play, the insolvent debtor likens his overdue bonds to weapons that threaten to injure him. Each one of these plays also explores the relation between affective ties and monetary obligation. While such common features are significant, I am less interested in providing a descriptive account of them than in investigating what these iterable textual and performative practices can tell us about a given play's function. For this reason, this is not a study that interprets literature as reflecting the legal aspects of debt litigation. Rather I offer a series of local readings of the ways that a given dramatic text grapples with the problem of debt. I do not wish to ignore the ways that the genre of the debt play is informed by preexisting definitions and expectations about bonds that audience members bring to each play. Nonetheless, even as writers call on popular ideas about debt to exploit an ensemble of dramatic conventions, once the bond is inserted into dramatic narrative, it stakes a unique claim upon what *and* how a play means.

As each play acknowledges, debt is a problem that extends beyond the mere exchange of coins. Thus all six plays demonstrate an urgent need to resolve, even if this entails mystifying, contradictory ideas about ownership and self-ownership in the context of an unduly harsh penalty for forfeiture. While each chapter may be read as an individual case study of the particular way that a given play examines a specific aspect of debt bondage, taken together these chapters suggest a growing resignation toward—or at least more developed formal modes of accommodating—the risks associated with borrowing money. A diachronic perspective, whereby we track early modern drama's evolving modes of engagement with different elements of the bond, reveals the outlines of our own imagination of debt. As we move from the late Elizabethan to the early Carolinian period, we can more sharply discern dramatic literature's role in rationalizing what Graeber describes as the conversion of an economy of credit into an economy of interest.

The first third of *Of Bondage*, examines the ethical problem of property-in-person that debt bondage broached and analyzes two plays that address the ways that the bond's penal condition shaped the relationship between money and justice. Organizing my argument in these first two chapters around the concepts of "payback" and "forfeiture," respectively, I show that despite the fact that the legal remedy for forfeiture was construed as a form of restitution that would stand in for and thus in theory prevent retaliatory violence, the compensatory logic of debt could not fully repress the link between monetary satisfaction and corporal punishment. Even those who maintained that incarceration was intended to secure custody of the debtor acknowledged that the objectionable conditions of prison made forfeiture an occasion to exact revenge. Chapter 1, "*Timon of Athens*, Forms of Payback, and the Genre of Debt," historicizes *Timon*'s infamous narrative discontinuity by reading the play as a conceptual exercise in competing notions of justice in exchange. Economically inflected readings have dominated recent critical assessments of the title character's inexplicable shift from altruism in the first two acts to misanthropy in the last three. Such analyses persist in approaching *Timon* as a characterlogical study, even though the problem with the play extends beyond that of the two Timons. Few critics, for instance, address the impressive amount of stage time devoted to the character of Alcibiades and his plot to avenge Athens. In an effort to forge a connection between the play's main action and its subplot, I make the case for *Timon* as a botched revenge tragedy. The bond, as I argue, is identified in this play as an instrument for restoring social order on the condition that its users abandon an idea of payback as punishment. Thus the play resolves the threat of waste—of lives, bodies, and things—that debt bondage portends by successfully juxtaposing bonds to the excesses of the revenge pact and the sterility of not-owing, both of which are identified as unproductive and asocial. The play's stake in the notion of debt bondage as a necessary and reasonable alternative comes to light only when *Timon* is situated in the context of its performers' own experience of debt bondage in the hands of their manager, Philip Henslowe. His reliance on bonds rendered him a notoriously ambivalent figure known for munificence and mercilessness. Historical accounts of his moneylending activities, however, can trace their own ambivalent depictions of Henslowe to the period's confused ideas of recompense as repaying in kind in the form of money and unkind repayment in the form of pain.

In Chapter 2, "Shylock and the Slaves: Owing and Owning in *The Merchant of Venice*," I argue that the dramatic energy of *The Merchant of Venice* is driven by the circumstances of the desperate debtor, and I identify forfeiture, rather than usury, as the central concern of this play. My analysis of the legal, economic, and theological implications of debt bondage elucidates the ways the play works through complex problems of ownership and self-ownership that bore immediate relevance in light of mounting cases of default. By showing that the play participated in ongoing legal debates about partial and absolute possession of property, I analyze its theory of ethical ownership, which it advances by comparing the coterminous entitlements of the debt transaction to an arrangement of second- and third-party possession of land known as *usufruct*. Absolute dominion with its attendant right to destroy hovers over the economic and affective transactions in the play. The decision of the trial rests upon the play's ability to reconcile to what extent—if at all—the practical consequences of forfeiture can buttress precepts of shared possession grounded in legal theory and theology, as well as the state's investment in these concepts, at the very moment that the penalty for debt raises the distressing prospect of human chattel. By overlaying the logic of economic contract onto the marriage contract in its second half, the play transposes the marriage bond into a debt bond and forestalls comic closure.

The next two chapers of *Of Bondage* consider the debtor's coeval status as the object of property and subject of contract in light of an evolving legal hermeneutic that was increasingly interested in theorizing the role of the debtor's intentionality in the adjudication of forfeiture. Chapter 3 focuses on the term "satisfaction" and Chapter 4 on the term "redemption," as these chapters explore economic exchange as a means by which the debtor may achieve some degree of social and political agency. While the plays I analyze feature trial scenes, as do *Timon of Athens* and *The Merchant of Venice*, *Michaelmas Term* and *The Custom of the Country* emphasize the contingent aspects of debt bondage by suggesting that the hold the bond has on the debtor's person may be loosened by his participation in heterogeneous, local economic communities. Chapter 3, "*Michaelmas Term* and the Problem of Satisfaction," demonstrates that the intrusion of the bond transforms this city comedy into a play about writing and the will. By the late sixteenth century, the negative aspects of common law were coming to be associated with its rampant textuality. As the period witnessed a significant shift from oral assimilation to print, which allowed for the proliferation of legal commentaries, manuals, handbooks, and writs, contemporaries decried the democratizing of the law to those untutored in its finer points. Middleton's engagement with the written culture of the law is not merely informed by the details of jurisdictional procedure but marked by a sensitivity to its elastic philosophical and affective underpinnings. In 1602, Edmund Coke and King's Bench justices determined that the insolvent debtor was no longer guilty of malfeasance for actively detaining his creditor's property but of nonfeasance for failing to perform his promise. Confusingly, the debtor emerged as the subject of law not by having enacted a crime but by having failed to act. In effect, he was tried for his passivity. Proof of his guilt rested on his having signed onto the bond, which served as evidence of his will. While critics object to the preposterous passivity of Middleton's protagonist, the country gull Richard Easy of Essex with whom city gallants have their way—erotically and economically—this character, I show, embodies the problematic connection between satisfaction and consent, issues that came to the fore in the 1602 decision on *Slade's Case*. Performed before an audience of law students, Middleton's play exploits the bond as a contested form of legal writing by dramatizing the role of the hand in establishing the debtor's liability. As this play suggests, the courts' intensified interest in the intentionality of the debtor did not resolve the nebulous matter of economic agency but rather amplified the hand's ability to both affirm and vitiate the priorities of contract.

Common law debates over whether the imprisonment of a debtor was itself satisfaction of an unpaid loan or whether the incarcerated was a human pawn that could be redeemed at a later point continued into the first decade of the seventeenth century. In this same period, justices determined that the indentured servant bound for Virginia could be classified as an animated gage, a hostage delivered over to slavery but subject to redemption. Unlike the debtor, the servant was not incarcerated, but he was held in custody by his planter until his debt was satisfied. The indenture thus functioned both as a labor contract and a *prima facie* debt bond. Chapter 4, "Freedom, Bondage, and Redemption in *The Custom of the Country*," examines an immensely popular play by Fletcher and Massinger, set in Lisbon, the hub of a global slave trade. Reading this play as a meditation on the relationship between indenture and enslavement generally and as it played out in the Virginia colony more particularly, I show that tragicomedy was the most apt form for working through the antimonies of contractual coercion engendered by debt bondage. The problem of the play is the transformation of expropriation into legitimate exchange. Temperance serves as the affective analogue for the legal process by which the impersonal exchange of bodies gives way to a phenomenon whereby subjects willingly alienate themselves. Within a colonial context marked by an insatiable desire for imagined profits, contract offered a means of proscribing market behavior so that interminable speculation could be contained within the bounds of rational calculation. In this play, temperate men engage in self-enslavement as they abandon the variable position as an object of property for the more predictable one as a subject of contract.

The final chapter of *Of Bondage* considers the "pit," the disease-ridden dirt hole in the basement of London's Compters or debtor's prisons. The pit is where all so-called desperate debtors ended their days. Imprisonment for debt occupied a prominent place in the English imagination for the six-hundred-year period during which civil incarceration and not personal bankruptcy determined the adjudication of insolvency. Imprisonment was the fate of those who defaulted on as little as ten shillings as it was of those who owed hundreds of pounds. In every case, the incarcerated was responsible for his own maintenance. Chapter 5, "Prison Prose, the Pit, and the End of Tricks" examines Middleton's *A Trick to Catch the Old One* and Massinger's update of Middleton's play, *A New Way to Pay Old Debts,* as products of an early modern carceral imagination, which evolved significantly in the period between the two plays. These plays show the ways that the threat of—as well as actual—imprisonment for debt confers status on the debtor. More particularly, each play envisions prison as an environment that inspires witty literary production, which itself compensates for impecuniousness by magically exalting cultural capital over material capital. While in both plays the debtor's body is identified as a generative site, Middleton and Massinger express very different attitudes toward wit as a weapon of ambivalent potency in the face of the deprivation of liberty. By the time of Massinger's play, social ties are imagined and experienced as forms of bondage, as perpetual debt offers the structuring principle of a civic order in which the hazards of imprisonment and the inconveniences of repayment may be endlessly deferred.

Conclusion

The idea of property as intrinsically linked to personal autonomy predates early modern common law and is explored by Aristotle, who cites one of property's functions as providing the prerequisite for civic engagement.[57] This ancient conceptualization of property as conferring onto its holder a form of autonomy that guarantees him "an independence that embroiled the individual in as few as possible contingent relations with others" strongly influenced early modern thinkers, as well as the later framers of the American constitution.[58] Indeed, the slogan of the American Revolution echoed the presumption of property-in-person stated in the Magna Carta, by which it declared that "a man is a slave if his property can be taken without his consent."[59] The staying power of this sentiment suggests that even before a person could be construed as a form of property, there had to be an initial conception of liberty that rested on the notion that to have one's property forcibly taken reduced one to the status of a slave. What then does the idea of property-in-person, an idea at the foundation of both English and American ideals of citizenship, mean when money is considered property and the body of the person who has borrowed money may be construed as an equivalent form of property? Reflecting on C. B. Macpherson's premise that the historical trajectory has arched toward possessive individualism, Stephen Best elucidates a coterminous vector marked by "property's drift in the direction of the commodification of personhood," such that personhood "appears increasingly *subject* to the domain of property."[60] Theatrical investigations of what happens when a debtor is unable to honor his bond provide a window onto the specific ways that forfeiture pressured the tenets of self-possession. The notion of property-in-person, a mainstay of English law, was rehearsed and revised through theatrical performances of debt bondage, which interrogated the presumed equivalency between the defaulted debtor's body and the money he owed.

The late sixteenth-century penal debt bond was a monetary instrument that set in motion a series of precedents that for centuries in England and America would haunt the legal, philosophical, and moral problem of what the law would come to refer to as living property. English common law provided colonists with a template and indentured servants unable to pay off their debts were subject throughout the colonies to sudden seizure and incarceration. The sources of the legal rules governing slavery in the American South continue to be widely debated, yet the strategies of divestment put in place by the common law adjudication of forfeiture recommend the figure of the debtor as the heretofore unacknowledged precursor of the African slave. While historically monetary measurements had been applied to women, servants, colonial migrants, and local vagrants, the notion of the body as a redeemable investment first became legally tenable in debt law. The crucial link between debt bondage and slavery inheres, however, not only in the figures of the debtor and slave but also in the shared logic subtending both systems. The debtor's body anticipated a novel species of money developed further by elaborate networks of global investors that regarded the body of the slave as at once useful and as a form of transferable and speculative property.

An environment in which thinking about human bodies as hybrid entities that could be both persons and property was already taking shape in the sixteenth century, as suggested by the statement of one English slave trader who referred to Africans as "pieces of merchandise."[61] Almost one hundred years after Shakespeare reminded his listeners that Shylock "dearly bought" Antonio's flesh, the case of *Butts v. Penny* granted a ship's captain rights of recovery of property (*trover*) for a captured cargo of African slaves.[62] Even Chief Justice Holt's attempt to overturn the decision on the case rested upon an equivocation, as he concluded "by common law no man can have property in another but in special cases."[63] Indefinite incarceration for forfeiture on as little as a few shillings continued in England well into the nineteenth century, during which time the so-called natural rights of freeborn Englishmen were enjoyed only by those able to pay their debts.

Chapter 1

Timon of Athens, Forms of Payback, and the Genre of Debt

> The desire for vengeance is a desire for essential equilibrium. . . . The search for equilibrium is bad because it is imaginary. Revenge. Even if in fact we kill or torture our enemy it is, in a sense, imaginary.
>
> — Simone Weil

Reparations

A joint endeavor of Shakespeare and Middleton, composed sometime between 1605 and 1608 and never performed during either writer's lifetime, *Timon of Athens* has been dismissed for centuries as "no play but a shew," a hodgepodge of schematic episodes, and an embryonic *King Lear*.[1] Hoping to penetrate this opaque portrait of insolvency, editors have recently put *Timon* into conversation with other works by Middleton featuring reversal of fortune like *Michaelmas Term* and *A Trick to Catch the Old One*.[2] As a result, economically inflected readings have come to dominate assessments of Timon's sudden shift from altruism in the first two acts to misanthropy in the last three.[3] Theodore Leinwand argues that Timon's naïve belief that he is exempt from the rules of the marketplace leads to extravagance and then self-loathing.[4] John Jowett reads the play's fractured narrative as reflecting the chasm between Timon's pleasure in abundance and pain in remittance.[5] While such interpretations foreground the exigencies of early modern England's culture of credit, Timon remains at the center. The play's obscurity, however, extends beyond the problem of the two Timons. An inexplicable amount of stage time, for instance, is devoted to the character of Alcibiades and his plot to avenge the Athenian state. So long as we look to Timon to unlock the mystery of *Timon*, we will fail to convincingly connect the play's main action to its subplot. In an effort to remedy this problem, this chapter reads both halves of the play's narrative schism as mediated by the ethos of payback. As such, as I will show, the play is both an elaboration and amplification of the social and legal consequences of not simply credit arrangements in general but the specific monetary instrument, the penal debt bond. By approaching this play as a formal engagement with the bond, I illuminate the stakes of staging the complex process of remuneration in a theater financed by debt.

Moneylending, debt litigation, and the ever-present threat of imprisonment were not merely potent metaphors for unequal social relations in the period's drama—they were the harsh realities around which players, writers, and theatrical managers negotiated their lives as commercial artists. The building and leasing of the playhouses were financed on bonds. As William Ingram reminds us, the Theater in Shoreditch would not have existed if James Burbage had not indebted himself. After having devised a bond of "many Hundred poundes," he and his brother Richard had "at like expense" built the Globe, with "more summes of money taken up at interest, which lay heavy on [them] many yeares."[6] Costumes, properties, and playscripts were obtained on bonds, and it was through the bonds devised by playhouse owners that theatrical labor was secured. Moreover, players such as Nathan Field, Henry Chettle, Robert Daborne, John Duke, and William Haughton, as well as writers such as Ben Jonson, George Chapman, John Marston, John Lyly, Cyril Tourneur, Thomas Middleton, Thomas Dekker, and Philip Massinger, moved in and out of debtor's prison with alarming frequency.[7] The problem of payback thus plagued not only the imaginative but also the material world of playing.

The entrepreneur Philip Henslowe has come to embody our historical imagination of the theater's involvement with the credit economy. In addition to a cache of documents detailing his career, his account book provides ample evidence of his dependence on debt bonds. Recent scholarship has emphasized the extent to which the professional playing companies, like the ones Henslowe managed, relied upon monetary instruments regularly used by those who conducted business in the suburbs and Liberties where the theaters were located.[8] Yet despite the fact that Henslowe was a creditor who loaned on bond, an association with usury has tainted his legacy.[9] While we have no evidence indicating whether the bonds he devised with individual players inspired gratitude or resentment, Henslowe himself appears to have been aware of the ambivalent aspects of bonding. He acknowledges in his diary, for instance, "When I lent I wasse a frend & when I asked I wasse unkind."[10]

Debt bondage sustained the business of playing, yet the coercive conditions of bonding could cast a shadow over the theatrical enterprise. On a practical level, incarcerated players could not perform. On the level of ideology, it would be impolitic for a play to depict debt as leading only to imprisonment or death, since to do so would vilify its own conditions of production and undermine the legitimacy of the bond. So long as debt proved a necessary evil, managers such as Henslowe sought to rationalize bonds (the Lady Elizabeth's men ultimately regarded his use of them as retaliatory), and writers such as Shakespeare and Middleton aimed to neutralize their retributive elements. Perhaps no one more than the player (or his manager) had such acute insight into the penal debt bond as a problematic but practical response to an economy marked by instability of value and a chronic shortage of coins.

Timon indexes its own historical moment at which "a bewildering variety [of monies] jostled for recognition," rendering money an unstable fiscal and social phenomenon.[11] As Peter Holland observes, the play is plagued by "considerable confusion about how much a talent is worth," as various forms of wealth float free of any stable ground of reference.[12] In this respect, Shakespeare and Middleton's play concur with early modern economic manuals that acknowledge it is "not so much what money is worth in it selfe, as how it is valued by publike auctoritie, custome, and estimation . . . or common use therof."[13] Custom and estimation varied wildly, as coinage was valued in specie not in tale, meaning that the worth of a coin was determined by the precious metal from which it was composed rather than by royal fiat. Yet in the absence of any consistent means of rating gold and silver, the integrity of coins, which were all too often clipped and counterfeited, was always in question. Paper monies, such as goldsmiths' receipts and bills of exchange, also remained indeterminate without the existence of an institution to authorize monetary worth. Debt bonds relied on what was arguably the most unstable currency of all—trust—and in an attempt to maintain authority, anchored value in the body of the borrower.

Creditors who loaned on bond could not charge interest because common law regarded money transferred by means of contractual arrangement to be a nonfungible form of property. Consequently a loan secured on bond was regarded "as a thing that is very like a piece of land."[14] As Francis Bacon explains, "For a bargain changes the property of each part, and therefore in action of debt it is alleged that the defendant detains the money or thing demanded as if it were his before; to wit, that the plaintiff had the property of it by the contract. . . . and therefore when the plaintiff demands only that which was his before, it cannot be said that he is deceived by the defendant; but that the defendant detains that of which the property was in the plaintiff."[15] Technically, a creditor could not abdicate ownership over the money he lent, which according to debt jurisprudence could not be wasted or used up as a fungible, like food or wine. In reality, however, debtors spent the coins they borrowed. At the same time, the law allowed an unsatisfied creditor rights in his debtor's person, which as collateral was considered a form of property like the original loan. This meant that while a creditor could not use or destroy his debtor, for instance by forcing him to perform labor or by murdering him, he could detain his debtor indefinitely.

The legal remedy for forfeiture was construed as a form of restitution that would stand in for and thus, in theory, prevent retaliatory violence. Yet the penal logic of forfeiture could not fully repress the historical link between monetary compensation and corporal punishment. As legal scholar Allan Farnsworth reminds us, the ancient instance of credit arose out of blood feud. In Anglo-Saxon culture, a murderer could buy off the vengeance of his victim's kinsmen by paying a larger "wergild" than he could afford. If he provided a security, he could pay in installments. In most cases the security took the form of another person, who remained a hostage held by the victim's family until the debt was settled. Over time, the debtor was allowed to serve as his own surety.[16] The accretion of common law, an institution based on precedent, kept the primitive aspects of forfeiture thinly covered over by its civilized precincts. As such, residual ancient ideas about wergild seeped into the early modern conceptualization of penalty for forfeiture. In early modern England, when a borrower had no other asset at his disposal, he became a pledge or "an animated gage."[17] An unsatisfied creditor could take action against "the body of the defendant; or against his goods and chattels," but when an insufficient borrower "bound" his "bodie," his person became a "forfeit."[18] Once attachment had been initiated, the law rigidly upheld the distinction between movables over which the creditor had no legal right, such as jewelry and clothing that the debtor wore at the time of arrest or any objects that he carried in his hands including coins, and the one form of property over which the creditor had a claim, the debtor's body.[19]

Even those who maintained that imprisonment was intended to secure custody of inmates' bodies rather than enact retribution acknowledged that a creditor could use the objectionable conditions of prison as a means to exact revenge.[20] Appeals to the city authorities, members of Parliament, and the central government for relief of imprisoned debtors argued that to detain the insolvent tainted the reputation of the creditor by making him vulnerable to accusations that he expected his debtor to discharge his debt by dying.[21] Writers such as Thomas Dekker sardonically portray the man who lends on bond as "a cheater of life," who declares of his debtor: "'He shall rot in prison!' or 'I will make dice of his bones!', words unworthy of a Turke, unfit for a Christian. No man speaks them, but a monster; no man, but a Devil; no devil, but a thing without a name worse than a devil who, having no power given him to torment, will snatch Divine Vengeance into his own hand."[22] If usury was imagined in the period as an event that wounded the body of the debtor with its biting force, the bond was perceived to be just as violent an instrument in hands of "hard-hearted creditors" who, unable to obtain monetary satisfaction, were willing to settle "only for blood."[23]

The divide between revenge and justice was never absolute, and *Timon* rips the veil off a system of debt inflected by violence. In this play the event of forfeiture exposes the clash of competing paradigms expressed by the related notions of paying back and paying for.[24] In accordance with the ancient custom of payback, the avenger owes a debt of blood that will be satisfied only by his inflicting harm onto the wrongdoer. This model of payback informed economic arrangements in which the debtor perceived himself as wronged by his creditor, whom *he* wanted to make pay. A culture of credit in which lender and borrower were often one in the same person made inroads, however, toward substituting reparation for retribution. Here a third party such as the state intervened and determined that the debtor was the wrongdoer who refused to pay for what he owed. Yet as a practical and imaginative means of grounding value, the bond complicated prevailing notions of justice in exchange. If bonds enabled a mode of distributive justice predicated on the dispensation of bounty, they also exposed the fragility of equity in an economy in which debasement always threatened to undercut wealth. In Shakespeare and Middleton's play, characters look to bonds to restore equilibrium when bounty turns to waste, even as this monetary instrument introduces the possibility of greater ruin by setting in motion the wheels of vengeance.[25] The play, however, eschews the vengeful aspects of debt bondage by staging the alternatives as even more destructive to the social fabric and moral economy of Athens. The avenger, we are shown, is excessive in his desire to get even, and in this respect, is ultimately no better than the misanthrope, who by having settled all accounts owes nothing to anyone and thus belongs nowhere.

The Gift of Debt

There is a long tradition of characterizing Philip Henslowe as the model for Shylock, but a more apt comparison might be between Henslowe and Timon. We are confronted with not one usurious figure but rather two Henslowes; one who is munificent and the other who is uncompromisingly misanthropic. For decades we have been told that, unlike the Burbages, Henslowe kept "his actors in subservience and his poets in constant need by one single method, viz., by lending them money and never allowing their debts to be fully paid off."[26] More recently, however, theater historians have emphasized that Henslowe's resources proved a boon for the development of early modern drama and that by exploiting a credit economy, he was able to underwrite creative and commercial risks that advanced the theatrical enterprise. One shortcoming of the sharer system, as Carol Chillington Rutter points out, was that it did not create the conditions for the expansion of capital but could only keep pace with daily expenses.[27] Availing himself of what his contemporaries regarded as a "new form of contractual agreement," Henslowe introduced into the world of the theater an instrument that was associated not with rapacious moneylenders but accomplished merchants.[28] His use of the bond would, however, become the ground of conflict between him and his players for decades. While we are now inclined to discount assertions that "both Heywood and Dekker lived for years in a kind of bondage (shared by many of their fellows)," or that Henslowe kept his actors "at his mercy," even revisionists take pause when it comes to assessing Henslowe's role as a creditor.[29] Neil Carson champions Henslowe as "a benign and efficient businessman," but when the discussion turns to debt bondage, he acknowledges that Henslowe "occasionally threatened to prosecute players for bonds in his possession and used this power to influence the sharers."[30] In regard to the protracted dispute between Henslowe and the Lady Elizabeth's men, Carson speculates that by 1615 Henslowe had "learned how to protect his capital by sequestering or impounding costumes" and that he regularly held on to playbooks as "security for outstanding loans," as well as devised more bonds "to guarantee the performance of various obligations" (Carson, 32).

Historical overviews of early modern credit networks have emphasized that lending on credit promoted social cohesion and communal goodwill.[31] The conjoining of justice and friendship was, however, a tenuous prospect in Henslowe's time. Scholars have recently reminded us that the end of the sixteenth century ushered in the period during which common law courts were coming to repudiate relationship in favor of strict contractualism, which meant that coercion was just as likely to serve as the ground of promise as trust.[32] No monetary instrument lent itself to coercive tactics more readily than the debt bond, which, because of the proprietary nature of its penal condition, came to be described in early modern juridical discourse as an obligation secured "*in terrorem*."[33] The increasingly hostile relations between Henslowe and members of the Lady Elizabeth's men reveals that after benefiting from the issuance of many bonds, they balked at the "*in terrorem*" aspect of their bonds.

Like any savvy playhouse owner, Henslowe devised bonds in order to obtain control over what was arguably his most precious commodity: the player's body.[34] Arguably, it was Henslowe's perception of his players themselves as his most significant financial investment—a kind of property whose value he held in reserve and for which he needed to provide insurance—that allowed for a conceptual ease in their slide from employees to debtors. The lynchpin of the player's contract was its monetary penalty, and the bonds Henslowe drew up with those who played at the Rose Theatre, for instance, obligated each player to forfeit the impressive sum of £100 if he left the playhouse before the term of his indenture expired. The penal condition of the performance bond figures prominently, for example, in the contract between Henslowe and Thomas Downton, devised on October 6, 1597: "Thomas dowten came & bownd hime sealfe unto me in xxxx *li* a some sett by the Receving of iii *d* of me before wittnes the convenant is this that he shold . . . come ii yeares to playe in my howsse & in no other a bowte London publickeley yf he do with owt my consent to forfet unto me this some of money above written."[35] Typically the bond between playhouse owner and performer also mandated that the player regularly attend rehearsal and performance; that the player not remain clad in stage costumes outside of the playhouse; and, in one instance, that the player not show signs of inebriation.[36]

The provisions of the player's bond were suited to the specific needs of the theatrical enterprise, yet from a legal perspective this particular kind of bond was no different than a conditional debt bond. The commonality among various bonds produced, according to legal historian A. W. B. Simpson, "the strange result" that the terms of their liability made all conditional contracts in essence "debtor-creditor forms."[37] Operating outside of a context of breach of promise, the efficacy of the bond lay in its ability to leverage the player's body as property on pain of forfeiture. In the 1615 "Articles of Grievance" company members drafted when relations broke down between them and Henslowe and his then partner Jacob Meade, Henslowe is singled out for having appropriated funds, stock, and playbooks. In the second half of the document, entitled "Articles of Oppression against Mr. Hinchlowe," Henslowe is charged with binding hired men in his own name, entering players' personal debts against the company's accounts, and requiring an exorbitant amount of money for security for players' bonds. Henslowe's use of bonds seems to have produced a scenario in which the threat of retaliation dampened the spirit of distributive justice, and as much is suggested by players' assertions that Henslowe threatened on several occasions to "break" the company or disband it through forceful means.[38] Conflating the corporate body of the company with the individual body of the player/debtor, they stress, ominously, that Henslowe "wthin 3 yeares . . . hath broken and dismembered five Companies" (Greg, *HP*, 90). The term "break" most immediately conveyed a scene of corporal violence involving the cutting, tearing, and shattering of limbs and bones.

Even though the debtor used up or destroyed the legal property of the creditor, the notion that the action of bonding jeopardized the physical person of the borrower became entrenched in the early seventeenth-century English imagination. Outrage about the authority that the bond accorded the creditor over the person of the debtor dominates sermons and popular tracts from the period. Samuel Cotesford, for example, rails against "merciless Creditors" who "value not the precious life of a man at the rate of an Oxe or a Horse: But for farre lesser summes, does keepe many able and active men in Prison, till they either dye or become unable to serve the Common-wealth" (sig. A2). Writers underscore the suffering of the debtor by likening him to a slave, which allowed them to detail the abuses of a legal system that subjected the debtor's body to isolation, disease, and death. Even though the English "brag that we have no Galleys, nor Galley-slaves," Cotesford asserts that his nation fosters "cruel-hearted men" who care "not so much for [their] money" as to "have [their] will" over the debtor (sig. A2). Bonds made "broken men" because their provisions rendered those who could not meet their obligations, in the eyes of the law, "credit-cracked," or in other words disabled and destroyed by forfeiture (sig. A2).

Attending closely to the complaints drafted by members of the Lady Elizabeth's men reveals the extent to which Henslowe's bonds came to be associated with an ethos of payback. For instance, through the action of bonding the playhouse owner appeared to significantly expand his purview beyond that of a landlord or consultant to the sharers. As long as the company remained indebted to Henslowe, he legally owned its stock. The players' articles against Henslowe accuse him of having "taken all bounde of our hired men in his owne name" and of "turn[ing] them over to others to the breaking of our Companie" (*HP*, 89). Another item objects that "Uppon everie breach of the Companie hee takes newwe bonde for his stocke; and our securities for playinge wth : him Soe that hee hath in his hands bonds of ours to the value of 500^{ll}: and his stocke to; w^{ch} : hee denies to deliuer and threatens to oppresses u^{s} : with" (*HP*, 89). Moreover, according to members of the Lady Elizabeth's men, Henslowe had the audacity to publicly state, "should these fellowes Come out of my debt, I should have noe rule wth : them" (*HP*, 89). The Lady Elizabeth's men agreed to pay Henslowe one-half of the gallery profits as rent and to commit the other half to their outstanding debt, which in 1615 they claimed amounted to £126.[39] In such situations of financial duress, "breaking" a company allowed a playhouse owner to recoup individual forfeitures, as well as company debts, by retaining the extremely valuable costumes, properties, and playbooks. Indeed, in 1615 Henslowe did break the company. He dismissed the hired men and sold the remaining stock for £400.

After performance bonds, conditional debt bonds dominate Henslowe's transactions with players who rotated in and out of debtor's prison, such as Richard Jones, Thomas Downton, William Bird, and Robert Shaw. Nathan Field, Robert Daborne, John Duke, and William Haughton also seem to have regularly borrowed money from Henslowe, as did Ben Jonson, George Chapman, Thomas Dekker, Thomas Middleton, and Philip Massinger. As Natasha Korda reminds us, Henslowe's accounts reflect the professional players' and writers' propensity to spend liberally on drinking and dining, as well on the costs of play readings at inns and taverns.[40] Henslowe clearly had a vested interest in covering his players' existing debts or ensuring their discharge from prison so they could honor the terms of their performance bonds. Yet in consolidating their loans, he made himself sole creditor. Moreover, the liberty and life of the borrower remained at the discretion of even the most merciful creditor, who could release his debtor only with the issuance of another bond known as a "quitclaim," which effectively voided the original bond and extinguished the proprietary right the lender had in the borrower.[41]

Henslowe's dealings with William Bird suggest how a creditor could exercise more power over his debtor in some instances by holding back from imprisoning him. Henslowe's true intentions remain elusive. Yet it is safe to say that he did not lend money expecting nothing in return. As much is implied by his having systematically recorded his transactions so that he could enforce payment at a later date if he needed to. From 1597 to 1602 William

Bird repeatedly looked to Henslowe for "redey money" (Carson, 11). All told, Bird borrowed £30 from Henslowe, repaying all but £4 by 1602 (Carson, 11). On March 8, 1598, Bird, along with Spencer and Downton, borrowed 30s. on bond and another £6 on bond on April 9, 1598.[42] In this same period Bird, Jones, Shaw, and Downton took the liberty of pawning some of the company's properties, such as "a rich cloak," to pay off their personal debts (*HD*, 2: 242). Henslowe issued several more loans to Bird, at which point he began taking articles of Bird's clothing and jewelry as security. Carson suggests that this was "more of a formality than a serious attempt to protect his investment" (12). Yet even after Bird reduced an outstanding debt of £28 to £4 10s., and Henslowe drew up another bond voiding Bird's debt, he was careful to record in his book that Bird was acquitted only of "all debtes & demaundes" not made on "covenentes" (*HD*, fol. 89v). By keeping the written bonds active, as Henslowe acknowledges, he reserved the right to "clayme & challenge of him [Bird]" at a future date (*HD*, fol. 89v). Out of the twenty-one loans Henslowe issued to Bird, almost half (nine) were sealed bonds.

Perhaps no other institution in the period than the theater was more familiar with the ambivalent function of the bond as an instrument of justice. Evidence suggests that entrepreneurs like Henslowe were as involved with the details of debt litigation as the day-to-day business of managing the company. In 1578, for instance, John Brayne (brother-in-law of James Burbage) devised a bond with James Burbage for £400 to guarantee the lease of the Theater and a share of the property. Burbage was subsequently arrested for debt in 1579, and then again in 1582 (Ingram, 203–4). While bonds may have cemented networks of mutual trust, they were just as likely to generate profound and abiding social antagonisms, as well as occasions for exploitation. As Lynn Johnson explains, while some cultural authorities maintained that affective ties could serve as "a kind of Covenant," those who were developing theories and practices of economic self-interest countered the role of fidelity in the performance of justice (50). In the case of borrowing and lending on bond, proponents of the common law doctrine of consideration "explicitly repudiated relationship in favor of strict contract that depended on a single transaction, not a continuous round of accruing obligation and expectation" (60). Here punitive measures stepped in where inner virtue flagged. Ideally, reciprocal debts could be contracted over months, or even over years, eventually to be reckoned or cancelled out against each other. Yet those who ran playhouses lent money at a moment marked by an unprecedented rise in debt suits. If the bond's threat of retaliation compromised its potential as a means of dispensing bounty, then the increasing incidence of debtors using up the coins they borrowed added to the challenges of establishing a reliable economy in a cash-poor society. Henslowe, himself both a lender and a borrower, was, we should remember, no less vulnerable to creditors looking to his body as a form of durable, transferrable value.

The Gift of Death

It is tempting to speculate that the alternatively munificent and misanthropic Philip Henslowe served as the basis for the character of Timon. Yet by reading *Timon* against the backdrop of a theatrical enterprise steeped in debt, my aim is not to assert any immediate influence or recommend any particular document as a literary source. I am less interested in drawing homologies between Henslowe's *Diary* and Shakespeare and Middleton's play than in demonstrating that the business of playing offers a window onto both the necessity and the punitive force of bonds. It is the retributive aspects of payback that Henslowe's legacy bears the weight of and that *Timon* attempts to accommodate. Only by first understanding the players' objections to bonds on grounds that they served as instruments of retaliation can we appreciate the strategies *Timon* employs to neutralize the exploitative elements of bonding. The two problems plaguing *Timon*, the disjunction between the first and second halves of the play and the inclusion of the character of Alcibiades, that seem to indicate structural weaknesses may in the final analysis index the play's cogency. Timon's self-banishment and Alcibiades's plan to overtake Athens work in tandem to provide an overview of revenge as an elastic conceptual category by which to understand payback as both pain and reward. Thus these retributive actions set the stage for equivalence in exchange to emerge as the only viable response to a crisis of value. Drawing heavily on the Aristotelian notion that money's primary responsibility is to create balance in society, *Timon* anticipates the guiding principal of the three prominent mid-seventeenth-century so-called "neo-Aristotelian" mercantilists, Gerard de Malynes, Edward Misselden, and Thomas Mun. While each had very different ideas about how to use money to ensure social cohesion, all were in agreement that when there are enough coins in circulation, money can play its proper role as a means of harmonizing competing interests among different segments of society.[43]

A play infused—both on the level of rhetoric and theme—with monetary issues, *Timon* frames its action with an extended meditation on the confused hermeneutics of value, which is explored specifically in relation to the activity of artistic production. In a series of interchanges members of the play's chorus, made up of a painter, poet, jeweler, and merchant, establish that they have traveled to Timon's court so that he can confer value upon their respective creative products. For the jeweler, Timon must "touch the estimate" of his gem.[44] Although it is of "good form" and has luster (1.1.19–20), the jewel's worth will be determined ultimately by the person who purchases it. "Things of like value differing in owners," the jeweler explains, "are prizèd by their masters" (1.1.179–80). The poet waits for his poem to be appraised, since it too holds no intrinsic value but is "as a gown which uses / From when 'tis nourished."[45] By summoning the cloth pulp from which the poem's page and gowns are made and by introducing the word "use," meaning to wear in both the sense of display and wear out, the poet reminds his listeners that all property is fungible. Gowns and poems present a conundrum; since they can only be possessed through use, to enjoy them entails wearing them out or destroying them. The ephemeral nature of the theatrical endeavor is glanced at obliquely insofar as it too is an artistic product financed by debt for the sole purpose of consumption.

Here we are introduced to the "nourish-use" nexus that comes to inform the metaphoric economy of the play, exemplified by images of Timon himself as a form of fungible property that his borrowers use and use up. For the poet, Timon is like a tree that provides the gummy sap that feeds him, since his poetry is "a thing slipped idly from [him]" when "'tis nourished" by Timon's revenue (1.2.22–24). Flatterers are later depicted as those who have come to "taste Lord Timon's bounty" (1.1.287). One bystander explicitly likens the interdependency of credit networks to a group of men feasting on their lender when he exclaims: "What a number of men eats Timon, and he sees 'em not! It grieves me to see so many dip their meat in one man's blood" (1.2.39–41).[46] This image reverberates with Bassanio's description of his cannibalistic relationship to Antonio's detained body when he confesses to Portia, "I have engaged myself to a dear friend, / Engaged my friend to his mere enemy, / To feed my means."[47] As Karen Newman notes, the "magic of bounty" functions as "a periphrastic epithet for Timon, an apostrophe that summons him to behold the 'spirits' his generosity 'hath conjured to attend!'"[48] Importantly, Timon is not named at the outset of the play, and his impersonal introduction suggests that those who depend on him perceive him as an inanimate resource as much as a flesh-and-blood person. In early modern usage the word "bounty" referred to fungibles exclusively, items such as food and wine that were typically dispensed as gratuities or gifts to be enjoyed (*OED*).

Although Timon is described as "a worthy lord" (1.1.9), a person whose own value, in the jeweler's estimation, is "most fixed" or certain (1.1.10), even he, whom the poet envisions as the embodiment of "bounty" (1.1.6), cannot stabilize a baseless economy. Timon holds up the jewel before the court cynic Apemantus and asks him, "What dost thou think 'tis worth?" (1.1.223), to which Apemantus replies, "Not worth my thinking" (1.1.224), reminding Timon that the gem itself holds no inherent value beyond that with which thinking invests it. Apemantus goes on to emphasize that while the poem the poet offers may represent value it too cannot embody it. He warns Timon that the poem "feign[s] him [Timon] a worthy fellow" (1.1.234), since as Apemantus wryly notes, "he that loves to be flatter'd is worthy o' th' flatterer" (1.1.237–38). Unmoored from any extrinsic ground of worth, poems, jewels, and even Timon himself remain vulnerable to arbitrary alterations in taste.

Initially Timon seems immune to the fluctuating nature of value and secure in his position as benefactor. Even those who bring Timon gifts ultimately depend on him to confer the worth of their offerings, and thus Timon is recognized as the sole dispenser and arbiter of value. For many critics, such munificence allows Timon to assert social authority and serves as a thinly veiled form of exploitation.[49] The play certainly supports the notion that by making his recipients endlessly grateful, Timon subordinates them. Throughout the first half of the play Timon is perceived by his beneficiaries as using bounty to "subdue[ ] and propertie[ ] [men] to his love and tendance" (1.1.61). One borrower comes to Timon because "his means [are] most short" and his creditors "most strait" (1.1.102), and Timon "ransom[s]" him (1.1.108–11). This borrower's desperation, however, "ever binds him" to Timon (1.1.110). Even after this man is released from debtor's prison, his hopes of achieving liberty are dashed when Timon won't allow him to pay off his bond, and as a result he remains perpetually "bound / To [Timon's] free heart" (1.2.5–6). When Timon gives Lucullus money so that he may marry for love, this loan has the effect of indenturing the man, who can only accept Timon's money as "a bond in men" (1.1.153). In this case, the oath of bonding is achieved through Lucullus's formal declaration: "never may that state or fortune fall into my keeping which is not owed to you!" (1.1.158–60). Timon's disinterest in any arrangement based on reciprocity is demonstrated further when he resists relieving two lords who confess to him that "we are so virtuously bound" (1.2.228) and "so infinitely endeared" (1.2.230).

Despite their polite protestations, Timon will not permit his borrowers to reciprocate the gifts he bestows. Such refusals demystify credit relations, showing them to be in essence legal arrangements whose terms are determined by the magnanimity or, alternatively, the pettiness of the lender. Yet Timon's disinterest in reciprocity need not be read only in cynical terms. For Timon, debt bondage constitutes the social and for this reason, default signals the apotheosis of community rather than its breakdown. As Timon explains: "O you gods, think I, what need we have any friends, if we should ne'er have need of 'em? They were the most needless creatures living, should we ne'er have use for 'em, and would most resemble sweet instruments hung up in cases, that keep their sounds to themselves. Why, I have often wished myself poorer, that I might come nearer to you. We are born to do benefits; and what better or properer can we call our own than the riches of our friends?" (1.2.88–103). On the one hand, by regarding his followers as proper to him, Timon erroneously understands himself as possessing his friends. On the other hand, Timon understands that debt structures the social to such a profound extent that to not make use of one's friends is an asocial proposition. In such a case, they become instruments whose sweet sounds are never heard. This image, with its emphasis on aurality and performance once again harkens back to the theatrical medium, positing Timon as a manager figure, whose charge is to showcase his instruments to which he is permitted access by the terms of his bonds. Thus the creditor-debtor relation is envisioned as having a productive function insofar as destitution animates the bonds among men. Timon's logic also, though, points to the insurmountable problem of a social economy in which possession entails use. Only by "hav[ing] use for 'em" can Timon enjoy his friends, even as such enjoyment ultimately depletes them. Timon is, however, unable to recognize his friends as deposits in reserve or investments to be "sounded" or redeemed at a later date. If, "for Timon, economics corresponds to waste," as Leinwand argues, this attitude is by no means particular to Timon.[50] Debt functions in this play as the ultimate gift, one that in the giving exposes the fragility of a system of distributive justice.

If the character of Timon has not heeded the poet's lesson that possession understood as right of use leads to debasement, the play goes to great lengths to demonstrate the injustices of a world plagued by the indeterminacy of value. Timon's downfall is foreshadowed when the poet expounds what one critic has identified as "the central fable of the play."[51] Fortune, as the poet explains, is "a sovereign lady" on a hill (1.1.73) who has "beckoned" Timon "from the rest below . . . to climb to his happiness" (1.1.79, 81). There remain others below, though, who are "better than his [Timon's] value" (1.1.83–85). The scenario involving magnanimous but fickle Fortune anticipates Timon's dilemma insofar as the value Fortune confers upon Timon is predicated upon her enjoyment of him.[52] In a world in which valuation is inextricably tied to possession, Timon, like others before and after him, will inevitably be "spurn[ed]" and left "to slip down" (1.1.93–94). The moral of this fable is borne out by the credit crisis of the second act, at which point Timon's bonds are overdue and his borrowers come to the realization that their creditor is all used up.

Act 2 opens with various characters appearing with handfuls of documents, as the stage directions indicate: "Enter a Senator with papers in his hand." The stage directions for Act 2, Scene 2 read, "Enter steward [Flavius] with many bills in his hand." Another character's speech is punctuated by the stage direction, while "giving him [Timon's servant] bonds" (2.1.33), another presents Timon with "a note of certain dues" (2.1.12), while the lines of a third are prefaced with the stage directions "presenting a bill" (2.2.18). Timon is six months overdue on a bond for "five thousand" talents (2.1.1). He owes another creditor "nine thousand" talents, and yet another eleven thousand talents. His land, which he previously "put to [the] books" of his creditors for collateral (1.2.200), is "all engaged, forfeited and gone" (2.2.151). His total outstanding debt comes to over "five-and-twenty" thousand talents (2.1.2–4). Repeating verbatim the poet's question that opens the play, "How goes the world?" Timon incredulously asks his servant Flavius, "How goes the world, that I am thus encountered / With clamorous demands of broken bonds / And the detention of long-since-due-debts?" (2.2.40–43). Flavius's reply echoes that of the painter in Act 1, who explains to the poet, "It [the world] wears, sir, as it grows" (1.1.4). As Flavius suggests, the world is like a gown or poem, always in the process of becoming worn out by those who enjoy it. Flavius elaborates, "Though you hear now too late, yet now's a time; / The greatest of your having lacks a half / To pay your present debts" (2.2.147–49). Without the proper mooring of value, Flavius stresses, "too late" collapses into "now," and the "greatest having" is simultaneously the greatest "lack. " The motif of waxing and waning is reiterated by another servant who comments that Timon's "days are waxed shorter with him," since his "prodigal course / Is like the sun's" (3.4.11–13). Even Timon comes to see himself as diminished when he compares himself to a moon "wanting light to give. / But then renew I could not, like the moon; / There were no suns to borrow of" (4.3.68–70). This waxing and waning is reflected further in the fluctuating amount of money Timon owes. The talent, as Peter Holland notes, which was worth 6,000 drachmas and equivalent to £50 sterling, seems to be precipitously depreciating as the play progresses, as we move from a world in which three talents provide an impressive dowry for a gentleman's daughter in the first act to Timon's request for 1000 talents, which by Act 3 has become an incalculable sum, represented by Timon's servant's desperate plea for "so many talents" (3.2.36–37).

Signaling a crisis of value, expressed in part by Timon's diminished ability to ground worth in the authority of his person, the play proceeds systematically to undermine the validity of all representational media. The objects that once conveyed Timon's magnificence are stripped of their allure and transmuted into gaudy props. Timon's sumptuous feasts that hosted "riotous feeders" and where "every room" once "blazed with lights and brayed with minstrelsy" (2.2.164–66) give way to an impoverished banquet of covered dishes of "warm water and stones" (3.6.86–87). The only property Timon has at his disposal is the "empty coffer" (1.2.193), which his steward passes around to collect loans from those who are stunned to see "nothing, but an empty box" (3.1.16). Timon's debased court is reflected in the impecuniousness of his words, as Flavius observes:

> What will this come to?
> He commands us to provide, and give great gifts,
> And all out of an empty coffer;
> Nor will he know his purse, or yield me this,
> To show him what a beggar his heart is,
> Being of no power to make his wishes good.
> His promises fly so beyond his state
> That what he speaks is all in debt; he owes
> For every word. He is so kind that he now
> Pays interest for't. (1.2.191–200)

At the juncture at which the absence of value becomes glaringly apparent, jewels, poems, paintings, talents, and masques reveal themselves to be vaporous entities that may evaporate like "smoke and lukewarm water" (3.6.88–89). Critics have commented on the all-male world of the play and it is tempting to read such moments as extended considerations of the uncertainties troubling an all-male theatrical enterprise founded on debt.[53] In the context of the failure of all signifying modes, the bond enters the picture as a form of writing that can effectively mediate value by grounding it in the body of the insolvent debtor. Insofar as the bond allowed the lender to claim property in the person of the borrower, its proprietary logic potentially overrode the instability of use. Yet as collateral, the body of the borrower was construed as a form of nonfungible property, like land, which meant that the lender could not possess or enjoy his debtor. Thus even as the bond anchored value in the person of the debtor, it did so at the price of instilling an ethos of payback.

The theme of revenge emerges at the moment of Timon's insolvency, even as the role of avenger floats free of any one person as it detaches and reattaches itself to various characters. As a result, revenge becomes less a particular character's fate than a dark mood that permeates the play. Initially a spotlight is cast on Timon's wronged creditors, who are themselves caught in intricate webs of lending and borrowing. The word "revenge" is first introduced in a statement of false clemency by one creditor's servant who observes of Timon, "he's poor and that's revenge enough" (3.4.63–64). When Timon proceeds to "try [his] friends" (2.2.189), he finds that the general understanding holds: when bonds are overdue "men must learn now with pity to dispense / For policy sits above conscience" (3.2.89–90). Added to the list of those who are unable to remit Timon because they would have to borrow more to repay him, and he is now too great a credit risk, are others who have to call in their loans because they are under pressure to repay their creditors. One of Timon's lenders marvels at the complex network linking him to Timon and both of them to other lenders:

> I must serve my turn
> Out of mine own. His [Timon's] days and times are past,
> And my reliances on his fracted dates
> Have smit my credit. I love and honor him,
> But must not break my back to heal his finger.
> Immediate are my needs, and my relief
> Must not be tossed and turned to me in words,
> But find supply immediate. (2.1.20–27)

Timon's "friends" regret having to reject him in his time of need, and those who have recently received aid from him ruefully acknowledge that this "is no time to lend money, especially upon bare friendship without security" (3.2.41–43).

While Timon incorrectly assumed that value emanated *from* his person, the bond anchors value *in* his person. The play reserves its most sensational imagery for the scene in which Timon is confronted by his creditors who become agents of vengeance as Timon describes his bonds as bills, as the pun implies, long-handled axes that threaten to slice him into pieces. As Timon's creditors descend upon him, they verbally impale him. One declares, "here is my bill," and another announces, "Here's mine," while several others follow in quick succession with "And mine, my lord," "And ours, my lord," and "all our bills" (3.4.85–89). In attempting to fend off the cluster of bills *cum* weapons, Timon protests that they "knock [him] down," "cleave [him] to the girdle!" and "cut [his] heart in sums!" He imagines that his creditors will be satisfied only when they "tell out [his] blood" "five thousand drops" (3.4.91–98) for the five thousand talents he owes. Perceiving the action of debt as having rendered him prey, Timon comes to envision the world as a dog-eat-dog wilderness such that "the commonwealth of Athens is a forest of beasts" (4.3.347–48), where the bear is "killed by the horse" and the horse "seized by the leopard" (4.3.342–44). The yoking of debt and vengeance has come to ironic fruition, as anticipated by one creditor's observation that "No meed but he repays / Sevenfold above itself; no gift to him / But breeds the giver a return exceeding / All use of quittance" (1.1.290–93). Here the word "quittance" puns on "quit," the legal term for the discharge of debt (achieved through the issuance of a quitclaim) and the synonym for revenge. "Quit," which promised the countering of one crime with another, was the term used by avengers such as Middleton's Vindice, who regards vengeance as "murder's quit-rent."[54] Timon is finally compensated for the gifts, or meed, he has bestowed extravagantly in the form of a return that exceeds the prospect of his enjoying quittance, either as discharge from his debts or the satisfaction of his achieving revenge, since his creditors now intend to pay him back.

The locus of revenge does, however, shift away from the avenging creditors to Timon when he takes up the mantle of the injured party. Timon arranges a final banquet at which he proclaims, "Uncover, dogs, and lap!" (3.6.84) as he presents his expectant guests with plates of warm water and stones (3.6.85), which he then throws in their faces (s.d., 3.6.94) before physically "assault[ing] them and driv[ing] them out" (s.d., 3.6.102). Duly impressed by "the quality of Lord Timon's fury" (3.6.107), Timon's guests speculate that he has gone mad (3.6.116). Timon's subsequent exile and suicide may also be plotted on this course of vengeance when we read his choices as a churlish response to the senators' formal apology and vow of "consent of love" by which they hope to "entreat [him] back to Athens" (5.1.138–40). After harshly rejecting their request that he return to aid his fellow citizens by guarding the city against Alcibiades's army, Timon feigns concern by leading the emissaries to believe that he will join them after all. He then, however, abruptly turns only to reject them even more forcefully when he explains that he "cares not" (5.1.170) and that they should go hang themselves (5.1.211). He dismisses those who have come to make peace with the final declaration, "Graves only be men's works, and death their gain! / Sun, hide thy beams! Timon hath done his reign" (5.1.222–23). He owes them nothing. Going to his grave believing that Alcibiades will follow to the letter his instructions to raze Athens to the ground (4.3.111–30), Timon's death may be seen as a final act of retaliation in that he abandons his city at its moment of need.

Timon's eye-for-an-eye logic stands in contrast to Alcibiades's cool calculation of equivalence in exchange. The theme of revenge colors the extended argument between Alcibiades and the anachronistic Roman-style Senate in a scene that seems to come out of nowhere.[55] In the ensuing debate, in which Alcibiades attempts to defend a soldier who has been accused of misconduct, we are reintroduced to the problem of the groundlessness of value in a society in which certain authorities, in this instance the state, may dispense bounty, even as the prizes they award become debased through use. Having deemed it "necessary" that Alcibiades's soldier suffer the death penalty (3.5.2), the Senate vows to unleash the full force of "the law [that] shall bruise 'em" (3.5.5). Here members of the Senate resemble Timon's creditors, who use their overdue bills as weapons, as the play once again charts the course from distributive justice to retributive violence. The Senators, who initially endorsed the soldier to fight on their behalf, now resort to the language of vengeance when they proclaim, "we are for law . . . He forfeits his own blood that spills another" (3.5.89–91).

By introducing the distinction between deserts and bounty, Alcibiades is, however, able to interrupt the cycle of retribution. He insists that the "comely virtues" of the condemned soldier can pay for or "buy out his fault" (3.5.16–18) and, moreover, that his "service done" should be "sufficient briber for his life" (3.5.62–64). Attempting to remedy the state's arbitrary determination of the soldier's worth, Alcibiades points out that the same man who is rewarded for pugnacity on the battlefield should not be punished for behaving like a "sworn rioter" off the field (3.5.62). For Alcibiades, the soldier's good deeds should serve as collateral and thus animate the restorative principal of equivalence in exchange. Unlike bounty, they cannot be used up or debased but rather may be construed as an investment toward the future security of Athens. In making one final plea to the Senate, Alcibiades attempts to ground the soldier's value in his own person, which he offers up as surety:

> Though his right arm might purchase his own time
> And be in debt to none—yet, more to move you,

Take my deserts to his and join 'em, both;
And, for I know your reverend ages love
Security, I'll pawn my victories, all
My honors, to you, upon his good returns.
If by this crime he owes the law his life,
Why, let the war receive't in valiant gore. (3.5.80–87)

Holding fast to the notion of proportionate return, Alcibiades appropriates the language of payback and retools it to make the case for equitable reckoning. Revenge here is shown to be an offense that exceeds the original one in both quantity and intensity, thus it may be associated with the interest of usury. For this reason, Alcibiades depicts the state as an insatiable moneylender when he describes the "usuring Senate" (3.5.116) as shamelessly profiting off of him as its members hung back from war so they could "told their money and let out / Their coin upon large interest" (3.5.113–14). All the while, he explains, he fought to protect their way of life and became "rich only in large hurts" (3.5.115). He presents them with an alternative, however, when he offers his meritorious deeds in which justice inheres as guarantee for the soldier's payment in kind. Thus his pledge to "strike at Athens" (3.5.119) in order to rectify the wronged soldier and the losses he has incurred allows Alcibiades to transform himself—now a hurt body or debased bounty—into a form of nonfungible property that may be held in trust.

As the play's dramatic focus on Timon's banishment gives way to Alcibiades's conquest of Athens, *Timon* with its parallel intrigues, grand speeches, and ironic climax careens toward becoming a revenge tragedy. Ultimately, however, by effectively transmuting what appears to be the quasi-legal brutality of debt bondage into a state-sanctioned means of affixing relative worth, the play successfully resolves the conflict between Alcibiades and the Senate. Confronted in the final scene by Alcibiades, who now heads up a contingency of armed rebels, the Senate admits that the desire for revenge is a perverse form of appetency or "hunger for that food which nature loathes" (5.4.32–33). Like a mode of distributive justice whereby bounty can only be possessed through use, revenge is likened to destructive feasting. Within the course of surprisingly few interchanges Alcibiades miraculously transforms insatiable, self-consuming revenge from a mode of intemperance into a means of restitution. He is suddenly willing to spare Athens. Importantly, though, he does not cast down his weapon, but vows to "use the olive with my sword, / Make war breed peace, make peace stint war, make each / Prescribe to other as each other's leech" (5.4.82–84). The word "breed" serves as a corrective to both "use" and its euphemism "nourishment" as Alcibiades forges an imagistic connection between retributive and rectificatory justice by investing his sword with generative properties. His formulation recommends debt bondage as ameliorative, and he forswears the annihilations wrought by the violence of use.

In the end *Timon* successfully reconfigures revenge as redemption, an association that is anticipated by the play's final crisis of valuation in which the exiled Timon discovers a pile of gold. Hovering beyond the bounds of society, Timon the outcast roams the wilderness cut off from the social and cultural networks of daily life and bereft of intimacy and affiliation. If there is an afterlife to ostracism, something that remains once one has become civilly dead, then it is the opportunity to transcend the cycle of credit. Timon is finally beyond of all systems of reckoning that conflate reward and punishment. Yet the cancellation of all bonds anticipates the cancellation of life. Not owing positions Timon as separate, a disposition that can lead only to his eventual extinction. Debt, it turns out, is the pretext of belonging insofar as it suspends equality between two parties who cannot walk away from one another so long as they desire restitution. While debt may be deferred justice, once exchange is brought to completion, there is no longer any need for relationship. Arguably, we are never so human as when we are most in need. Timon asserts what may be taken as the creed of the misanthrope, phrased as a mock prayer to pagan gods, when he declares his hatred for humanity:

> The gods confound—hear me, you good gods all—
> The Athenians both within and out the wall;
> And grant, as Timon grows, his hate may grow
> To the whole race of mankind, high and low! Amen. (4.1.37–41)

Rabelais too identifies debt as the web of humanity in the third book of his mock epic *Gargantua and Pantagruel*, entitled "In Praise of Debt." Once humans no longer owe anything to one another, Rabelais explains, the world becomes an uninhabitable environment where "None will save another; it will be no good, a man shouting Help! Fire! I'm drowning! Murder! Nobody will come to help him. Why? Because he has lent nothing: and no one owes him anything. . . . And, he would lend nothing either hereafter. In short, Faith, Hope, and Charity would be banished from this world."[56] No longer subject to the logic of the bond, Timon is dislodged from the entanglements of commitment, shared history, and collective responsibility.

Without a referential system by which its worth may be mediated, Timon discovers that gold, now merely a mineral of the earth, is useless. To paraphrase Henry Peacham, it lies "so heaped up" it "is like dung, which while it lieth upon an heap doth no good, but dispersed and cast abroad maketh fields fruitful."[57] Timon's paean to gold seems to mark the apogee of his madness as the play divorces this character from its own logic whereby it has by this point persuasively demonstrated that monetary worth is socially constructed. In digging the earth for nourishing roots, Timon discovers only a monument to the endpoint of a system of justice in exchange that inspires insatiable hunger, which is in turn likened to both cannibalism and starvation. Yet the pile of gold is the only real property in the play. Even as the gold conjures potential possessors—bandits, poets, and painters swarm Timon's hoard—only Alcibiades can extract its productive power by apprehending it as a reserve deposit and thus as an investment for future stability. Alcibiades animates the original sense of the word "pay," derived from the French word "payer," which comes from the Latin *pacare*. Here to pay means to pacify or to appease, as in to give someone something precious in order to restore peace or "come to terms with an injured party."[58] At this moment, the play gestures toward a functioning economy as one not hampered by the uncertainty of coinage or the debasement of things. Rather it is buttressed by the logic of investment that advances a notion of value neither dependent on exchange nor threatened by waste. Even as the play discredits those who naïvely invest in the notion of intrinsic worth and disavows the punitive force of the bond, it heralds a moderate approach to debt bondage, whereby economic agents mutually agree to place their trust in collateral that guarantees a future return.

Only the Alcibiades's plot can provide proper dramatic closure since it is through this character that the play is able to transform revenge into proportionate return by transmuting an eye-for-an-eye structure into a viable model of profit. Like Timon, Alcibiades is initially abandoned by the city that he served faithfully. Unlike Timon, however, he is able to rescue that same city and reinstate its social framework by animating the value of gold he finds by investing it in the bodies of his soldiers. Because Alcibiades functions as an agent of reform, the play does not end with a stage littered with corpses. Instead of carnage we are presented with a standing army and ensured the meting out of "regular justice" (5.4.61). The installation of a new regime promises that all violations—including forfeiture, we may assume—will be "remedied to [the senate's] public laws" (5.4.62–63). *Timon*'s resolution thus puts the onus of the proper management of debt onto the now-reformed state, since without any reliable means to ground value, only public restitution can curtail private vengeance. By the play's end economic exigency and equity are united. Bounty, associated with Timon, the one who borrows, has now been transformed into deserts, associated with Alcibiades, the one who pays for what is owed.[59] This is a model of paying back that represents not the excesses of getting even or the misanthropy of squaring accounts, but rather repaying as a means of rejoining humanity through the promise of indefinite return.

Conclusion

Timon of Athens is a play perhaps best known for Marx's discussion of its protagonist's paean to the power of gold. Money in this play, as Marx observed, is "the bond of all *bonds*"—"the true *agent of separation* and the true *cementing agent*."[60] But even before Marx, Aristotle commented on money's ability to function first and foremost as an instrument of justice, bonding each one to another and in this way keeping society intact. As Aristotle observed, "in associations that are based on mutual exchange, the just in this sense constitutes the bond that holds the association together."[61] This bond is money, which for Aristotle "acts like a measure: it makes goods commensurate and equalizes them. For just as there is no community without exchange, there is no exchange without equality and no equality without commensurability."[62] While Aristotle and Marx were attuned to the ability of money to foster social cohesion, as well as foment social disruption, their observations do not encompass the scope of *Timon*'s insights into the necessity of the bond and the ethical paradoxes its efficacy engendered. The lending of money in early modern England seemed to revolve around relations between persons, yet in the eyes of the law, loans executed an exchange of property, which produced new understandings of and dilemmas around property-in-person. The intentionality of lender and borrower alike, as *Timon* shows, was irrelevant in a world driven by an inexorable logic of satisfaction. Thus *Timon* is less invested in anatomizing character failing than in exposing the ways in which an economy of accumulated obligation challenged character consistency, exemplified by the problem of the two Timons—a problem that reverberates with that of the two Henslowes. At a juncture at which juridical tradition found its tenets strained by expansive networks of lending and borrowing, the rift between the bond's contradictory ideas of justice and the practical need for politic credit relations is played out in a drama that stands as a glaring example of *genera mista*. The bond must serve the purposes of commensurability but it can only do so by establishing a notion of proportionate reciprocity and repressing ideas of exact exchange. *Timon* has been identified variously as a tragedy, morality play, and satire. The one dramatic form, surprisingly, that has not been associated with *Timon* is the subgenre of revenge tragedy.[63] Reading *Timon* as a botched revenge tragedy, however, illuminates its awareness of both the terrifying and productive potential of debt, as the play explores how each may be managed by working through the problem of possession through use and competing forms of justice in exchange. In its magical resolution, this play belies the notion that *lex talion* had in this period given way to compensation systems based on state-delivered justice. Rather we are shown the ways that money and blood continued to coexist as options for recompense, so long as revenge and discharge of debt were articulated in related idioms.

Chapter 2

Shylock and the Slaves: Owing and Owning in *The Merchant of Venice*

> O, these naughty times
> Puts bars between the owners and their rights!
> And so, though yours, not yours.
>
> — Portia, *The Merchant of Venice*, 3.2.18–20

Since the publication of Walter Cohen's groundbreaking essay on *The Merchant of Venice*, scholars have cited its keen observations about the relationship between dramatic literature and the historical foundations of market societies. Critics rarely, however, refer to Cohen's contention that "the crisis" of *The Merchant of Venice* "arises not from [Shylock's] insistence on usury, but from his refusal of it."[1] Cohen's deft diacritical reading of Shakespeare's play as a mediation of the anxieties and opportunities of nascent global capitalism figures Shylock as an ambivalent avatar of new economic formations. For Cohen, this moneylender exhibits a surprising lack of business acumen when he insists upon "the penalty for default on the bond [which] is closer to folklore than to capitalism." The bond's "stipulation for a pound of flesh," he writes, "is hardly what one would expect from *homo economicus*."[2] The only logical explanation for Shylock's preference is that his craving for vengeance has overtaken his desire for profit. Shylock's hatred of Antonio in particular and Christians in general, Cohen and his successors suggest, make him an irrational market participant.

This chapter revisits the question of why Shylock chooses flesh over money in order to show that his decision is neither fiscally irrational nor driven by personal vendetta. In a juridical context in which flesh and money were regarded as comparable forms of property, to distinguish between them was to pose a false dichotomy. In the final analysis Shylock's insistence on Antonio's flesh may not serve as a reliable indicator of murderous intent. It does, however, remind viewers of his right to destroy that which he owns, and thus sheds light on an irresolvable tension at the heart of a culture of credit in which forfeiture and the practice of using human beings as collateral were all too common.[3] When we attend closely to the legal and economic frameworks shaping Shylock's situation, what becomes clear is that the dramatic energy of this play is fueled not by the machinations of a predatory usurer but by the desperation of an insolvent debtor.[4]

The monetary instrument that stands at the center of *The Merchant of Venice* would have been immediately familiar to members of Shakespeare's early seventeenth-century audience. Antonio and Shylock enlist the services of a notary to assist them in devising a debt bond, which, as Shylock explains, must be honored "on such a day, in such a place, [with] such sum or sums as are expressed in the condition," or "the forfeit [will] be nominated" (1.3.137–41). In other words, if Antonio repays the loan on time, he will be exempt from the bond's penalty.[5] In the early modern period, this kind of lending was, as Craig Muldrew has shown, "by far the most important form of indebtedness after sales and service credit,—certainly much more important than moneylending."[6] Usury, it turns out, has been our preoccupation, and it has circumscribed the parameters of inquiry and delimited the assumptions we bring to bear about the kinds of monetary and moral economies *The Merchant of Venice* explores. Conditional debt bonds were all but ubiquitous as was the occurrence of default.

The Merchant of Venice's fascination with bonds and the difficulty of honoring them may be gleaned from the frequency with which the word "forfeit" appears. A term inextricably connected with both the words "justice" and "mercy" throughout the play, "forfeit" appears in fifteen different contexts. Shakespeare calls our attention to "forfeit" at the moment of the signing of the bond, in which "the forfeit [to] be nominated" is "an equal pound of [Antonio's] fair flesh" (1.3.140–42). In Act 3, Antonio stresses that he "oft delivered" Shylock's borrowers from their "forfeitures" (3.3.22). Shylock is depicted as insisting on his "forfeiture," "justice," and "his bond" (3.2.281). Yet when the word next appears, "forfeit" is no longer distinguished from "justice" and the "bond" but serves as a synonym for both. At certain moments, forfeit becomes synonymous with the borrower's flesh, as for instance when the Duke urges Shylock to exercise mercy and "loose" or waive his right to "the forfeiture" (4.1.24). Shylock, however, is determined "to cut the forfeiture from that bankrupt there" (4.1.122). By the end of the trial Shylock's wealth is "forfeit to the state" (4.1.360). In the final act, the characters are safely ensconced in Belmont and putatively insulated from the commercialism of Venice and the legalism of the court, yet Portia discovers that her ring has been forfeited. The ring plot is not resolved until Antonio pledges his soul as "forfeit" (5.1.250).

The play's interest in forfeiture situates it squarely in a society confronted by a significant increase in the number of debt suits. This flurry of legislative activity was less reflective of an expanding population of vengeful creditors than the predictable outcome of more and more people borrowing on bond. Derived from the medieval Latin *foris factum*, the word "forfeit" from the late fifteenth century onward meant the sum of money one paid as a penalty for committing a crime. By the beginning of the seventeenth century, "forfeit" was becoming a common enough term that the word had evolved from a noun into a verb, as it came to refer to the act of failing to meet the terms of an economic obligation (*OED*). In this period, suits based on forfeiture accounted for over 80 percent of the cases brought before the court of Common Pleas; by 1640, suits of debt would account for 88 percent of Common Pleas and 80 percent of King's Bench cases.[7] By 1650, attorney and chronic debtor William Leach would petition Parliament on behalf of the 20,000 men and women languishing in London's prisons, the majority of whom were debtors.[8]

Forfeiture was a serious matter that portended the violation of the debtor's liberty and, in some cases, his death. The debt bond's conditional clause stated that the creditor had the right to seek remedy in the event of nonpayment if he lent freely, meaning without interest. In turn, when a debtor failed to meet his obligation, he understood that he was no longer exempt from the bond's penal condition. While an unsatisfied creditor could take action "either against the body of the defendant; or against his goods and chattels," as Muldrew stresses, in this period most actions were taken against the debtor's person.[9] The injustice of a system that permitted the creditor to apprehend his debtor on his own initiative, without the benefit of a jury trial, led Francis Bacon to conclude that only the most hard-hearted lenders refused interest: "As for mortgaging, or pawning, it will little mend the matter; for either men will not take the pawns without use, or if they do, they will look precisely for the forfeiture. I remember a cruel monied man in the country that would say, the devil take this usury, it keeps us from forfeitures or mortgages and

Bonds."[10] Once imprisoned, the debtor, like all other prisoners, was expected to pay his way. Insolvent debtors who could not afford the mandatory fees for housing, food, or even a mattress, bed linens, and candle tallow, were, according to one writer, "cast into utter darkness": "destitute of libertie, meat, drink . . . and clothing to their backs, lying in filthie strawe, and lothsome dung, wursse then anie Dogge, . . . wishing and thyrsting after death to set them at libertie, and loose them from their shackles, gives, and iron bands."[11] Unless someone came to the debtor's aid, imprisonment was perpetual. The destitute relied on scraps from the almsbasket and were housed in an open dirt pit, known as the "Hole," where they would likely die of starvation or "gaol-fever," which was typhus, a common epidemic spread by lice.[12]

Despite the difficulties people faced in meeting their obligations, the bond was fast becoming the monetary instrument most commonly utilized by borrowers for sums from a few shillings to hundreds of pounds.[13] The popularity of the debt bond stemmed from its attractiveness as an alternative to usury, allowing those with little or no ready cash access to an interest-free loan. Moreover, unlike oral agreements, sealed bonds enabled lenders to seek legal recourse in the event of nonpayment. Bonds were equitable instruments because debt law was a direct outgrowth of property law. Thus the same rules of contract applied to the exchange of money as to land, goods, and animals (which were not distinguished by common law).

The idea of money as a nonfungible form of property, like land or chattels, meant that loans on bond could not be negotiated through either substitution or exchange. Here, debt parted conceptual ways with usury. In contradistinction to debt, the usurious transaction was an all-or-nothing proposition because in charging interest, the usurer acknowledged that money was a fungible form of property. That usury initiated the transfer of ownership, rather than the leasing of something, was based on Aquinas's definition of usury, which English common law absorbed, as *mutuum* or mutation. In essence, a usurious loan entailed giving away one's property so that another could consume it.[14] Aquinas and the scholastic thinkers objected to charging interest since the lender was, in effect, asking the borrower to pay for something that by definition the borrower would use up. Unlike the one-time payment of a luxury tax, for instance, the establishment of a perpetual, escalating charge for the right to use that which at a certain point no longer existed seemed patently immoral. This perspective underwrites the fifteenth-century statute devised to regulate the rate of usury such that lending would remain a profitable enterprise so long as the lender was perceived as exercising discretion in taking "for the same lone any thing more besides or above the money lente."[15]

The conception of money as nonfungible property, however, posed its own problems around use. So long as the creditor retained ownership over what he loaned, he also held onto the *jus abutendi*, the right to abuse or waste his property. The notion of absolute ownership, which Blackstone defined as "that sole and despotic dominion which one man claims and exercises over the external things of the world, in total exclusion of the right of any other individual in the universe," was defined by fee-simple in land.[16] In an agrarian context, dominion included the prerogative to do whatever one wished with one's assets. As Blackstone acknowledged, "if a man be the absolute tenant in fee-simple . . . he may commit whatever waste his own discretion may prompt him to, without being impeachable or accountable for it to anyone."[17]

When the property in question was money, unregulated waste profited no one and threatened social welfare. For this reason, a functioning credit economy had to navigate between the taint of use, on the one hand, and reckless abuse, on the other. A preferable alternative was the logic of investment, whereby value resided neither in exchange nor use, but in future return. By encouraging networks of dependents and co-investors, the adjudication of lending and borrowing promoted an ideal of collective possession. This shared imaginary of profit was in keeping with popular understandings of possession as always partial in nature. As legal scholar David Seipp explains, in early modern England "one did not say 'this is my property,' as we use the term now. Rather, one said 'I have property in it' or 'the property of it is to (or with) me.'"[18] Here the language of trust, in which multiple owners of a plot of land had simultaneous stock in a given property, provided a conceptual framework for an arrangement in which each economic agent was accorded the right to enjoy the "fruits" of a loan, *jus fruendi*, over time. The structural arrangement of debt bondage, *The Merchant of Venice* shows, mirrored an arrangement of second- and third-party possession of land known as *usufruct*. By the middle of the seventeenth century John Locke would come to identify *usufruct* as the righteous response to the morally dubious aspects of property ownership, even as he and others championed the tenets of possessive individualism.[19] *Usufruct*, with its discrete apportioning, was the earthly working out of a celestial order in which God, the "proprietor of the whole world," entrusted men with all they possessed.[20] Thus even as individuals were coming to recognize the benefits of absolute property, they were exhorted to remember that all men were second and third possessors, insofar as "man's propriety in the creatures is nothing but the liberty to use them."[21] Debtor and creditor benefitted from the connection between debt and property when credit transactions recognized both parties as not only having participated in a transfer of goods but also as having a shared interest in the loan that they cultivated, as they would in the same plot of land, herd of domestic animals, or crop.

Reading *The Merchant of Venice* as a debt play, rather than as a usury play, does not merely offer an important historical corrective to the tendency to conflate these distinct monetary forms. It also elucidates the ways that this play is less interested in the sin of usury than in the intricacies of use as it works through the complexities of ownership and its attendant problem of waste that bore immediate relevance in an expanding credit economy marked by a rise in debt suits. In an effort to sort through the controversial aspects of possession in debt, Shakespeare's play pitches the issue in its highest key by dramatizing the moment at which the body of the debtor stands in for the monetary loan. At this instance, an ideal of ethical ownership becomes crucial, as the play poses the question of what sort of property Antonio's body should be and, concomitantly, what kinds of possession it may entail.

The decision of the trial in *The Merchant of Venice* hinges on the extent to which the bond emerges as a legitimate alternative to both usury and dominion. Thus the debtor's body becomes the proving ground of the bond's ability to invoke theological precepts of the origins of possession, which observe the sanctity of human life, while at the same time support the state's investment in penalizing the insolvent. As Seipp explains, the case of the human pledge was counterintuitive in common law jurisprudence: "Notes of arguments on hypothetical cases mooted in the Inner Temple in the 1490s record law students or lawyers speaking of lords having property in the bodies of their villeins and of guardians having property in the bodies of their wards. Nonetheless, it is fair to say that persons themselves . . . did not form a paradigm or even a noticeable instance of the language of 'property' in the courtroom."[22] Yet the occasion of forfeiture strained the law's elegant distinctions between fungible and nonfungible property, as well as between ownership and use. Debt was considered a "real" action, one founded on property (*in rem super proprietat*) rather than founded on possession (*super possessione*), because the bond guaranteed restitution and thus offered the creditor surety that usury could not.[23] Nevertheless, though the remedy for forfeiture was recuperative, in reality no court could (or would) aid the creditor in *rei vindicatio* or in locating the particular "*thyng*," for instance, the actual ducats that had been lent. Still, the law maintained that the debtor who failed to meet his obligation be punished for unlawfully detaining his creditor's property, which, of course, he had no way of recovering. The dilemma of forfeiture could only be resolved if the debtor's collateral functioned as an equivalent to the original loan. But what did this mean when the creditor retained the right to waste his property, which in this case was the debtor's person? *The Merchant of Venice* is driven by this question as it explores the circumstances under which a creditor may or may not possess his debtor, as well as the social, political, and theological implications of this conundrum.

Cattle and Chattel

The complexities of ownership in the case of debt come to the fore at the initial meeting between Shylock and Antonio, at which Shylock inexplicably narrates the Old Testament story of Jacob's industrious management of his uncle's sheep. By analyzing Shylock's description of Jacob's ingenious animal husbandry through the lens of Aristotle's discussion of usury as the unnatural breeding of money, readers are inclined to regard Laban's ewes and rams as the gold and silver coins that Shylock imagines Jacob breeding for profit.[24] This story may also be interpreted as a parable of possession, illustrative of the concurrent but discrete entitlements that underwrote debt transactions. While the Laban scenario is typically read as a dramatic digression, upon closer inspection it appears to be concerned with the difference between having and using property. In this respect, it contributes to early seventeenth-century disputes over compromised or graduated ownership that bore directly on debt jurisprudence as an outgrowth of property law. One person's harvesting crops in another's field was one of the most common controversies confronting lawyers struggling to determine whether property in grain, for example, was affected when another person cultivated or altered that thing through his own industry, for instance, by expanding the crop or using the grain to make malt. Puzzling over what it meant to simultaneously have and not have property in something displaced or transmuted, early modern common lawyers drew liberally upon Roman law and theological debates on the origins of possession.[25]

In relaying this Genesis story, Shylock too calls on biblical exegesis to aid him in the vexed issue of *muem et tuum* in lending money. The bible's relevance lay, however, not in its providing a directive for justifying ownership but rather in its tacit recommendation of human law as a supplement to God's in determining property rights. As Tudor lawyer Edmund Plowden wrote, the perspective of English common law was that "God committed all worldly things to the order and disposal of men, and so while God made men lords of the earth and possessors of all things in it, just how much of the earth and of the things therein one man should have, and how much another, God left to be ascertained and settled by mankind, by laws to be made by them for that purpose."[26] The Laban tale is thus at once an appeal to the "natural" acquisition of property, the myth that God originally left property equally to all persons, and an argument for human intervention in deciding its possession.[27]

For Shylock, Laban and his ewes provide a vehicle to explicate the difference between a borrower who takes a loan on interest and one who signs onto a debt bond where ownership is acquired by degrees. The sheep, which under certain circumstances could assume the status of fungible property, would be categorized as nonfungibles as part of Laban's estate. Their status is confirmed by their method of transfer, as Laban and Jacob devise what Shylock explains was a "compromise" (1.3.69), or a written bond (*OED*). Through this bond, Laban entrusts Jacob the right of use. In turn Jacob receives partial "hire" or wages (1.3.71) and is permitted the profits from only the "streaked and pied" or "parti-colored" lambs (1.3.70). As one who holds the animals under a lease, and who thus has "good property for a time," Jacob is obligated to be a "constructive trustee," who accounts for the profits received from a given property but whose primary duty is to conserve and protect it.[28]

The conditions of possession that determine Jacob's arrangement render him a third possessor, as Shylock indicates at the monologue's opening when he explains that Jacob was "the third possessor; ay, he was the third" (1.3.65), someone with rights to enjoy the property of another for a limited duration, with the obligation of preserving it. While Jacob may have been the third possessor of the birthright of Abraham, as this line is typically glossed, he is also the third possessor of his uncle's chattel, since Laban owns what he has in trust from God. This tripartite arrangement will be mirrored by Antonio and Shylock's agreement, in which Shylock, like Laban, owns what has in trust from another. In this case, the first possessor is Shylock's kinsman Tubal who entrusts Shylock with the staggering amount of three thousand ducats.[29] As second possessors, Laban and Shylock receive what they have without interest; in turn they prove to be good shepherds of their resources. They neither hoard nor consume their property but animate its productive potential by leasing it out. In theory, Antonio too stands to benefit if he follows this model, since by entrusting the money to Bassanio, Bassanio may win Portia and then satisfy his creditors.

Shylock completes the conceptual frame of his transaction with Antonio by reminding him of the double meaning of the word "interest." In response to Antonio's insistence that Jacob took "interest" (1.3.66), Shylock impatiently replies that Jacob did "not take interest, not as *you* would say / Directly interest" (1.3.67–68, emphasis mine). By 1600, "interest" was not only the word for money paid on a loan but also the legal term for having title in property (*OED*). Shylock implies that while Jacob had an "interest" in his uncle's property, in the colloquial sense of the word, he did not have "direct interest" in it, as exemplified by title. Shakespeare reminds his audience of the embedded nature of their own property relations, since early modern landowners did not have direct interest in land. As tenants in fee, English landowners were subject to all the public duties incumbent on freeholders, but in the event that they did not have a mature male heir, their land devolved to the Crown. What they owned was an abstract entity called an estate that the law defined as an allotted period of "time in land."[30] Thus, Antonio may borrow Shylock's money, but as a third possessor what he has in the final analysis is an abstraction—a loan—an allotted period of time during which he may have use of the money.

In advancing a notion of graduated ownership, the English legal system eschewed, as Seipp explains, "the image of one individual owner, or even one family, excluding all others and taking all increase from a parcel of land [which] would have been a vast oversimplification, and probably an unrecognizable image for holders of large or small parcels."[31] Concurrent but separate stakes in the same nonfungible property that was the hallmark of property law subtended a credit system in which debtors and creditors could indeed "thrive" (1.3.85) so long as, in the words of Shylock, "thrift" was considered a "blessing" (1.3.80). Here Shylock's reference to thrift evokes not merely the general virtue of marshalling one's resources but also to the specific notion that as co-investors neither he nor Antonio should abuse the property they have in common. Indeed, because they have rights in it, they also have duties to perform toward this property, and their common legal bond persuades them to preserve their assets for future tenants. In this way, economic obligations produce "merry bonds" (1.3.85) insofar as they are premised on the legal distinction between "use" as interest and "use" as trust. As Francis Bacon emphasizes, through devising a bond the owner of some thing signs onto an agreement "that the other shall have, hold . . . [and] take the profits thereof *for a time certaine*."[32]

Despite the pains Shylock takes in outlining the property status of his loan, a delineation incumbent upon the notion of *usufruct*, Antonio's failure to meet his obligation pressures an ideal of ethical ownership based on second- and third-party possession. The moment of forfeiture gives rise to a crisis that generates a host of political, theological, and practical questions about the status of the insolvent debtor's body, since the bond's condition dictates that Shylock owns what is owed to him. On the face of it, the remedy for forfeiture need not present any such problems. As legal historian A. W. B. Simpson notes, "The penal bond for securing performances was a sophisticated form of self-pledge, and Shylock's bond with its forfeit of a pound of flesh neatly illustrates the fact that the best pledge of all is the body of the contractor, which in early law he could have used as security."[33] Once the case comes to trial, Balthasar is the first to admit, "this bond is forfeit, / And lawfully by this the Jew may claim / A pound of flesh" (4.1.225–27), acknowledging before the court that Shylock's claim over Antonio is not a deviation from debt jurisprudence but an amplification of its proprietary logic. As Balthasar emphasizes, "the intent and purpose of the law hath full relation to the penalty" (4.1.243).

While the bond's penal condition may present a clear legal argument, Antonio's fate is not simply a monetary matter; it is also a moral one. By this point, the play has established that as collateral Antonio's body is, like the original monetary loan, nonfungible property. As Shylock admits, while that body is alienable, it is "not so estimable, profitable neither, / As flesh of muttons, beefs, or goats" (1.3.158–59). Antonio's own sense of his body as thing that may be owned but not used is confirmed by his self-description as "a tainted wether of the flock" (4.1.114), whereby he depicts himself as a castrated ram. As a nonfungible form of property, over which the lender retains ownership, it appears that it is well within Shylock's rights to destroy him. As anthropologist David Graeber points out, cattle served as money in ancient cultures not because people used oxen as a medium of exchange, but because they measured the value of things in accordance with that which was one of the most significant offerings to the gods. Cattle represented absolute value because they were destructible.[34]

Shylock argues his case strenuously when he compares Antonio to "asses . . . dogs and mules" (4.1.89) and insists that flesh "is mine, and I will have it" (4.1.92). In an attempt to justify his prerogative, Shylock is forced to engage an analogy, which defines ownership as dominium:

> You have among you many a purchased slave,
> Which, like your asses and your dogs and mules,
> You use in abject and in slavish parts,

> Because you bought them. Shall I say to you,
> "Let them be free, marry them to your heirs!
> Why sweat they under burdens? Let their beds
> Be made as soft as yours, and let their palates
> Be seasoned with such viands?" You will answer
> "The slaves are ours." So do I answer you:
> The pound of flesh which I demand of him
> Is dearly bought, is mine, and I will have it. (4.1.88–92)

Here Shylock points out that while the slaves are useful, their value resides in their "abject" and "slavish" treatment, or their abuse, which, arguably, over time leads to their wasting. Importantly, what you get when you purchase a slave is the right to dispose of him in any way that pleases you. Hence, no one can tell a master what to do with his own assets, for instance, by insisting that his slaves be permitted to sleep on soft beds, eat fine food, and enjoy conjugal pleasure.

The connection Shylock forges between the defaulted debtor and the slave has rhetorical force and speaks to an association alive and well for those watching Shakespeare's play. In *The Orator*, a series of late sixteenth-century exercises for law students translated from French into English, the penalty for forfeiture reduces the debtor to a slave, since once his body is bound, he is beholden to a creditor who will commit him "unto a most lothsome prison or unto an intolerable slaverie."[35] In his *Debt Book*, Henry Wilkinson likewise reminds readers, "It is a servile thing to be indebted . . . By debt a man's state and person are in a manner mancipated to the lender."[36] Forfeiture called up the specter of chattel bondage because of its exploitation of the insolvent debtor's person. Shylock's comparison between the insolvent debtor and the slave, however, obfuscates the question of ownership and use, since slaves were and were not considered property, and, more particularly, could be used on legal grounds but not used up on moral ones.

Unlike the crime of debt, the crime of slavery was marked by a violation of God's organic, nontransferable property—it made that which should not be alienable exchangeable. Yet Shylock's claim resonates because it acknowledges the law's ability to make and unmake persons. No one in early modern England would deny the humanity of slaves, even as historically the common law proved capacious enough to define chattel as including both animals and slaves. The debtor, too, occupied a nuanced legal status, one that called to mind historical precedents in which property and personhood jostled for primacy. Importantly, instead of simply relegating debtors to the position of slaves, the play establishes a metonymic relationship between the two, as their perceived lack of resemblance allows them to be plotted on a conceptual continuum. While it may be inappropriate to compare debtors to slaves, a wayward merging of these two figures keeps both in sight and begs the question: under what circumstances may those who are treated as property (the defaulted debtor) still be regarded as having property (in themselves)? Once the figures of the debtor and the slave are put into tension, we are inclined to consider their propinquity, not merely in legal but also in metaphysical terms. Even as the play dismisses this comparison, at the same time it animates it, keeping the debtor and the slave suspended in approximate likeness. By considering both indebtedness and enslavement as extreme states, Shakespeare raises the unsettling possibility that both stand as exceptions to the sacrosanct principle of civil liberty.

The persuasive energy of Shylock's comparison of Antonio to a slave may also be fueled by retributive anger. Earlier in the play, Shylock admonished Antonio for humiliating him by "spit[ing] upon [his] Jewish gabardine" in retaliation "for the use for that which is mine *own*" (1.3.103–4, emphasis mine). From Shylock's perspective, Antonio erroneously assumes that Shylock's money is a fungible form of property, which he uses but does not own. Antonio's inability or refusal to recognize Shylock as a proprietor, in effect, strips Shylock of the entitlements that this may entail. Shylock responds to this misprision by performing himself as Antonio sees him—as a dispossessed person. Thus he takes on the persona of a slave and mockingly describes himself as forced to grovel before his clients, to "bend low, and in a bondman's key with bated breath . . . whisper humbleness" (1.3.114–15).

On a more practical level, by likening Antonio to chattel, Shylock shifts our attention from his status as a moneylender to the situation of the desperate debtor. By refusing offers of monetary compensation and insisting upon his forfeit, Shylock asserts his authority as a creditor, one who owns what he loans, and thus makes strides toward preventing his witnesses from perceiving *him* as a slave, as Antonio has done. Yet, as will become clear in the second half of the trial, his persistent demand for Antonio's flesh stresses the ethos of qualified ownership underwriting debt bondage. There is no question that Shylock's claim to Antonio's person is legitimate, and its very legitimacy necessitates that the state devise an extralegal intervention to check the unsatisfied creditor by granting him partial possession of what is his due. Even as Shylock may own Antonio, as will come to light, he can never possess him, as long as possession implies use. At the same time, his ownership can never be absolute insofar as absolute ownership always threatens waste. Debt bondage, this play shows, brought new urgency to the state's role in preserving inalienable right to life, even as the state paradoxically continued to alienate the debtor from his own person by imposing indefinite incarceration as the penalty for default.

Ultimately, Shylock pursues the wrong line of reasoning not because he is inhumane but because he deviates from the logic of investment, which recognizes value not in the exchange or destruction of property but its imagined future profit. In this respect, Shylock, ironically, overlooks the very conceptual framework that could plausibly rationalize an extended analogy between debtor and slave, insofar as the bodies of each are construed as holding value in reserve that may be redeemed at a later date. Instead, he offers a comparison that would have seemed dubious even by Shakespeare's audience's standards. By the early seventeenth century, the institution of slavery within England was more an evocative concept, in which the slave marked the endpoint of a continuum of mastery and servitude. As such, the slave was a figure that drew attention to social processes of inequity, rather than a representative of a particular fixed status.[37] As early as 1555, Africans served as domestics in England and worked in wealthy households throughout the seventeenth and eighteenth centuries. While African domestics, unlike English servants, were "bought and sold . . . as merchandise," English law was loath to declare that a master had property in his slaves, even as common law courts protected his rights over their labor.[38] The medieval system of *villeinage*, which recognized the bondservant as part of the manor lord's property or *demesnes*, gave way to serfdom, an institution in which the serf was bound to live and labor on land belonging to his lord to whom he rendered services.[39] With the exception of foreign captives and those subject to penal bondage, all persons living within England continued to be regarded as first and foremost subjects of the monarch, even if their rights were curtailed by the custom of the manor, or the household or guild, where they served. This understanding of English custom informs Blackstone's assertion that "pure and proper slavery does not, nay cannot subsist in England; such I mean, whereby an absolute and unlimited power is given to the master over the life and fortune of the slave." [40] The body of the debtor, like that of the slave, is conceived as *quasi* property, a nodal point of various legal relations and social networks, and thus something over which neither debtor nor creditor can be considered the owner in any absolute sense.

The Jew Is Forfeit

The courtroom conflict between Shylock and Portia has been seen as representative of a debate between justice and mercy or between the letter and spirit of the law, even as a dramatization of the contrasting judicial approaches of the more equitable Court of Chancery, on the one hand, and the stricter Common Law courts, on the other.[41] But critics have bypassed the immediate dilemma informing the disagreement between Shylock and Balthasar: what does it mean to own what one is owed when the thing in question is a human being, or what legal scholars deem "an animated gage"?[42] Although Shylock regards this to be a transparent question that will yield a straightforward answer, his assumption is shown to be naïve; this is hinted at by the etymology of the word "debt," which derived from the Latin *dēbitum*, past participle of *dēbēre*, derived from *de*: from and *habere*: to have, meaning to be away from having or to not have something (*OED*). The word confusingly suggests that the person who took on a debt possessed but did not have that which he had been loaned, while the person who enabled the loan no longer had that which he continued to own. Shylock believes he is now due his forfeit because it never occurs to him that he could own something that he may never have. The second half of the trial takes up this conundrum as it investigates under what conditions ownership may give rise to possession and thus to the civil entitlements propriety implied.

In order to set in motion the terms of this debate, as well as lay the ground for its monumental resolution, the play first establishes that the full enjoyment of civil liberties hinges on fiscal solidity. Indeed, property, proprietary, and personhood appear at first blush to be tightly linked. We are shown Antonio being marched off to debtor's prison and are left with the impression that even if Shylock relinquished his claim to his forfeit, Antonio would nonetheless remain incarcerated, having defaulted to various creditors "who grow cruel" (3.2.313–14). The drastic state of Antonio's reputation is confirmed by Tubal, who reports of Antonio's "divers" unsatisfied creditors (3.1.84–85). While much critical attention has been devoted to the specificities of Antonio's bond with Shylock, little has been made of Antonio's general state of insolvency at the play's opening, at which point he is *already* "without money or commodity" (1.1.177); all of his ships have "miscarried" yet again (3.2.313). Antonio's situation would probably not be surprising to those audience members who understood that the impressive amount of capital needed to fund cross-oceanic expeditions made merchants notorious debtors.[43] As economic historian A. G. Frank emphasizes, the "unprecedented expansion of credit: loans, securities, [and] bonds" and the predominance of "negotiable obligations" meant that the merchant-borrower often had only his person to pledge as collateral.[44] Antonio enters into the arrangement that he does with Shylock, after all, because his body is his last remaining asset. While Shylock speaks out of anger, his depiction of Antonio as a credit risk is accurate: he notes that Antonio, like a spendthrift, "hath squandered" many "other ventures" (1.3.16). Later, Shylock aptly identifies Antonio as a "bankrupt [and] a prodigal" (3.1.33).

At the play's opening, Bassanio's liberty is also threatened as he too faces forfeiture on several outstanding bonds. Simply put, he is not merely in debt, he is destitute. Having been "left . . . gaged" (1.1.129), Bassanio, as this phrase's passive construction suggests, has been forced to pawn all of his remaining property, resulting in his having "disabled [his] estate" (1.1.122). Antonio is not Bassanio's only creditor; as Bassanio admits, "To you, Antonio, I owe the *most*, in money and in love" (1.1.130, emphasis mine). The prospect of *his* creditors growing cruel—and not simply a desire to purchase apparel to court Portia—creates in Bassanio an urgent need to obtain ready cash. As Bassanio admits, he is desperate to "get clear of all the debts [he] owe[s]" (1.1.133); like Antonio, he finds himself in a situation in which he has only his body to offer as a pledge.

The play amplifies the catastrophic nature of the situation confronting the two debtors by depicting the bond as an instrument of torture. In expressing his resignation to the legitimacy of Shylock's claim, Antonio stoically interprets the bond as a humane hastening of the trajectory of Fortune. In what he believes to be his final words, he comforts Bassanio:

> Grieve not that I am fall'n to this for you,
> For herein Fortune shows herself more kind
> Than is her custom. It is still her use
> To let the wretched man outlive his wealth
> To view with hollow eye and wrinkled brow
> An age of poverty. (4.1.261–66)

Here Antonio juxtaposes Fortune the usurer that habitually but gradually consumes all matter (including the human body) as fungible property and Fortune the creditor that efficaciously executes her right to destroy what she owns, relieving her charge from prolonged suffering.

Antonio's philosophical response to the bond as an instrument that hastens his death is more measured than that of his contemporaries who inhabited the early seventeenth-century stage. In Thomas Middleton's *Michaelmas Term*, a witness to the signing of a debt bond compares observing this activity to watching a condemned man speed up his own death by assisting the executioner in disemboweling him: the debtor is now "Alive, [but] in state and credit executed," as he "help[s] to rip up himself."[45] Devising a bond is likened to a "quart'ring out," and the creditor to "the executioner [who] strides over him [the debtor]," whom with "his own blood writes."[46] Upon realizing that he is "encounter'd / with [the] clamorous demands of debt [and] broken bonds," Shakespeare's Timon perceives his overdue "bills" as long-handled axes that threaten to "knock [him] down" and "cleave [him] to the girdle," "cut [his] heart in sums," let his blood "five thousand drops," and "tear . . . and take" his flesh.[47]

The notion of the bond's proprietary provision as bodily inscribed inspired depictions of it as an instrument of torture, but such an awareness also led to representations of the deed itself as interchangeable with the debtor's body. The debtor Tangle in Thomas Middleton's *The Phoenix*, for instance, regards his bond as "that most dreadful execution" and commands his creditors to "quickly dip your quills in my blood, off with my skin, and write fourteen lines on a side."[48] In *The Merchant of Venice*, Bassanio conflates Antonio's body with the letter he writes that confesses his inability to honor his obligation, a redaction of the metonymic linking of body and bond.[49] He explains to Portia: "Here is a letter lady, / The paper as the body of my friend, / And every word in it a gaping wound / Issuing life-blood" (3.2.261–64).

While dramatic representations of debt bondage traded in the macabre association of the debtor's blood with the ink with which he signed his life away, *The Merchant of Venice* moves beyond this familiar trope, taking up the theological implications of the blood-ink nexus, to cast the debt bond in metaphysical terms. The bond's invocation of ink as blood that heralded its potency "*in terrorem*," this play suggests, presents a means by which to neutralize its destructive energies.[50] For as Balthasar shows, if the bond's ink may be likened to the debtor's blood, his blood is always already ink, as the blood of all Christian debtors binds them to Christ. Here the state intervenes to introduce the decorporalizing logic of equivalence: it recognizes the value of the debtor's body as inhering not in his individual fleshy substance, but in his body's generic function as a placeholder for material and spiritual worth that may be extracted at some later point in time.

The trial advances toward its conclusion once Balthasar succeeds in making a metaphoric substitution where the debtor's body stands not for his bond with his creditor but for his contract with God. The court decrees that coursing through the body that Shylock assumes as his dominium is *Christian* blood, which, for Balthasar, resurrects Antonio as corporate property. Here law and theodicy come together in a shared investment in the fiction of blood as property, a crucial metaphor in defining persons as members of civil society and spiritual communities alike. From a legal perspective, forfeiture of property implied corruption of blood, a negative birthright that blocked inheritance. The law that had the authority to declare one civilly dead, also, however, had the power to bring persons back to life by endowing them or their heirs with renewed "credit or capacity," which could be made inheritable.[51] Thus to be reborn in law was to be restored in blood, whereby one's heirs were allowed to regain the privileges of birth and rank. Balthasar's drop-of-blood stipulation changes the trial's outcome, but its distinctiveness lies not only in its legal inventiveness but also in its peculiar diction. Declaring that "the bond doth give [Shylock] here no *jot* of blood" (4.1.303, emphasis mine), Balthasar engages the quotidian discourse of contract.

At this instance, Shakespeare parts ways from his source, Anthony Munday's 1580 *Zelauto; Or, the Fountayne of Fame*, a play that also features a Jewish creditor and his bond. In *Zelauto*, the judge stymies the creditor when he explains, "It is no reason if you have your bargayne: that you should hinder them with the losse of one droppe of blood."[52] By substituting the word "jot" for "drop," Balthasar situates his listeners in the world of manuscript production. The term "jot" meant "the least letter or written part of any writing" (*OED*). To produce a "jot" was to make "the smallest mark with pen" (*OED*), and to "jot" something down was to "write it down in the briefest and most hasty form" (*OED*). A jot of ink was a scrivener's error and the minute trace of the material production of an official document. By drawing our attention to the inky matter of the bond, and by conflating it with the blood of the insolvent debtor, Balthasar discriminates between earthly and spiritual deeds, as he grants Shylock rights to only one.

The trial's resolution brings us back to the parable of Laban and his ewes, as it turns out that Antonio, a self-described castrated ram, is property in which several parties have concurrent but discrete interests. Shylock, it is determined, is a third, and not a first possessor, as the trial confirms a tripartite view of the individual as compromised of person, body, and soul, with each entity claimed, respectively, by the law, the state, and God. In this way, Christianity automatically repositions any one who assumes dominion over himself as a mere custodian who holds his own body in sacred trust for the benefit of those who have an interest in it. Those who attempt to claim absolute ownership over another Christian are acknowledged as partial owners. This trifurcated vision of humans as apportioned property, moreover, imagines Christ himself as the Ur-creditor. A Pauline interpretation of the crucifixion as divine enslavement—where the sinner is not emancipated by Christ's sacrifice but dies anew in Christ, his new master—underwrites the "classic ransom theory of atonement" that cast all Christians as debtors.[53] As St. Ambrose explains, "Let no one be startled at the word 'creditor,' . . . He [Christ] gave to me a new kind of acquittance, changing my creditor because I had nothing wherewith to pay my debt."[54] Despite the play's invocation of a Pauline perspective, it is the earthly court of equity, more particularly the common law court, that has the authority to ameliorate improperly managed custody.

The judgment is merciful in that it informs the court's decision to advocate for an arrangement that reflects the relation of all Christians to God, who is the first possessor and from whom all believers are *usufructs*, receiving spiritual blessing and material wealth in trust. The bond that opens the trial raises the specter of chattel bondage, as the remedy for debt grants the creditor rights in the person of debtor. Yet it turns out that value is at once grounded in and abstracted from the debtor's body. The deed of trust that closes the trial represents a less violent but no less coercive form of written contract, one that confirms the idea of the forfeit as a kind of investment. Echoing the play's earlier images of the debt bond as an instrument that hastens death, the clerk's order to "draw" the deed (4.1.389) engages a verb that conjures torture and manipulation, as much as drafting. The signing of this final bond makes Shylock "not well" (4.1.391) and ultimately reduces him to silence. As his wealth becomes "forfeit to the state" (4.1.360), Shylock pleads with the judge to "take my life and all!" since to "take my house when you do take the prop / That doth sustain my house. You take my life" (4.1.370–71). Shylock construes his place in Venetian society not by ethnicity or religion but by what he owns, which as the word "prop" suggests, functions as the ballast of his civil existence. His plea indexes an awareness of the tight link between the person and property, as well as his fear that their unhinging will lead to his dispossession and a life of slavery.

Yet even as the outcome of trial is punitive, its judgment does not destroy Shylock, or even reduce him to a state of enslavement. Shylock's ethnicity, it turns out, is by no means a stable marker of either entitlement or dispossession, but rather a dense transfer point for intersecting definitions of insider and outsider. Shylock will not be cast beyond the city walls, a scapegoat that must be purged like Marlowe's Barabas, but instead subjected to a form of "institutionalized marginality" signaled by forced conversion.[55] In keeping with an ideal of ethical ownership, Shylock is granted partial interest in "one half of his goods," while Antonio is given "the other half" of Shylock's property "in use" (4.1.378). If at the beginning of the trial, Shylock the unsatisfied creditor symbolizes the potentially narrow binding powers of economic obligation, by the trial's end, Shylock the *converso* embodies the inclusive underpinnings of a viable network of credit. The converted Shylock will no longer remain segregated from Venetian society, as he is in the first part of the play in which he abhors intermarriage with Christians and maintains distinctive dietary rituals (1.3.27). Rather, his new status as a Christian allows him to assume a productive role in an economy that does not bar him from the contractual privileges of debt bondage but inhibits him from asserting exclusive dominion over God's property. The outcome of the trial, then, is neither *pro* nor *contra* Shylock but, more importantly, an assertion of legal metaphysics that demonstrates the ways that litigation can resurrect persons by recognizing blood as the ur-form of communal property. In restoring Antonio's credit, jurisprudence and faith work in tandem to support the state's investment in a credit economy based on the collective belief in the speculative value of the debtor's body.

Bonds and Bands

As a play that has a notoriously ambivalent relationship to its generic conventions, *The Merchant of Venice* attempts to fulfill its comic contract through the formulaic resolution of matrimony, yet its romantic tone proves unsettling. The final act does not offer a portrait of domestic harmony but rather a troubling disjunction between form and matter, exemplified by Jessica and Lorenzo's litany of ancient lovers' broken vows, the crisis of the misplaced wedding bands, and Antonio's isolation. On the face of it, the contractual arrangement of marriage based on a peculiar combination of mutual consent and hierarchical regulation would seem to offer an ideal solution to the fraught economies of persons and property vexing the play. Yet even as it seems to invest in the legal fallacy of matrimonial domination, the play insistently stages its ongoing interest in the relation between person and property as a problem aggravated by the circumstances of debt. Arguably, Balthasar has a particular stake in the problem of property-in-person not because he/she is Christian or any more ethical than his/her interlocutor, Shylock, but because he *is* a she. Balthasar/Portia is a woman soon to be married and, significantly, an exceptionally wealthy, independent woman poised to be paired with a debtor whose worth, by his own admission, amounts to "worse than nothing" (3.2.258).

Both Bassanio and Portia's father conflate Portia's person with the estate of Belmont. Yet each finds himself frustrated in his respective desires to count her as property over which he has exclusive dominion. Although seventeenth-century members of the aristocracy sealed bonds dictating their daughters' spouses, or left detailed instructions as part of their probate arrangements, domestic tracts in the period argued that limits be placed on patriarchal authority. By the time Shakespeare's play was performed, such directives about a woman's marital choice would have been considered extreme.[56] A more liberal attitude was advocated by those household manuals that compared paternal control in matrimony to the "most unnatural and cruel" demands of slave owners.[57] Fathers who sought to determine the terms of their daughter's marriage, contemporary writers Dod and Cleaver stress, are like men who would "sell their children for gain and lucre . . . and so bring them into bondage."[58]

Just as the notion that a woman was the property of her father was being challenged, so too was the assumption that a wife was owned by her husband. While fathers and potential husbands may have had a claim on a woman's legal persona, they had no rights over her actual person. David Seipp emphasizes that not only were married women not considered property, but a woman's interests in property, albeit limited, could not be denied altogether. Probate evidence from the period indicates that women had more control over disposition of land and chattels than common law admitted.[59] This was especially true in cases where the wife was of a higher social status or possessed greater wealth than her husband. As Natasha Korda reminds us, we need not assume that single women's and widows' financial interests in and management of their capital simply evaporated when they married. Scholars have shown for some time that "there were important ways in which wives were able to circumvent [the] rigidities of the common law—such as trusts for separate estate, which were in use by the 1580s and spread rapidly thereafter."[60]

Portia stands poised to be transferred to the winning suitor, the portrait hidden in one of the three caskets seemingly symbolizing her objectification, yet Bassanio's choice ends up widening rather than suturing the conceptual rift between ownership and possession driving the play. The matter of possession as a potential problem has been anticipated by Portia's speech framing Bassanio's gambit, in which she makes an equivocal declaration of the correct chooser's potential winnings:

> One half of me is yours, the other half yours—
> Mine own, I would say; but if mine, then yours,
> And so all yours. O, these naughty times
> Puts bars between the owners and their rights!
> And so, though yours, not yours. (3.2.16–20)

While Portia seems to suggests that her father's arbitrary rules bar Bassanio from assuming what is his due, her generalized tone places the blame squarely on the "naughty times," suggesting that the constraints of their historical moment have rendered direct interest or absolute ownership a predicament. Korda points out that Portia's tone is "chiding": the construction "Mine own I would say" signals "a volitional resonance" that allows us to see how she scorns the legal stricture of her father's will.[61] His dying wish also appears anachronistic, if not foolish, in the context of a thriving culture of credit. If what Korda refers to as "the (il)logic of coverture" (141) renders Portia a self-owner whose rights are denied, the concept of qualified ownership allows her to recognize Bassanio's interest in her without abnegating her own self-interest.

On winning Portia, Bassanio immediately becomes indebted to his new wife, who positions herself as a creditor rather than a prize to be handed over. In response to Bassanio's victory, Portia sets about the task of assessing her worth. Using phrases such as "I wish myself much better" (3.2.153) and "I would be" (3.2.154), she animates the idea of conditional property as she presents herself as an investment that will accrue value over time, but which may only be redeemed at a future point when she will be "trebled twenty times . . . / A thousand times more fair [and] ten thousand times more rich" (3.2.155–57). Bassanio too perceives their relationship as contoured by the exegesis of debt and correctly identifies the "gentle scroll" encased within the lead casket (3.2.139) as a "note," the word for banknote or bill of dues (3.2.140). This note turns out to be a bond that must be "confirmed, signed, and ratified" (3.2.148) by Portia, the person who will provide him the necessary funds. Anticipating the blood-ink nexus that will figure centrally in the ensuing trial, Bassanio intuitively senses at this moment that blood speaks, as his bond with Portia necessitates that he forgo verbal oaths. Having become "bereft . . . of all words," he confesses his "blood . . . in [his] veins" is the sole medium he has at his disposal with which to seal the deed (3.2.176). But more than a medium like language, Bassanio recognizes blood is the only available form of property he has at his disposal to offer as collateral. Bassanio's inflection of his romantic proclamations with images of debt bondage echoes Salerio's rhetorical flourishes. In the previous scene, he compares Lorenzo's relationship with Jessica to that of creditor and debtor when he observes that men can barely wait to "seal love's bonds new-made," whereas they are less inclined "to keep obligèd faith unforfeited" (2.6.7–8).

In keeping with the logic of debt, Portia gives herself in trust to Bassanio, who in turn is awarded partial ownership. Portia, whose name carries an aural resonance with the word apportion, proceeds to allocate various parts of her estate, as she grants Bassanio the "sum of something" (3.2.158), while she retains ownership over some other things. Here she offers a graduated version of *muem et tuum*, so that even as she dutifully catalogues Bassanio's right to her "house [and] these servants" (3.2.170), she reminds him that until the marriage is consummated, he cannot have her.

Yet in bestowing upon Bassanio his band, a phonetic variant and synonym of the word "bond," Portia abandons a perspective that honors ethical ownership as she assumes a proprietary attitude. Through the terms of the contract she devises, she establishes herself as both the owner and possessor of Bassanio. Although she declares that "myself and what is mine to you and yours / Is now converted" (a legal term of art and a loaded word within the context of this play) (3.2.166–67), one hundred and fifty lines later she employs the exact phrase that Shylock will use in defending his right to Antonio's flesh when she construes Bassanio as property in which she has interest: "Since you are dearly bought, I will love you dear" (3.2.311). Her conditions seem nothing less than draconian when she warns Bassanio "when you part from, lose, or give away [the band] / Let it presage the ruin of your love" (3.2.172–73). An inversion of the typical situation in which fidelity is a condition imposed on the wife by the husband, and not the other way around, Portia uses the band/bond to establish herself as arbiter ready to condemn or forgive her erring husband.[62] Bassanio apprehends the stakes of the agreement, and, in rendition of the formulaic condition of Shylock and Antonio's bond, imagines the band as riveted to his flesh, a piece of which he understands he must sacrifice if he forfeits. He hazards that if the band parts from his finger "then parts life from hence. / O, then be bold to say Bassanio's dead!" (3.2184–85). Later, when Portia discovers that the band is forfeit, Bassanio imagines dismemberment as the inevitable punishment and exclaims in distress, "why I were best to cut my left hand off / And swear I lost my ring defending it" (5.1.177–78).

In order to resolve the problem of forfeiture in the Belmont plot, Portia must be compelled to relinquish her proprietary claim over Bassanio's flesh. Matrimony, like debt, offers Shakespeare's characters and viewers alike partial gratification, as the play enacts on a formal level what it has been addressing on a thematic one. All bonds, including the "comic bond" between players and audience, it turns out, must be qualified.[63] The problem of the missing bands that comes to light in the final moments of the play reintroduces an issue that seemingly had been laid to rest at the trial: can a band/bond that permits the alienation of persons be used to preserve life?

After the trial, the Duke prevails upon Antonio to "gratify" the lawyer to whom he "stand[s] indebted . . . over and above" (4.1.408). The newly manumitted Antonio is almost immediately "much bound," this time to Balthasar (4.1.405). Upon their return to Belmont, Antonio's status as bound persists, as Bassanio introduces him as the man to whom he is "infinitely bound" (5.1.133), only to have Portia correct her husband by reminding him that it is Antonio who remains the bound one, since he "was much bound for you" (5.1.135). It soon follows that the only way to resolve the crisis engendered by Bassanio's admission that he remunerated the lawyer with his band is for Antonio to once again offer himself as a "surety" for his friend (5.1.252). With Bassanio's attempts to justify his marital deception identified as a false "oath of credit" (5.1.244), the stage is set for another bond, as Antonio steps forward to pledge his soul as collateral:

> I once did lend my body for his wealth,
> Which, but for him that had your husband's ring,
> Had quite miscarried. I dare be bound again,
> My soul upon the forfeit, that your lord
> Will nevermore break faith advisedly. (5.1.247–51)

Here Antonio announces his readiness to "dare be bound again," and taking the band from Portia and giving it to Bassanio (5.1.253, s.d.) enacts the medieval ritual of tribute and a version of the traditional marriage ceremony. At this moment, Antonio offers his person to "Lord Bassanio" (5.1.254), asking him to "Swear to keep this ring" (5.1.254). Through this bigamous arrangement, marrying Bassanio symbolically to Antonio and literally to Portia, the two creditors in Bassanio's life are awarded dual ownership. If the strict terms of Portia's bond jeopardize Bassanio's person, the sacrificial terms of Antonio's will safeguard his life. Ultimately, the play upholds the bond as a structuring principle since it seems only to be able to envision a world in which obligation and property are reapportioned, as bonds are drawn and redrawn but never cancelled. The play ends with the announcement that three of Antonio's argosies have "richly come to harbor suddenly" (5.1.274–75). Yet this closing note of prosperity is compromised, for as long as the bond serves as the foundation of affective, social, and political ties, the next instance of forfeiture looms.

Conclusion

By staging the moment of forfeiture as an occasion to explore what constitutes ownership and under what circumstances it may give rise to possession, *The Merchant of Venice* elucidates the tensions between individual and community, acquisitive capitalism and the social character of credit, as well as the persistence of theological arguments that the human body was the property of God. Throughout the play, the disjunction between owing and owning is refracted through the figure of the defaulted debtor, on the one hand, and the unsatisfied creditor, on the other. Both creditor and debtor tested the emerging premises of possessive individualism as they revealed ownership and self-ownership to be a matter of degree rather than kind. Even as the law acknowledged that a creditor had an interest in his debtor's person, the state maintained that no debtor could forfeit his right to life. It was just such a formulation that justified the state's ability to function, ironically, as Fortune the usurer, rather than Fortune the creditor, by allowing "the wretched man outlive his wealth / To view with hollow eye and wrinkled brow /An age of poverty" as he languished in prison (4.1.261–66).

Chapter 3

Michaelmas Term and the Problem of Satisfaction

> Is not this a lamentable thing, that of the skin of an innocent lamb should be made parchment? That parchment, being scribbled o'er, should undo a man? Some say the bee stings, but I say 'tis the bee's wax; for I did but seal once to a thing, and I was never mine own man since.
>
> —Jack Cade, *2 Henry VI,* 4.2.75–80

> The unity of will attributed to the promising is itself the *effect* of a repression, a forgetfulness, a not-remembering of the satisfactions which appear to precede repression, and which repression makes sure will not appear again.
>
> —Judith Butler, *The Psychic Life of Power*

In Chapters 1 and 2, I examined the shadow side of late Elizabethan England's economy of obligation. The plays I discussed consider the ways that the bond's proprietary authority strains the relationship between money and justice. The legal implications of forfeiture, for instance, in *Timon of Athens* and *The Merchant of Venice* serve as the pretext of dramatic action but also a portal onto a more general exploration of the contested meanings of property and possession in an expanding culture of credit. What comes to the fore in both plays is the extent to which lending and borrowing on bond cast the human cost of default—the debtor's loss of his reputation, liberty, and potentially his life—as an ethical dilemma. In both plays, the solution to this dilemma lies ultimately with a higher authority such as God or the state.

I now turn to the common law of contract and its attempts to impose order on an often-volatile credit economy. By introducing a series of innovations growing out of the consolidation of customary and canon law, the early modern state aimed to resolve the problems endemic to the administration of various courts with overlapping jurisdiction. Most important for my argument was the law's gradual drift toward regarding the lender-borrower dynamic as a transaction between persons, rather than solely a property relation, which resulted in the courts remunerating the creditor for the damages he sustained, in addition to supporting his right to incarcerate the insolvent debtor. The legislative interest in wrongful harm, or what we now call tort, signaled a seismic shift in the adjudication of forfeiture, which, in turn, generated new kinds of problems. In looking to compensate the creditor, the onus was on the court to prove that in signing onto the bond, the debtor had intended to repay his loan.

This chapter and the next examine drama's role in exposing the hermeneutical instability of the common law of contract, especially in regard to the law's ability to distinguish coercion and consent in cases of debt bondage. The plays I analyze dilate the law's conceptual ambiguities around the debtor's intentionality and demonstrate skepticism about the legal doctrine that ratified the borrower's willful subjection to his creditor. An evolving legal process raised questions such as: is the debtor who haplessly devises a bond liable if it defaults? What does it mean that the debtor emerges as an accountable legal persona only by *not* performing the act of repayment? Moreover, when a debtor is someone whose will is not free, how then can a creditor receive satisfaction? Thomas Middleton's *Michaelmas Term* considers these questions as it elaborates the ways that the debtor's participation in his own subjection necessarily alters the meaning of compliance.

At the end of act three of Thomas Middleton's *Michaelmas Term*, the arriviste gallant Richard Easy of Essex has accumulated £700 in unpaid debts. Yet by the final act of the play his financial problem is resolved. With inexplicable ease, Easy's debt is cancelled and he regains his estate, a turn of events he attributes not to his own—or any other form of human—intervention but to the force of "writings." These writings consist of various financial documents such as debt bonds, the mortgage he forfeits, and the deed of discharge that the merchant Quomodo, who despite having plotted against Easy for the entirety of the play, mistakenly signs. Easy takes stock by reviewing the "good deeds" and "bad deeds" that have affected his fortunes. Here he does not reflect on his actions but the "writings," which in a chiastic crossing of agency and instrumentality, allow him to "keep" and "gave" his lands away, and, consequentially, "turn[ed]" to safety or have had their just "deserts":

> Here's good deeds and bad deeds, the writings that keep my
> Lands to me, and the bonds that gave it away from me.
> These, my good deeds, shall to more safety turn,
> And these, my bad, have their deserts and burn.[1]

While we might read Easy's speech as a condemnation of deceit, a warning against "bad deeds," an understanding of this speech in the larger context of the play reveals Middleton's aim to present us with the disturbing possibility that knowing the difference between "good" and "bad" deeds may not matter at all. This is because the distinction between the two becomes moot when the subject who authorizes such deeds exhibits a passivity that crosses sites of intention and disperses the potency of the will. In the final analysis, the unconditional efficacy of these writings stands in stark contrast to Easy's qualified volition. In this character we are presented with an acquiescence that exceeds its own purposes, that being the faithful reproduction of the debtor's intention in the form of the signature, as Easy's only confounds the distinction between adherence and resistance to the contractual premises of bondage.

If Easy's hapless fall out of and back into fortune seems preposterous to audiences, this character's passivity has presented an interpretative problem for critics. The inordinate focus on the play's predatory schemers masks a more anxious suspicion of a character that would resign himself to his own demise. Several scholars have argued that Easy mars the play, pointing out that in *Michaelmas Term* "thematic unity has not found its dramatic correlative in consistent characterization."[2] Paul Yachnin avers, "our sympathy for Easy rises no higher than it would for any other dumb beast led to financial slaughter."[3] Even when he regains his estate in the end, readers do not regard this as convincing comic closure. Richard Levin, for instance, wonders how are we supposed to "side with Easy and enjoy his triumph," since his cozeners have been so "brilliant" and he is known only for "passive gullibility."[4] The one critic who sees the appeal of Easy, Theodore Leinwand, argues that through this character Middleton showcases the allure of masculine submission in an urban context in which homoerotic bonds carry cultural caché for certain men. As Leinwand explains in Middleton's London: "A fluid economy of dupes, dupers, and dupers duped operates . . . according to analogous, perhaps even interchangeable financial and sexual principles. Beggar (y)/bugger (y) neatly conflates what everyone would escape and what everyone wishes on others, but it is also the occasional discreet object of desire."[5] Highlighting the interdependency of same-sex erotic and economic bonds that establish the play's sophistication, Leinwand observes that even as gallants move between dominant and submissive roles in their erotic partnerships, impecuniousness is consistently linked to sexual passivity.

Without losing sight of the homoerotic allure of men who are "easy," I want to consider the broader economic and social implications of what it meant circa 1600 to be "easily possessed" (1.1.49) by examining how the states of self-possession and dispossession were mediated onstage and off by one kind of "writing," the penal debt bond. The bond in early seventeenth-century England was not merely a financial instrument but also a form of writing that as a document of accountability entailed its own generic conventions, which, in this instance, impinge upon those of city comedy.[6] Through the character of Easy and his dealings with this form of monetary writing, *Michaelmas Term* offers a diacritical reading of the signature or the hand, which served as the material sign of consent. In early modern England, the word "hand" referred to both instrument and object. As an appendage, the hand became a tool of agency and an entity that initiated social joining through the act of clasping. As the signature, the hand became detachable; when the signer "put his hand" to a deed, he figuratively parted with it.[7] A fugitive mark, the signature as a substitute for the physical person of its owner always signalled an absent-presence. In the particular case of debt bondage, the signature's function as a duplication of its author was even more problematic. The hand that authenticated the borrower also inaugurated his deprivation.[8]

The rules of city comedy, a subgenre that arguably revolves around the giving of one's hand in marriage are, according to one critic, violated in *Michaelmas Term*, since Middleton undermines the "two central comic assumptions" driving the subgenre: the pursuit of procreation as a means of preserving the social order and civic freedom as a virtue.[9] In this city comedy the heteronormative trajectory of courtship is indeed interrupted by the quest to secure the hand of the debtor. Yet the generation of progeny and civic enfranchisement remain central to the play even as the introduction of the bond revises the connection between the two. The debt bond comes to stand for the product of pecuniary parthenogenesis between men. Nonetheless, even as economic obligation binds men, the bond proves to be an unreliable contract, since the hand of the male debtor, unlike that of the betrothed woman, attests to his coeval status as the object of property and the subject of contract.[10]

In what follows, my aim is to demonstrate how the intrusion of the bond transforms *Michaelmas Term* into a play about writing and the will. By the late sixteenth century, the negative aspects of common law were coming to be associated with its rampant textuality. As Subha Mukherji stresses, the period witnessed a significant shift from oral assimilation to print, which allowed for the proliferation of legal commentaries, manuals, handbooks, and writs, democratizing the law and increasing its availability to the unmonitored translation and application by those "far-removed from the 'collective mind of the profession.'"[11] Middleton's engagement with the written culture of the law is not merely informed by the details of jurisdictional procedure but marked by a sensitivity to its elastic philosophical and affective underpinnings. In what follows, I situate Middleton's play, which revolves around the compliant debtor Richard Easy and the devisement of his bonds, in the context of contemporaneous legal debates over the notion of consent in economic obligation that came to a head in *Slade's Case*. In 1602, Edmund Coke and King's Bench justices determined that the insolvent debtor was no longer guilty of malfeasance for actively detaining his creditor's property but of nonfeasance for failing to perform his promise. Confusingly, the debtor emerged as the subject of law not by having enacted a crime but by having failed to act. In effect, he was tried for his passivity. In the case of written bonds, the debtor's signature was the means by which he entered into formal commercial and legal networks and officially bound himself to their obligations. By dramatizing the role of the hand in establishing the debtor's liability Middleton's play, however, enacts Bradin Cormack's observation that "when a literary text uses law for metaphoric or narrative ends, it may also be testing the law's categories, and so come to reflect back at law an intensified account of the work that, less audibly, those categories do in the law itself."[12] As a play that recognizes the bond as a complex form of *legal* writing, *Michaelmas Term* exploits the dramatic potential of the courts' intensified interest in the intentionality of the debtor, which far from resolving the nebulous matter of economic agency amplified the hand's ability to both affirm and vitiate the priorities of contract.

The Pliable Hand of Capital

Changes in the scale and forms of moneylending at the end of the sixteenth century culminated in a marked rise in the use of the written bond and diminishment of informal verbal agreements. As Marjorie McIntosh emphasizes, "a new breed of lender" emerged in early modern England, one who did not take interest but who distinguished himself by his reliance on written bonds, which discouraged the possibility of extending credit for years on end.[13] Bonds were handwritten on parchment or paper and drawn to order, meaning they were not intended for use as general or all-purpose instruments. The language of the bond did not adhere to any strict formula, other than to specify the names of the parties, the amount of the loan, and the date and place of repayment, though bonds often included a phrase in which the debtor pledged his "bodie, land, and goods." The bond between Theylos Walcott and Richard Hale for £50, dated April 10, 1589, is representative:

> The Condicon*n* of this obligacon*n* is such that yf the within bounden Theylos Walcott his executors or Assignes/ or any of them doe paye or cause to be paid vnto the within named Richard Hale his executors or/ Assignes the some of ffyfty pownd*es* of lawfull mony of England on the tenth day of April wh*i*ch shalbe/ in the yere of our lord Christe A thousand ffyve hundred ffowr score & ten at the new dwelling howse/ of the said Richard Hale in the poultrye in london without delay that then this pute obligacon*n* to be voyd or els yt to/ stand in full force & strengthe.[14]

As this bond suggests, the debtor was expected to sign a written text that he had not authored and which was cast in impersonal legalese by an anonymous scribe, who had himself devised the bond as a "*persona fictiva*," meaning in the name of someone else. The scribe's use of the third person displaces the motivations of lender and borrower onto an unknowable but omnipotent generic authority. Even the seal, which established the integrity of the bond, could have been "loaned" to the debtor by the scrivener for the purposes of devising the bond.[15] Yet, as much as the bond promotes the ideal of the bound self as unfettered from the individual, the force of the bond lay in its claim to a specific body. The crucial rhetorical work of the bond was to identify the borrower as "bounden" and to remind the debtor of its penal condition, which in the event of forfeiture would "stand in full force & strengthe."

While a bond could be a "single" or "simple" bond, meaning an unconditional contract, all debt bonds were conditional. A kind of backward contract, the conditional debt bond detailed the penalty that would take effect if its condition had *not* been performed. For this reason, creditors executed bonds for a larger sum than the loan (usually twice the amount) and, importantly, this penal sum was not construed as interest. Rather than charging for the use of his money, as did the usurer, the creditor legitimately contracted to receive compensation for the loss he stood to suffer by the debtor's failure to repay on time. Those who repaid their loans by the assigned day would not have to pay the additional charge, in which case the lender would receive only the original amount he loaned. However, if the condition of the bond was not met, then the creditor was permitted to collect his penalty or seize his debtor's property and even his person. When an insufficient borrower "bound" his "bodie," he became the "forfeit," and while an unsatisfied creditor could take action against "the body of the defendant; or against his goods and chattels," as Craig Muldrew stresses, by the beginning of the seventeenth century, most actions were taken against the debtor's person.[16] The judiciary rationalized the creditor's right to detain his debtor on grounds that the writ of *capias ad satisfaciendum*—another form of writing that was scripted and sealed by a judge—ensured the debtor's appearance in court and prevented him from seeking sanctuary within the liberties of the city or his own home.

The bond was thus a form of writing that summoned the body onto the scene of personhood, a legal as well as a metaphysical category, with ambivalent effects. Advancing what Karl Polanyi describes as a "commodity fiction," the bond transformed something that is "obviously *not* [a] commodit[y]" into one by allowing the debtor's body and the coins he borrowed to assume an equivalency by means of convention only.[17] The homology between legal and commodity form rested on an abstraction, whereby the tension between alienable property and the inalienable self could be resolved only by the bond's recourse to the logic of the universal equivalent. If the validity of the bond depended upon the promulgation of this fiction, this fiction relied on the integrity of the bond. Any alteration rendered a bond void. Thus in order to perform its function, the bond, like other kinds of paper monies such as bills of exchange or goldsmith's receipts, had to transcend its own materiality. Early seventeenth-century legal handbooks, such as William West's *The First Part of Simboleography*, typically include a section on how to discern "good" bonds from "bad," which entails identifying the signs of scriptive authority that distinguish debt bonds from other forms of writing, such as "ordinarie letters, priuat notes, reckonings, and rememberances made by many for a mans owne priuat vse and memorie, and from all bookes of arts, histories, diuinties, philosophie, and such like."[18] Yet as long as lawyers debated the bond's scriptive features, this monetary instrument was denaturalized and exposed as a textual entity informed by various kinds of writings.

Leading up to the watershed decision on *Slade's Case*, justices acknowledged that the bond's validity could be compromised by the integrity of the debtor's signature. By the middle of the sixteenth century, the signature as the sign of consent was required of all legal deeds, which were signed on the front by the participating parties and endorsed on the back by witnesses and attorneys.[19] In this same period, however, early modern writing manuals understood the hand to have negligible authority. To sign a document was to engage in the acts of replicating and verifying.[20] The hand, from this perspective, was like the seal (itself a transferrable item), a means of conferring an office or function, which meant that devising a deed did not involve the manifestation of interiority but rather the projection of a persona.[21] Nonetheless, in civil law, the presence or absence of consent, as marked by the signature, determined the viability of contract. The legislative tension between the subjective will of the assenting party and the efficacy of contract was particularly pronounced in the case of debt because, as legal historian Randy Barnett explains, "an inquiry into the promisor's intent allowed him to avoid liability by fraudulently undermining otherwise perfectly clear agreements by generating and preserving extrinsic evidence of ambiguous or conflicting intentions."[22] In short, there was no guarantee that promise would be performed because it had been ratified by the hand.

Discussions of debt bondage in the period's legal manuals grapple with the ways consent was not equal to and could even exceed and resist contract. West in *The First Part of Simboleography*, the most widely read manual of the early seventeenth century which includes an explanation of all legal forms as well as commentary, considers a situation when an "act of man" and the compulsion of "right" or the law are at odds (sig. A[1]v). While West stresses that debt bonds should not "make any bodie or service ours," but rather "bind another to us, to give, do, or performe some thing" (sig. A[1]r), once the bond is signed, however, he acknowledges that right must override the signer's will, presumably since the debtor could subsequently attempt to amend or contradict the binding nature of his obligation. For West, the dilemma generated by competing interpretations of the debtor's intention compromises the integrity of economic contract. West attempts to head off just such a problem when he suggests to law students that while the borrower's "mind and will" are "necessarie" to the making of obligation, in the final analysis it is the "right" (or the formal constraints of contract) that renders the agreement enforceable: "For although to the making of Obligations, the mind and will of man be very necessarie, yet thereof ariseth the obligation, not for that a man willeth, but for y [the] right and fact granteth such obligation to arise" (sig. A[1]v). It is this perspective that leads West to determine that even if "a man wil not be bound," he "neuerthelesse is bound if hee commit any such thing by which right will haue him to be bound" (sig. A[1]v), a "thing" such as his hand.

West's assertion of the efficacy of the hand, which works in concert with right of law, undermines the ideal of contract as representing the binding parties' respective wills. Requiring the debtor to yield to the terms of the bond bolstered the view that contractual obligations could be imposed upon unwilling parties. West concludes that only "true contracts" are based on "true consent": "Therefore true contracts be those, which are by mutuall consent of both parties" (sig. A3r), meaning those deeds devised under circumstances in which "two or more, in one selfe thing, to give, or to doe somewhat" (sig. A2). Ultimately, the idea that the promisor's hand reliably indexed singularity of purpose was, as West admits, a chimera, and so the law had to intervene to adjudicate between honest and feigned intention, which mimic one another whether "utterd by mouth, or shewed by writing" (sig. A2v). Even as West maintains that a valid contract is one in which "our wills conioyne us" (sig. A2r) and contemporaries, such as legal theorist William Fulbecke, concur that "the chiefe ground of contract is consent," at this point in the development of common law, consent could not provide a stable foundation for economic obligation.[23]

With the 1602 resolution of *Slade's Case*, the notion that signing a bond entailed the undertaking of an assurance buttressed the authority of those lawyers who sought to locate the impartiality of the law in the primacy of the debtor's signature.[24] In one of the most significant decisions in the common law history of contract, Edmund Coke (for the King's Bench) prevailed over Francis Bacon (for the Court of Common Pleas) on whether forfeiture on a bond could be adjudicated in accordance with a civil consideration that recognized the debtor as having committed breach of promise.[25] While Chief Justice Pope's summation of *Slade's Case*, which had been argued on four separate occasions each Michaelmas Term between 1596 and 1602, that "every contract executory imports in itself an *assumpsit*" immediately altered the status of oral agreements, lawyers applied the decision to sealed bonds by arguing that they functioned as written *assumpsits*.[26] Those creditors who sued on *indebitatus assumpsit* based their case on the notion that promise was binding, and the fact that the debtor signed a bond proved that he had received a loan and had also ipso facto taken on or assumed the obligation to repay it on time.

Even as the legitimacy of the bond rested upon the authorizing function of the hand, the introduction of the notion of liability into action of debt only deepened the difficulty of determining the circumstances under which a written bond would stand as an accurate representation of the signer's will. Coke and the King's Bench justices opened Pandora's box when they recognized that credit relations were based on the exchange of words, as well as real property. Thus they regarded economic obligation as not simply verifying the transfer of things but as documenting a relationship between social actors whose interaction was only partially realized at the time of the bargain. For Coke, individuals entered into agreements knowingly, and their failure to carry out their terms constituted deceit. Yet while creditors could be hoodwinked by irresponsible borrowers, debtors could be tricked into signing onto bonds. By introducing an interval between promise and performance, Coke produced the need for the courts to consider the space between past and future actions of the bound parties. The gap between signing and enacting a deed altered the function of the hand as that which would primarily launch a relationship rather than guarantee its fulfilment.

Bacon and his Common Pleas colleagues saw *assumpsit* as extralegal evidence of the binding nature of an agreement and thus as irrelevant in the case of debt. For these justices, debt was *contractus est permutatio* (contract is the exchange of things), meaning that at stake in the case of default was returning to the creditor what had always belonged to him. As Luke Wilson explains, from the Baconian perspective, when a debtor forfeits on his bond: "Circumstances must be brought into line with the relations which obtain legally: the plaintiff *really* has the thing sued for, therefore he *should* have it. And since the transaction occurs in an instant, no interval can insert itself between promise and performance or open a space for agency there; and there can be no articulation of intentions, states of mind, and so on, only a condition which signified by its structure that money or goods bargained for are not in the possession of the person who has a right to them."[27] In cases of default, however, "the thing sued for" was the body of the debtor, which would stand in for the money or goods that had been lent. Unlike the actual coins, which legally remained in the possession of the lender, the creditor did not at any point own the body of his debtor. From a political-theological standpoint even the debtor himself could assert only a partial claim of ownership over his own person.[28] Despite Coke's victory, *assumpsit* while necessary was not sufficient in making economic obligation binding.

In the end, arguments pro and contra *Slade's Case* raised more questions than answers about the relationship between signature and intent. More particularly, *Slade's Case* aggravated the already complex role of the body as one of the crucial indices of self-ownership. Even as the hand rendered the debt bond a consensual document, the links between property and ownership—links that were tenuous before *Slade's Case*—were not any more likely to be secured by the presumed intention of each party. The meaning of the body as a material entity that could be either possessed or dispossessed would henceforth be subjected to the transactional force of the bond, a document whose legal mandates were influenced by the vicissitudes of the market but whose ethical presumptions were constrained by moral sanctions. Coke and the King's Bench justices hewed to the signature in an attempt to disavow the irretrievability of the hand and attempted to move from promise implied in fact to promise implied in law in order to create the appearance of unified intention and action. Yet, as the adjudication of forfeiture demonstrated from 1602 on, *Slade's Case* inadvertently made the hand the fulcrum on which to measure the relationship of body, will, and contract.

The Generative Hand of Capital

In the first decade of the seventeenth century, drama's ability to test and amplify the legal notion of embodied consent was most pronounced in theater's interest in the relation of law to desire, which, as critics have shown, found expression in plays produced for young men of the Inns of Court.[29] As a play that explores the relation between law and desire *Michaelmas Term* is exemplary. Its characters' general yearnings for wealth, status, and sex are expressed through the law, while they work to accomplish their specific goals by manipulating the law's incomplete conceptualization of monetary satisfaction as grounded in the debtor's body. By repeatedly drawing attention to the litigious activity of bonding, as well as to the frantic atmosphere of the first, longest, and busiest of the four court sessions of London's legal calendar when landed gentlemen flocked to the city, Middleton panders to his audience.[30] Performed by Paul's boys circa 1605, the plot of *Michaelmas Term* turns on legal trickery, which relies on its private theater audience's intimate knowledge of legal detail. More particularly, the evidentiary problem of the bond as a form of writing that constructs the agency of the signer makes up the play's dramatic crux, putting it in conversation with the recent decision on *Slade's Case*.

When we consider Middleton's play in light of not only the general problem of indebtedness but also a specific transitional moment in debt legislation, its staging of the interplay of economic and erotic power takes on new meaning as the hand—the bodily site of instrumentality—rather than the ass—the bodily site of waste—emerges as the corporal locus where struggles over dominance and submission are played out.[31] Throughout *Michaelmas Term* men give their hands to one another to create a document that is imagined as the offspring of those who have engaged in an act of consensual bondage. Not surprisingly, the play's symbolic economy is informed by the tropes evoking not only anality but also inception and pregnancy. Openness and fullness, often juxtaposed, signify respectively, the originary transactional moment and end result of monetary and erotic satisfaction enjoyed by men. Those who exploit the hand as a compensatory vehicle of an inscrutable will use it as a tool to "spread" themselves open (Ind. 65). While these men seem to thrive in Middleton's London, satisfaction, however, is elusive, since sundry currencies of value—notably semen and coins—cannot be retained when not all containers prove reliable.

The play's Induction is dominated by the Patriarch of the family of law, Michaelmas Term, represented here as an allegorical character cloaked in a judge's robe holding forth to the three other legal terms of the calendar year. Michaelmas Term inaugurates the play by invoking the inductive power of his hand, as he announces "my hand's free" (Ind. 9) and steps forward to address the law students in the offstage audience seated before him: "But, gentlemen, to spread myself open unto you, in cheaper terms I salute you, for ours [the Children of St. Paul's] have but sixpenny fees all the year long, yet we dispatch you in two hours without demur" (Ind. 65–74). By "spreading [himself] open" to the young men in attendance (both onstage and off), Michaelmas Term anticipates the "free-breasted . . . and somewhat too open" Easy (1.1.55) who will be tricked out of his fortune in main plot. Yet the distinction between Michaelmas Term and Easy hinges on the crucial difference between being "free," meaning a free agent able to have an agreeing mind to validate contract, and being "too open," or in other words, incapable of consent. Michaelmas Term is able to achieve satisfaction, whereby he experiences fiscal profit as bringing him a sense of bodily fulfilment. He envisions himself sated on the coins he has reaped from the "silver harvest" of the term (Ind. 11), and describes himself "drink[ing] deep" of his clients' cups (Ind. 46–48). A consensual receptacle, Michaelmas Term both takes in fiscal rewards and is able to "dispatch" or quickly discharge those who seek his services (Ind. 67). Suggestively overlaying the legal sense of the word "dispatch," to expedite a case through court, with the implied offer to get the young men in the audience off erotically, Michaelmas Term brags of his ample capacity to "grasp

[the] best part of the autumnian blessing / in my contentious fathom" (Ind. 9–10). Here he conjures the image of holding onto riches in his inner depths, as suggested by the word fathom, as the curled fingers of the grasping hand signal simultaneous openness and fullness, an image that resonates with the description to follow of the Exchequer itself as an over-stuffed "gap[ing] hole" that is at once empty and over-full (1.1.4).[32]

Characters like Michaelmas Term who spread themselves open up are shown to be generative like those men who are depicted as capable of taking in/on other men's loads. This idea is brought home in the play's Induction by the comparison of naïve newcomers to the city to "asses" or beasts of burden that scheming citizens use to bear their "load[s]" (Ind. 41–42). Once they deposit their goods, citizens turn their gulls cum asses loose "to graze again" (Ind. 41). In accordance with this symbiotic relationship, gulls are productive because they incite citizen's desires and are able to satisfy them by functioning as repositories of the riches citizens trick them out of. Here the ass functions as receptacle and is not associated with expulsion. This logic is redacted in one character's description of the prostitute's vagina as like a purse into which a gallant may safely deposit his semen. The prostitute's vagina is imagined not as sinkhole but a container where "that which [one] gather I' th' day, [one] put[s] into their purses at night" (1.1.240). Both the ass and the purse retain what is expended through scheming or erotic activity and may also serve as places from which one may yield a return.

While Quomodo aims to use the gullible Easy as his ass, in contrast to the other gulls the woollen draper has victimized in the past, Easy is not able to bear his load; while he is open, his hand is not free. By the end of Act One, he is well on the way to financial ruin. The young heir, new to London and desperate to appear urbane, borrows money from seasoned con artists to purchase expensive apparel and obtain entrée into dice games. Immediately upon his arrival, he is singled out by a group of gallants as "a fair-breasted gentleman, somewhat too open" (1.1.55) and as someone who appears "fresh and free" (1.1.120). The word "fresh," meaning new and pure, was also used to describe someone too eager and thus devoid of any discerning "appetite or inclination."[33] The pairing of the word "fresh" with the word "free" compromises the integrity of the latter term, as confirmed by Easy's self-description as "easily possessed" (1.1.49), a characterization that further circumscribes the meaning of his general announcement that he is "free" (1.1.49). As one who is ready for the taking, Easy is, in accordance with common law of property, ripe for enjoyment or use. Those new to the play's "man-devouring city" (2.2.21), as Gail Kern Paster notes, are represented as arriving with their "social virginity" intact, a virginity that will be inevitably violated (21).[34] Paster discusses the play's reference to "city-powd'ring," a metaphor for the "seasoning" of "the fresh bodied new comer" who becomes cured by experience as salt would work upon undressed meat (27). Here she interprets the literal meaning of the image to refer to the cosmetic powdering that once applied to the face and hair added a fashionable veneer over rustic lack, as well as to the powdery substance used in medicinal sweating tubs in the treatment of syphilis (28). As a metaphor for the impersonal urban forces that work upon the newcomer in harmful ways, we can add another referent for "powd'ring," that being the powder that scribes sprinkled over contracts, such as debt bonds, to dry the inky signature. The narrator of Middleton's satiric *Father Hubbard's Tales* laments, for instance, that the lawyer's fines "went off with such powder" that those unable to pay them were turned back to the country.[35]

If Easy's passivity signals his vulnerability, it also thwarts those who scheme against him since the law must step in to fill the void that would otherwise be occupied by his will. This problem is dramatized through the play's acknowledgment that the endorsement that renders the debt bond viable is too variable in regard to its legal implications. Through a series of credit transactions, the woollen draper Quomodo and his servant Shortyard bleed Easy of his fortune and, via the mechanism of the bond, use him as a repository as they dispense into him assets (both material and erotic) that ultimately derive from his own largesse. Easy is first duped by "the commodity game," a Ponzi scheme described within the period as attracting only the most naïve.[36] After having been manipulated into mortgaging his lands in exchange for an unsellable bolt of moth-eaten cloth, he is then enticed into cosigning several debt bonds for which his person serves as collateral.

Middleton's Easy, however, is not only gullible to financial ploys; he is also vulnerable to erotic manipulation. While the woollen draper Quomodo orchestrates Easy's penury, Quomodo's servant Shortyard instigates Easy's seduction by following through with his plan to "flatter, dice, and brothel to him [Easy]; give him a sweet taste of sensuality; train him to every wasteful sin that he may quickly need health, but especially money; ravish him. . . . Drink drunk with him; creep into bed to him; kiss him and undo him" (1.1.124–29). The image of Easy as "undone" and the victim of "ravish" or rape is evoked by his passivity in the protracted scene in which we witness Easy "putting his hand" to a series of bonds with his "good sweet bedfellow" (2.3.146) Shortyard at his side. Here he resembles the bankrupt protagonist of Middleton's

A Trick to Catch the Old One who describes his creditors as "ravishing" him and forcing him "to play the maid and take it!"[37] As a result of his misplaced trust in Quomodo and misguided affection for Shortyard, Easy forfeits all and narrowly escapes "the inconscionable trouble of law" (4.1.20), a euphemism for prison.

Shortyard's disingenuous response to Quomodo's suggestion that Easy cosign a bond to generate funds for his new companion hints at the depth of their intimacy. Shortyard falsely protests that he could never ask such a favour from his companion, since their "purses are brothers" and that "in a word [they] are man and wife; they can but lie together, so we do" (2.3.164–69). The servant's description of their relationship as akin to matrimony encourages Easy to regard the debt bond as a figurative marriage contract marking the culmination of their courtship. For Easy, this binding agreement serves as the material sign of what he haplessly assumes to be a mutual erotic and economic partnership. At the signing of the bond much is made of who shall assert himself by "enter[ing]" first, a literal reference to who will be the primary signatory but also a suggestive question as to who will first impress his stylus into the wax of the virgin document, signalling an indentation passively waiting to be filled. As the second signer Easy prostrates himself before Shortyard and Quomodo and assumes a position of legal, and by implication erotic, passivity. Easy's powerlessness is revealed in full when he realizes, and here he echoes the inscription of the conditional bond verbatim, that at the moment of its sealing, his "body, goods, and lands" have become collateral (3.4.226). Quomodo's wife Thomasine, who witnesses the signing, compares observing this activity to watching a condemned man speed up the process of his own death by helping the executioner disembowel him. She comments that Easy is now "Alive, [but] in state and credit executed," as he "help[s] to rip up himself" (2.3.221–22). Later she exclaims, "Now is he quart'ring out; the executioner strides over him; with his own blood he writes" (2.3.367–68). Construing Easy's act of submission as leading inevitably to a savage form of violation, whereby Quomodo and Shortyard will stride over Easy's body and then rip him limb from limb, Thomasine's imagined fate for Easy recalls that of Actean as she associates their legal consummation with the realization of other dangerous forms of desire.

Oblivious to the peril he faces, Easy anticipates the scrivener's announcement "ready for your hands, Gentlemen" (2.3.346) when he blithely volunteers, "here's my hand" (2.3.317) and coyly assures Shortyard, "you shall have your will of me for once" (2.3.360). The signing of the bond is staged in specificity, allowing Middleton to satirize Easy's presumption that the quality of his character may be discerned by the elegance of his handwriting. This supposition inspires Easy's vaunting question to the scrivener, "How like you my Roman hand?" (2.3.372). Roman hand, as Grace Ioppolo points out, was considered suitable only for the types of occasional writing women were expected to produce as opposed to the secretary hand of daily writing that remained the province of men.[38] Roman hand was also distinguished by being written "on the form of a Circle," with its letters carrying "a visible rotundity."[39] The association of Easy with the open "O" of the Roman hand, as well as the Roman fig sign, an obscene gesture made to represent the female genitals whereby the thumb was inserted in between the middle and index fingers, keeps us focused on Easy as a penetrable entity. Easy's rhetorical question provokes a sarcastic response from the scrivener who pushes the pun into the arena of the scatological by commenting, "Exceeding well sir, but that you rest too much upon your R. and make your E's too little" (2.3.373–74). Easy rests too much on his "R" or arse because he is lazy and/or because he assumes the bottom position in his sexual encounters. As a result of over-penetration, he has trouble making his E's, or "making his ease," the phrase for relieving one's bowels. Here the joke is on Easy who resembles his Roman hand, insofar as he is like an inscription that serves as the locus of various impressions that others press onto him. The joke, though, is also on his creditors who cannot profit from all that they deposit into this bottomless entity.

As the capricious losses and gains of property among men stand in for the romantic tribulations between men and women in *Michaelmas Term*, patrimony emerges as the means by which men attempt to advance themselves. The scheming woollen draper Quomodo, for instance, is motivated by his desire to have his son obtain standing as a freeman of the city and eventually a place at court. While Middleton offers a cynical perspective on Quomodo's fantasies, he does allow the arena of procreation to be expanded to include economic relations between men. Yet through the extended comparison of debt bonds and children, Middleton explores further the crisis that a confused notion of economic agency engenders. The character Michaelmas Term of the play's Induction has no biological children and so "makes those [his] heirs whom [he] has beggared" (Ind. 26) or buggered, as Leinwand suggests, by seducing men into debt bondage and ravishing/raping them with the penalty of default. In the main play, Quomodo, too, regards debt bonds as akin to progeny insofar as they bear his imprint and go forth into the world as legally recognizable extensions of himself. He explains to Easy: "As often as you give your name to a bond, you must think you christen a child and take the charge on't too. For as the one, the bigger it grows, the more cost it requires; so the other, the longer it lies, the more charges it puts you to. Only here's the difference: a child must be broke and a bond must not. The more you break children, the more you keep 'em under. But the more you break bonds, the more they'll leap in your face" (3.4.142–50). Bonds and children are alike, he explains, in that they are costly and require those who fathered them to provide maintenance. The difference between bonds and children resides in the fact that men may exercise their patriarchal authority over children by subjecting them to violence. Bonds, however, rebel against those who created them. They have the ability to discipline their fathers by stripping them of their authority through the demonstration of penal force.

Quomodo's procreative analogy captures the peculiar temporality of the creditor-debtor relationship, which as a commitment often made impulsively only comes to fruition in time. In plotting indebtedness along a temporal axis, the action of the play dramatizes time's claim on the debtor in condensed form. Easy stands ready to become dispossessed at some future point that inevitably arrives too soon. A perversion of a patrilineal order that endows heirs through the linear transmission of property, the debt bond takes the debtor out of time, disrupting the relation between father and son. Thus a customary tradition, such as primogeniture that discriminates past, present, and future, is upended, leaving in its place only the enduring presentist nature of the debtor's consent, whereby he sells himself off in perpetuity.

Bonds, as Middleton shows, are unlike children in one other crucial way. As much those creditors seeking to sue for damages would like the bond to assume a one-to-one correspondence to the debtor's intention, the bond inevitably takes on a life of its own. The most abject of all bonds, not surprisingly, are those that Quomodo describes as bastard bonds.[40] These are debt bonds that no signer will claim and without clear criteria for liability, are forfeit: "Faith, they are like the offsprings of stol'n lust, put to the hospital. Their fathers are not to be found; they are either too far abroad, or too close within; and thus for your memory's sake: The desperate debtor hence derives his name: One that has neither money, land, nor fame. All that he makes, prove bastards and not bonds" (3.4.166–73). Quomodo's extended metaphor of bastard bonds puns on the Greek word for "interest," which literally meant offspring and on "bastard-secretary," the hand used by scriveners to transcribe engrossed legal documents such as debt bonds.[41] He mines the metaphor by suggesting these bonds are juridically illegible just as bastard progeny are socially discredited.

Bastard bonds cannot satisfy their creditors, and if those who authored them have fled the country or remain hidden in their own homes, the law steps in as the Ur-Patriarch. Orphan bonds in this respect get a second chance, and so, arguably, do desperate debtors, who in disowning their wayward offspring commence the process of creating a new legal persona.

Easy's "ease" turns to dis-ease when those scheming against him disguise themselves as officers who inform him that in the absence of the first signer (Shortyard), as the secondary signatory he alone is liable for all overdue bonds. In an effort to avoid incarceration, Easy attempts to orphan his bonds by denying paternity. His denial, however, is met with the officer's insistence: "Is not your name there" (3.4.38), by which he identifies Easy as the author of the various bonds. Easy's insistence that he signed the bonds "for fashion's sake" (3.4.40) is met with the officer's sarcastic reply, "'tis for fashion's sake that we arrest you" (3.4.41). His creditor, Easy is told, is "a most merciless devourer," whom even if offered "money, goods, or land" would "rather have [his] body in prison" (3.4.80–83). The officer's warning echoes Quomodo's imagination of a man's credit as a physical entity that may be "wounded" (3.4.135) and invokes *Timon of Athens*'s insolvent protagonist who imagines his overdue bonds as weapons having the power to maim him.[42]

While Easy's attempt to orphan his bonds proves unsuccessful, Middleton provides a glimpse into the fate of orphans through his representation of two bastard figures, the prostitute Country Wench and the pseudo-knight Lethe. Each of these minor characters demonstrates that the abject status of the orphan necessitates the invention of a prosthetic or artificial persona, which in turn leads to freedom from liability but also exclusion from crucial civil networks. Cut loose from all original ties, these members of the younger generation have fashioned themselves into works of art rather than duplications of their biological parents. Country Wench is described as begot by "tirewomen and tailors" (3.1.5), and the "cockscomb" Lethe (3.1.99) is characterized as the product of some "monster [that] won his mother" (3.1.298). Both end up beggaring their parents, who in a perversion of biological and social orders become servants to their children. Like Easy, who is too free, each of these characters begins the play in a state of desperation and thus is no longer eligible to be bound economically, socially, or even by means of familial ties. Country Wench resorts to a life of prostitution because her father "spent [his] unshapen youth . . . and surfeited away [his] name and state in swinish riots," making him a beggar (2.2.21–24). The Scottish Lethe, newly transformed from the impoverished son of an itinerant tooth drawer, depends solely on his reputation at court and is thus impelled to live lavishly beyond his means to compensate for his lack of pedigree.

While Easy's father has not spent or denied his patrimony, Easy goes on to bastardize his own inheritance by trading land for disenfranchisement. After all of his property has been transferred to the Quomodo, he is pronounced "a free man" (4.1.52), which, unlike Michaelmas Term and his "free hand," casts Easy into a state of dispossession, unburdened of liability and obligation alike. Shortyard's disappearance puts Easy in a perilous position, and in the end, Easy is incapable of satisfying the men who duped him since his lands are held in abeyance until the legal details of a series of fraudulent bonds—seemingly beyond any one person's comprehension—are resolved. Easy's anxious speculation that "all that I beget hereafter I'll soon disinherit" (3.4.174) has turned into a dark prophecy as he comes to embody the sterility of contractual limbo, confirming one character's observation that no one "proves a deeper knave than a spent fool" (3.1.21). No longer perceived to be a generative source, Easy has shown himself to be too easy, which has compromised his ability to uphold his end of the obligations he forged. By amplifying the illusory nature of contractual consent, the play acknowledges the discontinuities to which debt bonds and their confused notion of economic agency may give rise. On the one hand, freedom to contract signifies the right to participate in binding legal agreements and, in this play, grants certain men immunity from expropriation. On the other hand, freedom from contract allows others to remain exempt and escape the burden of liability at the cost of disenfranchisement. *Michaelmas Term* can only achieve comic closure by introducing the creaky device of the jury trial, and at the final instance, an impartial judge intervenes to restore the economic and social status quo.

When Quomodo realizes that he has signed a memorandum releasing Easy from the action of debt, he seeks legal recourse and brings his case to court. Technically Quomodo is correct, the contract should be nullified since, in the words of West, if there is "any error of deceit in the consent or thing, for which the contract is entered into, that contract is either made altogether none [sic], or of none effect" (Sig. A3r). The judge, however, in accordance with *Slade's Case*'s logic of *assumpsit*, is not influenced by pleading on the case and instead defers to the document itself, which he interprets as providing sole evidence of the signer's intention to perform his promise. He reads it: "In witness whereof I have set to mine own hand: *Ephestian Quomodo*" (5.3.70).

Referring to Quomodo's hand, the judge comments, "'Tis firm enough your own, sir" (5.3.71). Quomodo is thus placed in a position in which to win his case he must surrender his agency by denying his hand and claim that he signed the bond as a "jest" (5.3.73). Thus even the intentional signer is undone by the law's strange logic of personhood.

Quomodo's fraught reconciliation with his hand is paired in this final instance with Lethe's troubling reunion with his mother. Through the intervention of the same judge, Lethe's mother is forced to acknowledge her wayward progeny. Like Quomodo, Mother Gruel refuses at first to claim that which bears her imprint and in defiance castigates her son by yelling at him, "call'st me mother? Out, I defy thee, slave!" (5.3.149). Only by force of the judge's decree does she assume maternity as the judge insists that she accept that this man is her son, demanding, "Wilt thou believe me, woman?" (5.3.156). She begrudgingly takes responsibility for Lethe when she inquires, "Art thou Andrew, my wicked son Andrew?" (5.3.158).

Quomodo's inventive scheming throughout the play has inspired dreams of the social authority that proprietary rights may endow. In the end, these dreams are deflated by the fluidity of debt bondage that shows how the hand that enables the fantasy of autonomous reproduction also attests to the impermanence of patrilineality. Because he has staged his own death as a means of testing the loyalty of his wife, son, and servant, Quomodo's appearance in court casts more than his hand into doubt. Here we are confronted with the dilemma generated by the existence of one natural person splintered into several juridical personae. Quomodo's hand has endorsed a series of legal documents, including the memorandum releasing Easy, but since it has been indiscriminately disseminated it does not function as an accurate replication of its signer's intent. As a result, Quomodo's hand cannot be sutured back onto his person. The trial shifts its focus from the adjudication of the debt to a case of mistaken identity, illuminating further the legal ambiguity subtending all written contracts, as Easy asserts to the judge, "We are not certain yet it is himself [Quomodo], but some false spirit that assumes his shape, and seeks still to deceive me" (5.3.12–13). The judge asks Quomodo the impossible question, "How are we sure y'are he?" (5.3.20), and proceeds to determine that the person before him is not Quomodo "but a counterfeit" (5.3.26), a word associated in the period with the scandalous proliferation of debased coins. Quomodo has produced bastard bonds and by denying his paternity he renders himself a legal entity that no longer counts. The play closes with the fracturing of will, identity, and body as Quomodo empathetically declares: "my deeds have cleft me, cleft me!" (5.3.93). Here Quomodo perceives himself as having been spread open against his will, and his distress and pecuniary loss register as a poetic reversal of his original aggressive intent, expressed at the play's opening, to use debt bonds to "cleave [Easy] the heir in twain" (1.1.104).

Conclusion

In the final analysis, Easy's passivity may be pleasing but it cannot satisfy.[43] This is because, as I have suggested, the implication of signing onto a bond was undergoing a gradual but nonetheless seismic shift as the result of the 1602 decision on *Slade's Case*. In *Michaelmas Term*, even as the bond seems to render consent tangible through the material artifact of the signature, at every turn the play exposes the incoherency of agency and the debt bond as a palimpsest, a document comprised of layer upon layer of uncertain causality, confused intentionality, and suspect liability. In the end, the separation of Quomodo's person and hand is the only possible resolution to the trial and the play because the depersonalization of the signature is ultimately what allowed the bond to function effectively as a transferrable monetary instrument. Thus in order for the bond to evolve into a generic promise that could bind the lender to an anonymous recipient across time and space, the link between material person and hand had to be severed. In turn, the signer had to see himself as an interchangeable bearer of universal will—his empirical self a contingent variable, no longer anchoring specific desires. The signer of the debt bond, in effect, had to become the abstract representative of the signature itself: a repeatable, conventional entity.

While my analysis has elucidated the links among dramatic narrative, economic practice, and legal debate, I have also aimed to reveal the ways in which formal encounters between bonds and playtexts generate a series of problems and possibilities for both dramatic and monetary forms of writing. As Mukherji notes, the law in this period was itself becoming an "upstart economy" by virtue of its promiscuous textuality.[44] And while it may have been easy to satirize the common law's culture of writing, the efficacy of the written deed was undeniable. Thus even as the bastard bond serves to potentially discredit the proper paternity of this form of monetary writing, such representations also speak to the play's—and the culture's—awareness of the bond as a form of writing engaged with various contested legal and philosophical debates about contractual consent. Just as we cannot deny the social impact of the bond in the early modern period, we should not dismiss the play's suspensions or deferrals of genre as structural weakness. Middleton's bypassing the signposts of romantic comedy stands as a violation of generic contract as he substitutes pecuniary parthenogenesis for heterosexual marriage. We may, though, look to those moments at which the play's logic becomes strained as instances at which it is (in)formed by the bond as Middleton exploits the tenuous nature of satisfaction in regard to both economic obligation and dramatic expectation.

Chapter 4

Freedom, Bondage, and Redemption in *The Custom of the Country*

If this be the English man's liberty, what is servitude?
—*A Petition Entitled Liberty Vindicated Against Slavery* (1646)

The Custom of the Colony

Perhaps *The Custom of the Country*'s reputation as the most obscene play ever to grace the English stage accounts for its immense popularity. Written in 1619, Fletcher and Massinger's play, when performed in 1628, outsold revivals of *Othello*, *Richard II*, and *The Alchemist*. *Custom* was performed twice more at court before the closing of the theaters.[1] While eighteenth-century audiences deemed it lewd—Pepys and Dryden were offended by its representation of an all-male brothel—modern critics have not found *Custom* to be either particularly scandalous or compelling. Over the past two hundred years, literary scholars have by and large remained silent on the topic of *Custom*, occasionally noting its debt to Cervantes's *Persiles y Sigismunda* and conformity to the conventions of the early modern chastity play.[2] The exception has been Carolyn Prager who, in analyzing the travails of the group of shipwrecked Italians that end up in Lisbon, draws our attention to the significance of a port city at the center of a thriving Mediterranean traffic in slaves. For Prager, *Custom* portrays coerced labor to illuminate the dangers of becoming spiritually bound to one's passions.[3]

As a play that features chattel bondage, *Custom* capitalizes on its audience's fascination with tales of captivity and self-sale of Christian men in the Mediterranean. However, at the historical moment this play was performed, the practice of Christians taking possession of other Christians was no longer solely a reality of the Mediterranean world.[4] By setting the play in Lisbon, Fletcher and Massinger allude not only to the dangers of an exotic port city known for its global slave trade but also to their own port city of London, which by 1625 had garnered a reputation as the hub of an international servant trade.[5] In 1606, in the earliest phase of English colonization in the Americas, the Virginia Company inaugurated an aggressive recruitment program aiming to entice, if not force, young Englishmen to work in the colony. Company members initially agreed to grant prospective servants a small parcel of land at the end of their term.[6] The prospect of a settlement, however, did not offer adequate motivation for the grueling work rumored to be imposed upon those who toiled in the colony's tobacco fields. Meanwhile, the company's policy of enforcing martial law on recalcitrant workers (as of 1609) frightened off new recruits. Company officials and port agents resorted to coercive measures in "recruiting" able-bodied young boys, including kidnapping and plying them with alcohol in order to trick them into boarding ships.[7] By 1616, London authorities facilitated the exportation of hundreds of orphans, felons, and impoverished youth, and by 1620, a staggering number of young men were being shipped to Virginia on a regular basis. The company's ability to advance men the cost of passage created an impressive overseas workforce based on an elaborate system of credit.[8]

Unorthodox strategies of recruitment shaped the perception and treatment of those young men who were neither daily wage earners nor live-in servants. Colonial workers were unlike their existing counterparts in England insofar as "the mechanism used to secure the investment in their voyage to the colonies had made them into property."[9] The employment conditions of those whose crossed the Atlantic were established by the terms of a signed contract that bound workers to planters they had never met, who had advanced them the cost of transport in lieu of compensation, either in the form of wages or livery (room, board, and clothing). The indentured servant, as David Galenson explains, "unable to borrow elsewhere the money necessary for the passage fare and provisions, borrowed against the future returns from his labor."[10] In this respect, the servant was his own surety insofar as he put up his person for collateral, making him, in the eyes of the law, "an animated gage, a hostage delivered over to slavery but subject to redemption."[11] The indenture functioned both as a labor contract and a *prima facie* debt bond: Its promissory element was subtended by the logic of *capias ad satisfaciendum*, the writ that allowed for the detention of the body of the borrower in the event of nonpayment.[12] The creditor-debtor relation thus set the stage for English servants becoming "the most liquid form of capital" in the New World.[13]

There are no explicit references to the Virginia colony in *Custom*; nevertheless, its guiding conceit—the "custom of the country"—indexes an emerging notion of property in person forged by debt law and solidified by New World indenture. Critics have assumed that *Custom*'s title references the first-night rite of bridal rape described within Fletcher and Massinger's Spanish source material. Yet at the beginning of the seventeenth century, the phrase "custom of the country" was used in the specific context of colonial indenture, in which it referred to younger, unskilled servants who arrived in Virginia without proper documentation.[14] The distinction between so-called "custom-of-the-country servants" and other indentured young men was negligible, however, since the conditions of servitude for all men, whether or not they arrived with papers, were ultimately determined neither by English statutory provisions nor by the recommendations of London authorities, but by "the Custom of the Country"—the phrase written on every indenture.[15]

Within England, customary law was based in place and had developed out of geographical disputes over the efficacy of local tradition; it was applicable only within a specific jurisdiction. Not surprisingly, custom had long been in conflict with the tenets of common law, and London's central courts, which were inclined to regard it as a tool of those wishing to assert their hegemony, summarily rejected claims to custom in legal disputes.[16] The tension between custom and common law surfaced in 1622 when the London Deputy of the Virginia Company admonished stockholders for not upholding the terms of their servants' bonds. English law mandated that "all contracts made in *England* betweene the owners of lande . . . & Servantes wch they shall send hither" be duly observed in the Americas upon pain of penalty. Company officials responded by pointing to the indenture's inclusion of the phrase "the custom of the country."[17] Overseers across the ocean saw themselves as answerable only to those laws "suche as might proceed out of every mans private conceit."[18] Here colonists asserted that the body of the servant was no longer under the jurisdiction of the English monarch but subject only to the laws of economic exigency.

Agents of the Virginia Company were among the worst offenders of good labor practices, as indicated by reports sent back to England. In a June 8, 1617, letter to Edwin Sandys, John Rolfe describes Virginia's servants as men who "cheerfully labour . . . their harts and hands not ceasing from worke, though many have scarce rags to cov[e]r their naked bodyes."[19] One servant bound to the treasurer of the colony writes of his master that "he maketh us serve him whether wee will or noe and how to helpe yt we doe not knowe for hee beareth all the sway."[20] In a letter Thomas Best sent to his brother on April 12, 1623, Best declares, "I am in great danger of Starvinge. My Master Atkins hath sold me for a £150 ster. like a damnd slave as he is for using me so baselie" (*RVC*, 4:235). The ambiguity of Best's statement is significant. Was he sold like a slave or rather is he saying that his master became "like a damnd slave" when he "us[ed] [him] so baslie"? His comment points to the flexibility of slavery as an evocative concept in this context.

Critics of the colonial enterprise seized on reports of suspect labor practices to demonstrate that authorities across the Atlantic left unchecked were keeping certain segments of the population in "extreme misery and slavery."[21] Calling on an early seventeenth-century understanding of self-restraint as a virtue, as informed by the Neo-Stoic notion of *sophrosyne* or moderation, detractors targeted colonists for their intemperance.[22] Francis Bacon, in his essay on New World plantations, insists that the colony's government be made up of "temperate" men only.[23] London investors questioned the legitimacy of the colony by accusing planters of using their servants "with more slavery then if they were under the Turke" (*RVC*, 1:334–35). The word "slavery," a slippery term in an evolving early seventeenth-century discourse of liberty, functioned, as Alison Games stresses, "as a code, a single word conveying horrors no Englishman should have to endure" and was used to refer to any government considered illegitimate or abusive.[24]

Tracts defending the colony, such as the 1620 *A Declaration of the State of the Colonie prepared for this Majesties Counsel for Virginia*, aimed "to show that Letters and Rumours are false and malicious [and] suborned to evill purposes" (3). In a report, entitled *A True Declaration of the Estate of the Colonie in Virginia*, company official William Barret celebrates rather than denies the unstable admixture of peril and profit that characterized working conditions beyond England. He poses the rhetorical question, "what is there in all this *tragicall comedie* that should discourage us with the impossibilities of the enterprise?"[25] For Barret, "from . . . Calamatie" comes the "abundant and sustaining life" to be found in the New World, a place where all "extremities" are rendered "wholesome and temperate."[26] In keeping with the company's goal of combating criticism and reframing the enterprise to attract skeptics, the acquisition of wealth is represented as inspiring temperate conditions, which calms the turbulent effects of an unpredictable environment and the baser impulses it inspired.[27]

If the language of temperance shaped defenses and detractions of the Virginia project, it took on new force in the period's tragicomedies, in which self-restraint is recommended to those cast beyond the disciplinary orders of their native country.[28] More particularly, scholars have demonstrated that as a genre that consistently imagined loss as gain, tragicomedy with its trope of turning and heralding of moderation was ideally suited to the contradictory impulses and implications of England's burgeoning mercantile and maritime efforts.[29] *Custom* participates in the tragicomic project when, in accordance with the standard Stoic precept, its characters claim adversity as a spur to virtue.[30] Yet, in its championing of self-restraint, this play moves in an unexpected direction. Even after passion gives way to interest, characters are not rewarded with self-possession but remain bound by debt.

By situating my analysis of *Custom*'s interest in metaphorical and literal bondage within the context of the English traffic in servants, this chapter shows this play to be equally invested in temperance as an economic disposition as a physiological condition.[31] Throughout the play, the accumulation of profit is predicated on the ability to honor contracts. Virtue is thus measured in accordance with a legal paradigm that recognizes predictable behavior as productive insofar as good character is equated with fiscal solidity. In this respect, the outlines of *Custom* reflect the contours of a domestic culture of credit in which most exchange relations were, as Craig Muldrew observes, "in some way proprietorial" and for this reason functioned best when cast in a moral framework.[32] As he explains: "The fact that wealthier tradesmen had to forgive so many debts to the poor also must have given them great deal of potential power in their communities through the employment of discretion. Deference was expected as the price of forgiveness, and as long as the wealthy could maintain the credit of their own households they could use the fact that they lost so much of their wealth through forgiveness to justify their authority" (309). As Muldrew notes, the continual forgiveness of debts was psychologically expensive for debtors and a costly means of maintaining authority for creditors. Attempts to instill discipline in male members of poorer households, which included the issuance of tracts against excessive drinking and disorderly conduct, were designed to shame chronic borrowers into exercising thrift. In the interest of stabilizing otherwise fragile chains of credit, as evidenced by the period's deluge of defaults, English lenders and borrowers understood the importance of cultivating circumspection so as to guarantee that each party in a binding agreement could be counted on to pay his debts.

If temperance was crucial to creditworthiness at home, it was absolutely essential in a colonial context. While probity allowed Englishmen and women inclusion in local economic networks, reciprocity between a reasonable creditor/master and a temperate debtor/servant allowed indenture to exemplify an ethical alternative to forced labor. Accordingly, throughout *Custom* arrangements of economic obligation are shown to be the by-products of individuals acting reasonably in accordance with their interests rather than impulsively in response to their passions, which in turn allows them to create and reinforce webs of interdependency that make up a cohesive community. If, as I argued in Chapters 1 and 2, Shakespeare recognized the bond's role in facilitating justice and maintaining social harmony within England, then Fletcher and Massinger understood that the bond had to do the same beyond England. The social and moral order of the body politic, increasingly understood as a global entity, depended on a credit economy in which relations of trust could be extended over time and across great distances. As long as unrestrained passion stood as an obstacle to fiscal proportionality, and the social harmony it enabled, the movement from excess to moderation became the precondition of consensual exchange in a transmarine economy.[33] Thus *Custom* realizes the bond as an instrument for achieving temperance insofar as the process of bonding is what enables characters to become morally and fiscally redeemable.

Bound to Serve

Although colonial servitude has long been regarded as an extension rather than an aberration of English apprenticeship, revisionist scholarship validates Edmund Morgan's observation that "servitude in Virginia's tobacco fields approached closer to slavery than anything known at the time in England."[34] New World labor practices mark a significant break with Old World ones. Planters, as Hilary McD. Beckles stresses, "freely bought, sold, gambled away, mortgaged, taxed as property, and alienated in wills their indentured servants."[35] Indentured servants could be used as stakes in card games and seized as property by colonial magistrates to satisfy their masters' unpaid debts.[36] While Englishmen who served in America may not have been slaves technically, in the absence of any established political-legal framework, they remained at the mercy of the custom of the colony. They were subjected to corporal punishment, denied wages, controlled by their masters both during laboring and nonlaboring hours, required to obtain a pass to leave the plantation, forced to seek permission to marry, and regarded "primarily as a capital investment."[37] Thus unlike servants who remained in England, whose oath of service granted their masters some degree of authority over their lives, New World servants entered into a labor relation in which their masters demonstrated a significant investment in the bodies of their charges.

The peculiar proprietary logic of colonial indenture mirrored credit relations at home, and the similarities between the arrangements are explored by writers who depict the experience of indebtedness as comparable to that of embarking on an oceanic venture. Henry Peacham in his advice manual to those new to London, *The Art of Living in London*, correlates indebtedness and indenture when he imagines the city as "like a vast Sea" and warns the naïve country gentleman to be "ready at every storme to sinke and cast away."[38] Having weathered the trials of a rapacious, commercial milieu peopled by con artists and creditors, Peacham fashions himself as "another Columbus or Drake," who upon coming to London is armed against those who lay in wait to "catch hold of [his] fleece" (A1). He explains: "Let a Gentleman . . . have a care to keepe himself out of debt . . . when he walkes abroad he is ready to be snapt up at every lanes end by Sarjeants Marshals men, or Baylies . . . in the meane time his creditors . . . will be ready to disgrace him; and if arrested, he shall be held to prison many times like a dogge" (A3). The author of *Pictures of Passions* compares debtor's prison to "an ocean venture," and in *The Compters Common-wealth*, William Fennor, prisoner of the Woodstreet Counter, subtitles his pamphlet, "A Voiage made to an Infernall Island long since discovered by many Captaines, Seafaring Gentlemen, Marchants, and other Tradesmen."[39] Dedicating his tract to "all cashiered Captaines, of other their inferiour Officers, heedless and headless young Gentle-men, especially elder brothers, forsaken Serving-men, . . . Broken-Citizens . . . or any other of what art or fashion soever that shall by chance, rather mischance . . . become tenants against their wile" (A3), Fennor attempts "to instruct young heires to keepe out of books and bonds, which oftentimes are the maine cause of their overthrow" (A3). Describing his experience as an incarcerated debtor as a "voyage" (A3), he aims to reach those who "have been passengers through this troublesome Ocean and know the danger, or to any that shall hereafter," as well as those that "have no desire to venture this voyage but will rather be contented to sit at home and read the discovery" (A3).

Thomas Powell in his *The Mystery and Misery of Lending and Borrowing* advances the most vibrant overlay of debt and indenture. The debtor, as Powell explains, is "a refugee" (201), whose only hope of escaping his predatory creditors lies in jumping a ship to "parts habitable and agreeable" (242). The ship he boards is called "the Pay Nought" (243), commanded by "Sir Oliver Overmuch who manned the same with person best qualified in the Art of Insolvency, the greater part whereof, himself had known" (243). The ship of debtors makes landfall on "a most spacious continent with a climate exceeding temperate" (25), where they set to work merchandizing the commodities they find there. The joke is on them, however, as it turns out that the "plantation" to which they have traveled is still London; they have voyaged only "4 degrees beyond the Temple [Bar]" (250).

In Fletcher and Massinger's *Custom*, the sea voyage is the means by which its characters escape a situation dominated by threats of bodily harm and enter into a new milieu, in which the rules of commerce both constrain and protect them. Through its concern with sexual purity in particular, expressed as bridal rape and prostitution, and corporal violation more generally, exemplified by forced enslavement, *Custom* showcases the fight to preserve bodily integrity in a context in which one's person takes on unprecedented value as the possession of another. The play begins with the stark dramatization of the Roman governor, Count Clodio, manifesting his appetite for virgins by his adherence to the antiquated practice of first-night rites (whereby a bride on her wedding night is deflowered by her husband's kinsmen), a custom that, as one character explains, "this wretched country hath wrought into a law."[40] The assertion of *ius primae noctis* that frames the play is depicted, as in Cervantes's *Persiles y Sigismunda*, as an iniquitous practice that offends social mores. Yet Fletcher and Massinger curiously substitute the traditional rite, in which defloration is initiated by members of the same clan, with the brutal assertion of ownership by a singular tyrannical authority. In *Custom*, the governor claims rights to the body of a virgin bride whose family desperately tries to satisfy him with monetary compensation. By highlighting the proprietary underpinnings of *ius primae noctis*, Fletcher and Massinger's version of this custom resonates with the English feudal practice involving the payment grooms made to ecclesiastical authorities to ensure that the church lifted its ban on first-night consummation. The English custom of *mercheta mulierum* became secularized as mandatory payment to the overlord, because, as literary critic W. D. Howarth explains, serfs "were the property of the overlord," and marriage to someone belonging to another manor signaled the loss of manor property.[41]

English villeinage had long been extinct by the time Fletcher and Massinger's play was performed, but, as historians stress, the concept of white slavery remained "unmistakably fossilized in common law."[42] The relation of manor lord to his serf and the sanctioning of bridal rape are linked at the onset of this play as equivalent abuses of authority and means of designating the bodies of others as property. The "custom of the country" thus functions as an overdetermined phrase, freighted by the historical baggage of medieval serfdom, and animated by travelers' tales of *ius primae noctis* in so-called primitive societies, but emerging most prominently in accounts of colonial authorities' exploitation of the gray area between English law and local custom.[43] In the acts that follow, the particular "unresistable" custom of bridal rape (8) is implicitly compared with the Portuguese tradition of enslaving foreign captives.

The crisis that frames *Custom* is sexual exploitation, but the opening scene establishes erotic enslavement as a metaphor for intemperate relations based upon various forms of corporal coercion. When Count Clodio refuses to take a monetary fine as a substitute for Zenocia's maidenhead and insists instead on observing the "black and barbarous" custom of *ius primae noctis*, the play links his overweening passion to an irrational refusal of payment (21). Zenocia's husband and brother-in-law stress that the count intends to subject her to his "intemp'rate, rude and wild embraces" (9). Described as a "maidenmonger" (11), Clodio is "a cannibal that feeds on the heads of maids / . . . / a cat o'mountain" that would make "a town bull" seem a "mere stoic," and "a Spanish jennet a most virtuous gentleman" (11). Even Clodio confesses, "I am hot and fiery / And my blood beats alarums through my body / And fancy high" (20). For Clodio, "to possess [Zenocia]" (8) is "to enjoy" or consume and use her up. He is thus likened to a slave driver who "would weary her" (10) and is described as a merciless overseer who "breaks young wenches to the saddle," "teaches them to stumble ever after," and "whip[s] off [their] heads" (11). Despite repeated offers, he remains resolute that "no money nor prayers shall redeem that [her body]" (18). Zenocia herself begs him to "set [her] own price" (918), and her father later pleads with Clodio to "let [him] pay the ransom" (22). Yet for Clodio only "[Zenocia's] body will content [him]" (18). When bride, groom, and brother-in-law flee Rome, Clodio deems their flight a crime of property, protesting to Zenocia's husband Arnoldo, "thou hast robb'd me, villain, of a treasure" (23).

Here the play's perspective on the social dangers of extreme passion remains in keeping with an Aristotelian notion of immoderation as inimical to civil order.[44] Aristotle advises those who occupy positions of authority to guard against "disproportionate excess" because their lapses create the conditions for those beneath them to slide into a state of "slavery."[45] This prescription for a temperate society is understood by a variety of seventeenth-century commentaries to rest in the hands of the ruler. They argue that "a monarch who abuses property rights is described in ways that define him as passionate ('lustful') rather than reasonable, self-indulgent ('sensuall') rather than disciplined, and governed by a desire for 'goodes' rather than a commitment to the good of his people."[46] *Custom* too identifies constancy among those that rule as necessary to instilling temperance in those who are ruled. A pose of self-retention is thus heralded as the quality that all people must cultivate in a commercial context in which selves are alienable. While the analogy between rape and tyranny was an early modern commonplace, the idiom of temperance was capacious and could be mobilized as an explanatory model for the need to moderate the nation's economic prosperity in accordance with the needs of social harmony.[47]

The mercantilist Gerard de Malynes, for instance, in making the case for the ideal quantity of money as an amount that does not lead to unlimited accumulation and its disruptive social potentials, draws an analogy between the proper balance between the store and circulation of coins and the correct proportion of blood flowing through the body. He notes that having "plenty of money" is just like having enough "blood in the body," "enough" being all that we need to nourish our limbs without achieving imbalance.[48] Similarly, the neo-Aristotelian economist Bernard Davanzati writes:

> For as *Blood*, which is the Juice and Substance of Meat in the natural Body, does, by circulating out of the greater into the lesser Vessels. . . . So it nourishes and restores as much of it as was dri'd up and evaporated by the Natural Heat: In like manner, Money . . . does, by circulating out of the richer Purses into the poorer, furnish all the Nation being laid out upon those things whereof there is continual Consumption for the Necessities of Life. . . . Hence, it may be easily conceived that every *State* must have a quantity of *Money*, as every *Body* a quantity of *Blood*.[49]

Sentiments such as these underscore the claim—one that matches Galenic medical theory—that society is a finite body that functions best when properly balanced. As Davanzati warns, "Blood stopping in the Head or the larger Vesssels puts the Body naturally into . . . Apoplexy," so then when money is "only in a few hands," then the state suffers from "dangerous Distempers."[50]

As Casey Evans has demonstrated, temperance in this period was conceived not only in terms of humoral, climatological, and alimentary balance but also in terms of temporal restraint, understood as the virtue of prudent delay. The temporal aspect of temperance, as Evans shows, appealed to those

English writers aiming to defend the ethics of New World conquest. More particularly, temperance became "an explicit term of economic evaluation, with which to judge the financial and cultural implications of colonial settlement in the New World," implications that would not be apparent to the English colonizer for quite some time.[51] In the English imagination, Spanish activity in the New World was the model of intemperance, marked by excessive appetite for worldly goods and temporal mismanagement. Spanish explorers impulsively returned to Spain after having cruelly extracted spoils rather than choosing to remain in the Americas to establish plantations. Debt bondage and its conception of the debtor's body as a redeemable investment dovetailed with English colonialists' ideals of delayed gratification, particularly because this ideal did not seek to extinguish the desire for profit but rather contain that desire within the bounds of deferred satisfaction.

The tension between the urgency of desire and the patience of deferral, which becomes heightened in *Custom* once the setting shifts from Rome to Lisbon, is managed in the play through the idiom of temperance. The interplay of sexual exploitation and threat of enslavement become even more pronounced at the moment at which the virgin bride construes the trial of her honor as a test of her "male constancy" (32). By turning the gendered language of sexual assault on its head, Fletcher and Massinger conflate the virtuous woman who desires to be inviolable with the male foreign captive who seeks to remain inalienable, or unpossessed by another. When pirates hijack the ship carrying the wedding party, the bride's husband and his brother leap into the ocean to ensure that they will "never" have to "taste the bread of servitude" (30). Yet when they come ashore, they are described as "disarm'd and ready to be put in fetters" (30). Arnoldo and his brother Rutillio are then subjected to a series of trials that threaten their respective rights of self-ownership.

In staging the careful negotiation of the ever-shifting boundary between voluntary and compulsory service, *Custom* represents the male body as vulnerable to an immoderate authority that seeks to drain it of its prowess. Once on shore, Zenocia is sold to the Portuguese Countess Hippolyta who is determined to "ravish" Zenocia's erstwhile groom Arnoldo (54). The occasion of Arnoldo's capture is marked by his signing a debt bond, when upon his arrival a Jewish moneylender recognizes the brothers as "poor and strangers" (34) and offers to assist them with a loan. The gold he provides, however, is not as he claims "bounty" that he "give[s]" "freely" (35). Instead, it is the "earnest of that which is to follow," and he explains to Antonio that this is "the bond which you must seal for 't is your advancement" (35). Having been granted an advance, Antonio is then expected to work off his debt by servicing the Jew's mistress, the ravenous, Amazonian Hippolyta whose "touches" are described as "fetters" and whose "locks" are "soft chains to bind the arms of princes" (60). Arnoldo only narrowly escapes enslavement, when his demanding mistress declares, "Upon my conscience, I must ravish thee!" and attempts "to bind him" in literal chains (54). Like Clodio, Hippolyta strives to possess Arnoldo so that she may "enjoy [him] indeed" (54). When he flees her court, Hippolyta's exclamations echo that of Clodio, when she deems this as an offense akin to the wrongful seizure of property and has Arnoldo imprisoned for theft (presumably of himself) (55).

Hippolyta, however, undergoes a miraculous transformation after being advised by the governor of Lisbon that her bondwoman Zenocia cannot be counted as "a lawful prize," because she is "of that country we hold friendship with" (81). Suddenly willing to marshal rather than exhaust her resources, Hippolyta generously decides to "redeem all" (61), as she comes to recognize that "It is in vain / To strive with destiny" (104). Her conversion is confirmed when she assumes her place in Lisbon's credit economy and, as "recompense" for the suffering she has caused, forgives Lisbon "the hundred thousand crowns the city owes [her]" (104). She summarily "discharge[s]" Zenocia from her bonds (81) and "unloose[s]" the imprisoned Arnoldo from "[his] bonds" as well (65), allowing him to "redeem" himself in exchange for his bride.

Based on the Latin *redimĕre*, meaning to buy back, redemption was understood in the early modern period as both deliverance from sin as the result of Christ's sacrifice and the act of being purchased or ransomed by someone who served as one's redeemer (*OED*). By 1620, however, "redemptioner" had a very specific meaning since it was the word used for a young man who sold himself to a ship's captain for transport to the colonies, where he would be auctioned off to the highest bidder upon arrival. Redemptioners were Christian and of English or German descent, yet they were never incorporated into the households of their masters. Neither slaves nor live-in domestics, redemptioners had abnegated rights of self-ownership in order to satisfy the debt they had accrued for the cost of transport, room, and board.

In keeping with the colonial meaning of redemptioner, Arnoldo, although no longer enslaved to Hippolyta, remains indebted to her. While Arnoldo has been released from his shackles, he must now "pay dearly for her favour," as one character wryly observes (65). With a kiss, he publicly pledges himself to Hippolyta and asks that she "accept [his] ready service" (66). Formally acknowledging his debt to her, he agrees "forever to be fetter'd to [her]" (78) so that she may "command [him] through what danger" (78). This time it is with his voluntary submission that she "makes him [her] slave," as he "give[s] [his] freedom" over to her in acknowledgment of his debt (78). In the case of both Hippolyta and Arnoldo we witness the conversion of passion into interest, the word that in seventeenth-century philosophical discourse served as the generic term for that which trumped the chaos of potentially destructive human impulses.[52] In recommending temperance as the necessary disposition for participation in economic and legal bonds put under pressure by global expansion, *Custom* stages the dilemma posed by exchange relations that exposed the limits of an English notion of liberty founded on self-ownership.

Redeeming the Male Body

While Arnoldo has successfully tempered Hippolyta's urges, his brother Rutillio faces an even more dangerous trial when he agrees to serve in a male brothel. The main function of the play's infamous brothel scene would seem to generate material for a subplot involving the rakish brother of the morally upright protagonist. Yet this scene occupies a more central function in the play than previous scholarship has allowed in that it amplifies the perils of labor in an exotic locale by dramatizing the association of coerced sexual performance and compulsory service. Brothels appear frequently on the early modern English stage, but unlike the majority of plays featuring bawdy houses, *Custom* does not present a tale of female fall and redemption. Fletcher and Massinger instead use the male stews as a means to show the brutal effects of a market economy on the impressed young man. Although the brothel revolves around the laboring male body, in relinquishing rights to both his capacities and the product of his labor, the male sex-worker alienates himself. Undermining the fantasy of the stews as a proving ground for male stamina, here the brothel is a work site determined by the relationship between the dispossessed worker and the intemperate overseer.

Human traffic is initially posited as an alternative to penal bondage. When Rutillio is apprehended for having "wand'r[ed]" into the city's munitions storehouse (57), he is given the choice of either "six years tug[ging] at an oar i'th' galleys" (57) or allowing Sulpitia the brothel madam to purchase him for six hundred ducats. He gladly accepts the madam's offer to redeem him and vows to "give her [his] whole self," which she concurs she "has reason to expect . . . considering the great sum she pays for it" (58). Rutillio erroneously assumes that his potency will allow him to excel as a he-whore, and he boasts, "I am excellent at it" (58):

> Bring me a hundred of 'em: I'll dispatch 'em.
> I will be none but yours. Should another offer
> Another way to redeem me, I should scorn it.
> What women you shall please: I am monstrous lusty,
> Not to be taken down. Would you have children?
> I'll get you those as fast, and thick as fly-blows. (58)

From the play's first act, Rutillio's enthusiasm for sexual conquest is established as he admits his envy of the count's plan to enact the "admirable, rare custom" of bridal rape (6). When, however, it becomes evident that he has consigned himself to a life of "tug[ging] in a feather bed" (59), he moderates his passion, wishing to be "honestly married" so that he might be "civilly merry" (87–88). Work in the stews, it turns out, is another form of chattel bondage, since his clientele, the "men-leech[ing]" city-women of Lisbon, are relentlessly demanding and never satisfied (86).

Despite the brothel's labor force of able-bodied young men, demand pushes production to its breaking point. One worker bemoans the grueling conditions and warns the unyielding madam, "You do so over-labour 'em when you have 'em, / And so dry-founder 'em, they cannot last" (55). Another complains, "the labor [is] so much . . . and so few to perform it" (87). They curse the climate, which is described as sultry; the "dampish air" causing "a snuffing in [the] head" (86) and "too warm for [their] complexions" (87). The Danish and German men are broken: one is described as in "fitters," or fragments, and "chin'd" (55), or broken-backed, and another is hospitalized and no longer able to "labour like a thresher" (56). The English workers fare no better and are left to "draw their legs like hackneys" (56). In the end, even Rutillio complains bitterly:

> Now do I look as if I were crow-trodden!
> Fie, how my hams shrink under me! Oh, me,
> I am broken-winded too. Is this a life?
> . . . .
> I had a body once, a handsome body,
> And wholesome too. Now I appear like a rascal
> That had been hung a year or two in gibbets.
> Fie, how I faint.
> . . . .
> Place me before a cannon; 'tis a pleasure.

> Stretch me upon a rack.
> . . . .
> No galleys to be got, nor yet no gallows? (86)

A man who "draw[s] [his] legs after [himself] like a lame dog" and who is "too feeble" to run away (87), Rutillio is outdone at the prospect of pleasing "an old, dead-palsied lady in a litter" (84). The brothel, as he realizes, cannot serve as an opportunity for adventure and empowerment since value does not inhere in the skills he offers but rather in his body's capacity to endure. Pleasing the women of Lisbon proves more demanding than "labouring in [the] fulling-mills" (88), and he grows wistful at the thought of wage-labor whereby he could lease his person while still retaining proprietorship of himself: "Death, if I had but money, / Or any friends to bring me from this bondage, / I would thresh, . . . keep hogs / . . . Thatch for three half-pence a day and think it lordly, / From this base stallion trade" (89).

The madam's response to Rutillio's request for liberty parodies that of the planter cum slave-owner:

> If you be so angry,
> Pay back the money I redeem'd you at
> And take your course. I can have men enough.
> You lost me an hundred crowns since you came hither,
> In broths and strength'ning caudles.
> Till you do pay me,
> If you will eat and live, you shall endeavour.
> I'll chain you to't else. (88)

Through the figure of the madam we are shown the dire results of the gross mismanagement of liquid assets (in this case, of semen rather than cash or tobacco): A demoralized, and potentially rebellious, workforce and an enterprise always hovering on the verge of extinction. Labor performed outside the stable context of the guild or household devolves into a promiscuous arrangement when the worker's performance is compelled by threats of an emasculating authority, misogynistically coded as female.

The moral problem of male prostitution as presented in *Custom* spoke to the most startling example of colonial planters' assertions of prerogative over their servants, the practice of resale. Here, Rutillio's delusions of unlimited sexual potency mirror the misguided hopes of the beguiled young men who slavishly labored on plantations, clinging to the promise of recompense that would never materialize. The selling off of a servant's contract was not entirely unknown in seventeenth-century England, since, for example, with the permission of guild members, a master could sell his apprentice to another company member. But by the time Fletcher and Massinger's play was performed, the binding of an apprentice with the intent to sell him was considered a gross abuse of authority.[53] The colonial market in servants, however, explicitly identified servants as saleable goods, since, as Edmund Morgan points out, "by going to Virginia," a servant "became for a number of years a thing, a commodity with a price."[54] In a cash-poor colony, the bodies of young men, in the words of Virginian planter John Pory, were understood to serve as the colony's "principall wealth" (*RVC*, 3:221). In official reports and personal letters, young men tell of being equated with pounds sterling or pounds of tobacco (*RVC*, 4:235). Despite recognizing their servants as valuable investments, colonial masters apparently had no compunction about abusing or wasting this precious asset. Word spread quickly that "divers m[aste]rs. in Virginia doe much neglect and abuse their servants there with intolerablle oppression and hard usage" (*RVC*, 2:442), and that "Divers old Planters and others did allure and beguile divers younge p[er]sons and others (ignorant and unskillfull in such matters) to serve them upon intollerable and unchristianlike condicons upon promises of such rewards and recompence, as they were no wayes able to performe nor ever meant" (*RVC*, 2:113). On December 19, 1625, the Virginia Council oversaw a dispute between Captain Robert Newman and Thomas Weston over the sale of servants. Weston "demanded of Mr. *Newman*" "[what] commodities he would bringe from *Canada*, Mr. *Newman* replied yt the chieffest thing that he would bringe should be two or three servants & asked Mr. *Weston* [what] he must geve for the Transportinge A man from *Canada*, Mr. *Westone* said yt the said *newman* must pvide the men himselfe and give XXs for the ye Transport of A man, and find them Victualls."[55] A third party intervened to remind the judge that when Weston agreed to transport servants from Canada, Weston had set his price at "a hundred pownde," since he knew he could get as least as much for servants that "were sold here [Virginia] upp & downe like horses."[56] As late as 1648, it was, according to one colonial magistrate, "more advantageous" to import servants within the colonial territories than "any other commodityes."[57]

John Rolfe, who acknowledged that the "buying and selling of men and boies" was steady business in the colonies, tried to reassure his fellow Englishmen by reminding them that "in England" slavery was "a thing most intolerable."[58] As early as 1604, William Perkins broached the question of whether "a Christian may with safe conscience have and use a man as a slave," even as most Englishmen believed it to be un-Christian "to have any Christian man bound to another and to have the rule of his body, lands, and goods."[59] Thomas Smith, for instance, represented the common view that the "persuasion" of Christians was "not to make nor keepe his brother in christe, servile, bond, and underling forever unto him, as a beast rather than as a man," because Christianity had spread throughout the realm "a doubt, a conscience, and scruple to have servants and bondmen."[60] William Gouge in his treatise on domestic duties cites the Anabaptist argument that "it is against nature for one to be servant, especially a bond-servant to another," even as he avers "a politique inequality is not against a spirituall equality" and invokes biblical authority to justify "the *bounden* duties of service."[61] Gouge understood a servant's person to "properly belong to a master for the time of their service," such that the master had the right to "passe them over and give or sell them to another" (Gouge, 664). Yet even as he admits that "the customs and statutes of our land does also permit masters to make over [turn over] their servants from one to one: and on their death-beds to bequeath them to whom they will, even as their goods and possessions" (664), he decries masters who "have them [servants] beyond the sea" and who "aime merely at their owne advantage . . . so they may make gaine thereby" by selling them (Gouge, 665).[62]

If Fletcher and Massinger's play condemns Christian slavery, it recognizes the practical necessity of debt bondage. Rutillio's problem is solved not simply by his own change of heart but by the introduction of yet another economic arrangement. He is released from the "base trade" into which he has been impressed when he is redeemed by the once-hotheaded aristocratic Duarte, who, like Hippolyta, has undergone a miraculous transformation. Juxtaposed both to the lusty he-whore and the greedy madam, Duarte is the embodiment of temperance, exemplified by his magnanimous offer to pay the madam the entire balance due, despite the fact that Rutillio's debt has inexplicably doubled. The character of Duarte represents the process by which passion may be refined, as he gains an awareness of the virtue of exchange over and above possession. Once his extremities are calmed, Duarte's interest in profit overtakes his unbridled passion for pleasure. He effectively forswears obsessive self-love, exemplified by compulsive boasting and dueling, and in seeking to achieve a temperate existence based on an understanding of the self as embedded within economic and social networks, he demonstrates that appetite may be a useful means for the creation of consensual community.

Rutillio is redeemed, but he is not free. He ends his days as Duarte's stepfather when he agrees to marry his creditor's mother, the woman to whom he declares himself bound by "the infinite debt [he] owe[s] [her]" (41). (He has also accepted a loan of one hundred crowns from her [44].) Through his financial dependence on both mother and son, Rutillio is inserted into a credit economy that requires him to identify himself as "a creature bound [to them]" (107). In the end, the distinction between degrading labor and economic bondage turns on the temperament of the consenting parties.

In heralding economic obligation as socially restorative, Fletcher and Massinger echo Aristotle who advocates redemption as mediated by considerations of the status and disposition of the participating parties: "If, for instance, someone has ransomed you from pirates, should you ransom him in return, *no matter who he is*? Or if he does not need to be ransomed, but asks for his money back, should you return it, or should you ransom your father instead? Here it seems that you should ransom your father, rather than even yourself."[63] In this anecdote, Aristotle illustrates the ideal of proportionate reciprocity as distinct from both distributive justice, exemplified by the communal dispensation of wealth, and retributive justice. In this scenario, debt does not mean returning literally what one has borrowed but rather giving to each what is owed. Conjoining the concerns of social justice and economic obligation in Aristotelian terms, *Custom* rejects exploitation and equality alike, demonstrating that only a mutual arrangement between a rational superior and an economically beholden, self-possessed inferior can create social harmony.[64] *Custom*'s ideal of proportionate reciprocity, which speaks to a particular early Stuart notion of enfranchisement as *inequitable* entitlement, is figured as the heroic achievement of self-rule in the face of the internal and external chaos potentially unleashed by the unstable mix of slavery and servitude. In this respect, the play offers a psychological primer for a functional commercial society based on credit. Although a social order founded on the speculative prospect of redeeming one's bonds may inspire fantasy and passion, it also creates the conditions in which the subject may transcend his primitive appetites, allowing him to abandon barbarous custom and embrace the civility of mutual agreement.

Conclusion

Custom begins with the call to "make with all main speed to th' port" (23), and at its bleakest moments its protagonist muses, "my life's so full of various changes that I now despair of any certain port" (65). It ends, however, with "the evening . . . set clear after a stormy day" (113) and everyone's bark at last "having found a quiet harbour" (114). Thus a voyage that began with the lawlessness of desire, exemplified by threats of rape and piracy, ends with the assertion of the laws of commerce, expressed by relations of credit. Off the stage, no early seventeenth-century harbor was quiet as long as it was part of an oceanic world driven by pursuit of profit. The year of 1619, the date of Fletcher and Massinger's play, marks the first cargo of slaves sent to Jamestown.[65] Before African slavery became institutionalized, the English systematically subordinated their own. They disavowed the ethical problems of indentured servitude by mobilizing the fantasy that they were unlike non-Christian slave traders (particularly the Portuguese and Spanish) who depended on relations of domination based on a cash nexus and resorted to physical coercion to ensure a labor supply. As long as colonists could identify Portugal as the epicenter of human traffic, slavery would be demarcated as a foreign, specifically Catholic, institution. Thus members of the Virginia Company represented plantations with indentured servants as a far cry from the slave markets and galley ships that English emissaries and merchants encountered elsewhere.[66]

Yet at the moment of *Custom*'s first performance, the financial and legal scaffolding that upheld a thriving credit economy within England tied London to a world of commerce beyond its borders, leading one historian to describe the city in this period as "the hub of a metropolitan market system that revolved around port activity."[67] The port, a word derived from the Latin feminine *porta* and masculine *portus*, functioned as both an opening and an enclosure and thus served as an entrée and a haven. By connecting inland towns to the capital and by contributing to the development of an international city-center, port cities "shared other features with each other that they did not share with other kinds of cities, features that marked them as a breed apart."[68] Port cities contained larger and more diverse communities than non-port cities and offered a greater variety and volume of commercial goods, as well as a more effective distribution system for these items. In encouraging expanding markets, they also increased the need for raw materials and labor to convert these materials.

While critics have considered the relevance of early modern England's maritime culture to the period's dramatic literature, literary scholars by and large have not attended to the role of the port in facilitating urbanization. However, the oceanic world was not "other" to the world of cosmopolitan London, which was as much an island city as it was an ocean city. The Thames was the staging ground of both the country's and the city's commercial, military, and political activities and thus a spatial and symbolic extension of the capital. Those who worked for the commercial playhouses of London were part of a transmarine economy that entailed cycles of transport and profit beyond England. In order to understand how the theater responded not just to a capital city but also to a *port* city, we need to interpret *Custom*'s dramatization of the ambiguity of the port, insofar as oceanic travel leads to travail, in light of the ways global markets transformed local labor practices through the exigencies of urban credit.

Recent readings of plays like *The Tempest*, which as Daniel Vitkus suggests uses New World master-servant relations as an analogue for its own conditions of production, shed further light on writers' and players' awareness that the bonds that held theatrical laborers to their company heads operated much in the same way as those that held colonial workers to their overseers.[69] In addition to a specific play's representation of servitude as a labor relation determined by bondage, theatrical companies themselves were, scholars have shown, analogous in their investment structure to colonial joint-stock companies.[70] As I emphasized in Chapter 1, the players' bodies were not simply commodities to be used or exchanged, but an investment in which various stockholders had interest. *Custom* thus may be read as one of many elaborations of the connections among the perils of the port city, the plight of the player, and the function of the bond as a new species of promise.

Chapter 5

Prison Prose, the Pit, and the End of Tricks

A man is no longer a man confined but a man in debt.
—Gilles Deleuze, "Postscript on Control Societies"

Marke what imprisonment doth still produce,
Some greatly pine with griefe, some are profuse.
—Francis Mussell, *The Prisoner's Observation by Way of Complaint* (1645)

The last two chapters considered the bond as something other than a vehicle of entrapment. While bonds were endowed with proprietary power, they were also written documents authorized by the borrower. By signing onto a bond, the debtor participated in his own bondage, and, in this respect, the bond interpellated its debtor as an economic agent. The plays I analyzed in Chapters 3 and 4 advance their respective generic programs by exploiting the debtor's ambivalent role in an arrangement that straddled the uncertain boundary between coercion and consent. In Middleton's city comedy and Fletcher and Massinger's tragicomedy, debt bondage is represented as a flexible arrangement whose penal condition can be manipulated, if not mitigated, by the contractual underpinnings of the bond.

In this final chapter, I explore, most broadly, the cultural imagination of imprisonment for debt in a period during which civil incarceration and not personal bankruptcy determined the adjudication of the insolvent. More particularly, I examine two plays that represent penal confinement as liberating at the very moment that a rash of petitions submitted to Parliament characterize debtor's prison as the epitome of "bondage."[1] In *A Trick to Catch the Old One* by Thomas Middleton and *A New Way to Pay Old Debts* by Philip Massinger, the debtor maintains his dignity in the face of the inhumane conditions of prison not by reclaiming his person but by transcending the material conditions that threaten to debase him. In keeping with the period's seriocomic prose pamphlets, each of these plays depicts debtor's prison as at once degrading and reformatory. The redemptive powers of prison lie, however, not as one may expect in its serving as a site of spiritual conversion. Rather prison is the crucible that transforms the desperate debtor into the insouciant gallant. In Middleton's *A Trick,* the creditor may own his debtor's body but he is without monetary capital. The dispossessed debtor loses his liberty but gains in the process cultural capital. In this respect, Middleton's play mobilizes the key feature of debtor's prison literature: the notion of gain by loss, a logic, as Valerie Forman has argued, that was endemic to the concept of investment. If investment relied on a "narrative of transformative prosperity," then prison offered the site where the debtor's body accumulated worth, although not in ways profitable to his creditor.[2] By the time of the performance of Massinger's *A New Way to Pay Old Debts,* the bond that had for over a century been associated with the terrors of incarceration was seen as foundational for productive commercial and civic orders predicated on debt.

Imprisonment for forfeiture was not new in early seventeenth-century England, but, as Mark Benbow emphasizes, this "problem seems to have been intensified in . . . the first quarter of the seventeenth century."[3] This intensification reflected the culmination of the common law procedure that permitted creditors to take action against their debtors without the benefit of a jury trial. In 1617, William Fennor laments the 5,000 debtors moving through England's prisons annually, while a 1624 petition to King James and Parliament lists 3,000 debtors incarcerated in London that year alone. Another petition issued two decades later cites 10,000 "inslaved Christians" imprisoned for debt in England.[4] Indeed, the first few decades of the seventeenth century saw an unprecedented increase in debt litigation. For instance, in 1560, the number of cases in advanced stages in the King's Bench was 781, but by 1580, the number of cases had risen to 3,805, and by 1640, there were 8,109 cases in King's Bench and 20,625 in Common Pleas.[5] According to the Privy Council letters presented to the committee the Stuart government established to manage the overwhelming number of incarcerated debtors (the Commission for Hearing the Causes of Poor Debtors), the majority of those incarcerated had unwisely stood surety or been victims of "lewd and fradulous [*sic*] devices."[6]

Tricks had serious consequences in a legal context that did not discriminate between honest and dishonest debtors. Even though the 1602 decision on *Slade's Case* introduced the problem of the debtor's liability, the early modern judiciary had no interest in motive.[7] The courts, for instance, were under no obligation to distinguish those who were in debt as the result of misfortune or recklessness, despite the lament of a 1622 petition that it is "not agreeable to the role of justice to thrust all kinds of debtors into prison together in a heap without respect to . . . guilt of fraud or obstinacy."[8] Moreover, imprisonment was the fate of those who defaulted on as little as ten shillings as for those who owed hundreds of pounds. In every case the incarcerated was incapable of earning the money necessary to satisfy his debt, and his stay in prison added to his indebtedness since he was responsible for his own maintenance. London jails were owned and leased by city authorities that rented them out as franchises to wardens, who, in turn, charged exorbitant fees for rent and food.[9] The Royal Patent of 1618 emphasizes the illogic of a system that overwhelmed prisons with "the Bodies of those persons whose imprisonmente canne noe waie avail their Creditors, but rather is an hinderance to the Satisfaction of their Debts, for that, during the tyme of their Restrainte, they are in no wise able to goe aboute or attende their lawfull Busynes, but must of force consume themselves and that little they have miserably in prison."[10] Another petition on behalf of insolvent debtors presented to Parliament marvels that "A man who shall be arrested for some trivial debt of forty or fifty shillings, shall be compelled to lie in prison there till his very chamber rent amount to thrice the value of his debt. . . . there are as many men, very neere, that are condemned to perpetual imprisonment for their fees, as suffer that misery for their debts."[11] Whereas on the continent debtors could not be detained for more than one year, in England those who spent only seven years in prison were counted among the lucky.[12]

An indefinite term in one of London's Compter prisons or Counters (compter was derived from the word counter, which referred to the counting or keeping of records) was not, however, necessarily an excruciating prospect to those who had a reserve of cash.[13] Unlike the modern penitentiary, fashioned by the innovations of Benjamin Rush and Jeremy Bentham, which were built around the principals of confinement and surveillance, the early modern prison provided neither discipline nor isolation. To the contrary, prison life offered a community rife with conviviality. Once imprisoned, inmates were housed in accordance with their means. Those who could maintain the various fees were permitted to walk abroad, entertain guests, or even live within the

"Rule," the precinct beyond the prison walls that blended into the surrounding neighborhood. Thomas Dekker describes the porous boundaries separating prison and the outside world, as those with adequate funds lived large in a place that provided sanctuary from harassing creditors:

> Here they play at *Bowles*, lye in faire chambers within the Rule, fare like *Dives*, laugh at *Lazarus*, can walke up and down many times by *Habeas Corpus*, *&* jeere their Creditors: there they lye *Barricaded* (within King *Luds* Bulwarke) against Gun-shot: there they strut up and downe the Prison (like *Magnificoes* in *Venice*) on the *Rialta* brave in cloathes, spruce in Ruffes, with Gold-wrought night-caps, on their heades. They feed deliciously, plenteously, voluptuously; have excellent Wines to drinke, handsome Wives to lye with when they please, who come in, not like the Wives of Prisoners, but of the Best and wealthiest Citizens.[14]

While many prisoners continued to enjoy the benefits of prison, receiving visitors, moving about freely, and gathering to drink and play cards, this lavish lifestyle could not be sustained by the debtor.

In addition to the graduated comforts of the pay wards, which descended from the knight's all the way down to the two-penny ward, fine distinctions were made even among the so-called common wards, such that life in the beggar's ward offered a substantially different experience than time spent in the Hole, the most abject space in the carceral system. The destitute were ultimately relegated to the place where the most "miserable souls" received meager alms from the parishes and were left to "languish and dye."[15] In this dirt pit, desperate debtors lay naked and destitute on moldy straw awaiting a slow and painful death from gaol-fever (typhus) or starvation. The literature of the period describes this prison within the prison as a cold, vermin-infested, damp pit of twenty square feet housing up to forty or even fifty prisoners.[16] One writer tells of men packed shoulder to shoulder in a ditch that was "as hard as chennell," or cannel, a hard bituminous coal, their situation "worse then Dogs" in a "foule kennell."[17] The once-incarcerated debtor William Fennor describes the Hole as a virtual hell on earth: "He that would see the miseries of man, let him come into this place, the Hole, that stinks many men to death . . . in this place there are many men that for want of sustenance utterly perish . . . in this place a man shall not look about him but some poor soul or other lies groaning and labouring under the burden of some dangerous disease . . . they walk up and down like so many Ghosts for want of food to relieve them" (sig. L4). The threat if not the actual experience of the Hole profoundly influenced early modern writers, leading scholars to identify a distinct genre of penal writing in the first quarter of James's reign that has been distinguished as "one of England's most characteristic cultural forms in the period."[18]

Works by prisoners in this period typically attempt to exculpate or memorialize the author, address the conditions of incarceration, include appeals for release or the mitigation of hardship, and elicit sympathy in their readers. Debtor's prison literature, however, comprises a subgenre insofar as the predicament of the debtor was unique. Debtors remained the largest numerical group of imprisoned in the seventeenth century and unlike those facing criminal charges, were without hope of trial, transport, pardon, or even execution.[19] This may explain early seventeenth-century dramatists' obsession with the Counter, which as Jean Howard argues, offered the cultural site through which the theater could "elaborate a succession of probing and contradictory Counter narratives, ones attuned to both the dominant norms and the alternative social logics possible in the culture of debt and credit in which the theater itself was embedded."[20] While, like all prisoners, the debtor paid for his incarceration, he was a member of the only class of prisoner for whom this arrangement was temporary, making the experience of prison initially congenial but ultimately harrowing and life-threatening. Thus debtor's prison literature introduced new features into the genre of prison writing, that being an elaboration of the contradictory trajectory of indebtedness, exemplified by the stark duality of abundance and deprivation, which is in turn mirrored by the ambiguous situation of the incarcerated who may be temporarily socially endowed but is ultimately civilly deprived.

Writers describe the downward spiral of the debtor as he devolves from the better wards to lying "in Hunger and Cold," as creditors and prison wardens let him starve so that his "bones pay so derrely" and his only source of nourishment is scraps from the almsbasket.[21] The almsbasket was an open pannier strapped to the back of the "basket-man" who walked the streets crying out for "bread and meat for the poore prisoners," a well-known incantation throughout London. In reward for his efforts, the scrap-gatherer received payment out of the alms collected for the prisoners. Such donations of food and money were sporadic and inadequate.[22] In John Cooke's *Greene's Tu Quoque* an imprisoned debtor complains bitterly to Gatherscrap, the basketman, about the rotten odds and ends for which those new to Hole had to fight:

Hunger will draw me into their fellowship
To fight and scramble for unsavoury scraps
That come from unknown hands, perhaps unwash'd:
And would that were the worst: for I have noted,
That naught goes to the prisoners, but such food
As either by the weather has been tainted
Or children, nay, sometimes full-paunced dogs
Have overlickt.[23]

If off the stage, prison was a deadly serious matter, on the stage, the most sordid aspects of prison are transformed into something worthwhile. Comedy, in particular, not the genre one would immediately associate with the horrors of prison, relied upon and expanded the conventions of "Jacobean prison works" in general, and as I will show, debtor's prison literature in particular.[24] As part of an impressive group whose members had done Counter time Middleton was no stranger to prison prose. Imprisoned for a debt of £5 on December 23, 1608, and later sued by another creditor for £16 the following year, on July 18, 1609, Middleton was arrested by a third creditor for an overdue bond of £7 9s.[25] Middleton lent his authority on the Counter to several collaborations with Thomas Dekker, and one of their more popular prose pamphlets, *The Black Book*, is comprised of satiric portraits of the various types the writers encountered in prison. Middleton's own seriocomic *Father Hubbard's Tale* and *Micro-cynicon* (1599) both feature the downward spiral of the young spendthrift facing imprisonment for debt.

As in his prose pamphlets, Middleton's *A Trick to Catch the Old One* tracks the insolvency of its impervious protagonist, but despite having a reputation as his best-crafted comedy, this play baffles critics.[26] Performed by Paul's boys at the beginning of the seventeenth century, *A Trick* presents the sequential stages of the scheme the prodigal Witgood engineers to recover the property his covetous uncle has "lap[ped] into bonds."[27] By passing off his mistress as a wealthy widow to whom he is engaged, Witgood collects cash advances from those who greedily (and foolishly) expect a return on their investment. By the play's end, Witgood has regained his land, satisfied his creditors, and married a woman of his own choosing. Although much stage time is devoted to detailing the legal complexities of various credit arrangements, including mortgages, debt bonds, and quit claims, the plot remains accessible—so long as critics ignore those scenes featuring the abject lawyer and moneylender Dampit.[28]

Typically characterized as marginal interludes, constituting "a kind of Hogarthian 'Usurer's Progress'," the play's Dampit scenes revolve around this character's cynical railings, which are seen as exemplary of the "rogue exposures" and "characters" developed in the debtor's prison writings of Dekker and later perfected by Hall, Overbury, and Earle.[29] As a figure that at once complies with and challenges the audience's stereotype of the merciless creditor, Dampit does, however, do more than animate a stock type. The significance of his role comes to light when Dampit is understood as the play's "economic unconscious."[30] This "notorious, usuring, blasphemous, atheistical, brothel-vomiting rascal" is, as I will show, an extension of and foil to the play's protagonist Witgood, who is himself described at certain junctures as "a rioter, a waste-thrift, and brothel master" (1.3.28–29). Through the character of Dampit, the play gestures toward the horrors of the Hole—social abjection and physical deprivation—yet sustains the ideal of prison as a staging ground upon which the debtor finesses the rhetorical means to mystify his circumstances. Wit, as Dekker explains in one prison narrative, is "a Baum" and "a weapon."[31] It was, moreover, the specter of the Hole that inspired Dekker and Middleton to hone their authorial skills and enabled them to repay their loans through the profits they garnered from their "rhapsodic conceit[s]" and "flippant witticisms."[32]

A Trick presents wit as a crucial improvisational mode that allows its practitioner to transcend his material constraints—which includes the inky matter of the written bond.[33] However, even as the play juxtaposes the pit and wit, it reveals them to be mutually constituted. If the pit is the disease-ridden hole to which all desperate debtors are ultimately consigned, it is also the word for the open section of the amphitheater directly in front of the stage. In this period, the term "pit" obtained a more general association with the theater.[34] The play enacts the ways in which theatrical mimesis merges with the social process of credit, insofar as a credit economy is always based on illusion. Yet, in the final analysis, *A Trick* neither celebrates the seemingly magical properties of credit nor condemns its destructive elements when its fictive elements are exposed. More than simply an aesthetic effect, wit is shown to be an outgrowth of debt and as such, a mode that clears the way for the debt bond itself to function as an intensification and wider practice of wit's speculative logic. Neither the antecedent nor cause of wit, the bond operates in this play as wit's practical allegory in the sphere of social practice.[35] Thus *A Trick* does not offer a contest between the witty and the foolish, as one would expect from the genre. Instead Middleton's play stages the in-fighting among those vying to harness the power of wit, which like bonds themselves, advances a suppositional form of value that proves to have ambivalent worth in face of the deprivation of liberty.

The Pit

The early modern carceral imagination is distinguished by an ironic perspective that weds the imprisoned debtor to the feckless disposition he manifested when he lived free of fetters. The clever gallant who relied on tricks to deny his bonds and outsmart his creditors continues to engage cunning devices in prison where he ultimately turns to witty prose. Despite the physical and psychic oppression of imprisonment for debt, prison literature represents incarceration, generally, and a stint in the Hole, in particular, as occasions to sharpen one's rhetorical skills. In the Counter, wit offers an alternative currency to coins and bonds and serves as a means by which one may secure psychological if not actual liberty. Hence, many writers credit the Hole with providing the impetus for their literary career. In *Certaine Characters*, Geoffrey Mynshul, a King's Bench prisoner, confesses that his indefinite detention at the discretion of his unsatisfied creditor compelled him to find a way "to banish melancholy" and "wade through [the] tedious time."[36] As horrified as he was by his conditions, he was also inspired by them, and with the aim "to terrifie" young gallants on the outside, he set pen to paper to ensure that others would avoid entering "into debt any further than necessity urgeth & if they be forced to borrow to pay as soone as they can" (4).

The productive potential of the Hole is best exemplified by the story of William Bagwell, a former merchant and chronic debtor who chronicles how incarceration for insolvency led him to become a writer. Bagwell offers his readers a series of poems marked by what by one contemporary critic describes as "a mixture of Christian laments and psalm-like stoicism."[37] Bagwell explains that despite having maintained good credit for years, "I fell into many troubles, and then lost my selfe, and my friends, and my estate, credit, and trading, and after that to make up the Tragedy, I lost my liberty, being cast into prison for a small debt, which I was not able to pay."[38] The perpetuity of prison brought him to the realization that his life as a merchant was effectively over and led him to pursue a new trade as a poet. He admits that in the beginning he was "very unskillful," but when he could no longer pay his "chamber rent" and was "put into a worse place in the prison" (1), notably the Hole, his writing improved markedly. Once consigned to the Hole, Bagwell committed his "observations" about prison life, which took the form of little vignettes, to paper (1). He dedicates one "to the men, which are prisoners in the Hole" (21):

Your backs may want course rags your skin to hide.
Your bones in time by lying hard will ache.
Your flesh the live will not at all forsake.
Until you die: and then they'll turn you over unto the Worms. (21)

Yet even as Bagwell acknowledges the stench, the starvation, and the squalor, he recommends the Hole as the site of reformation for all desperate debtors:

from such lewd courses you are now restrained,
And to doe better things are you enjoyn'd.
Thus in your bondage you exercise more
Your selves in prayer, then you did before. (23)

The Hole as the place where one who has been "borne free" is most "likely to die a slave," paradoxically, creates the conditions for its inhabitants to realize their artistic potential and even attain creative, if not spiritual, freedom.[39]

Writers of the period obfuscate the dire conditions of the Hole by imagining prison as a place where one can reorient the delinquent compulsions that led to incarceration in the first place. In his "A Paradox in Praise of Sergiants, and of A Prison" (1607), Dekker's narrator explains that the mistreatment he suffers in the Counter results in the prolific production of "*Invectives*, *Satyres*, *Lybals*, [and] *Rimes*."[40] For Dekker, as for Bagwell, time in the Hole proved to be "the only best schoole . . . wherein is learnt *Experience*, *Experience* breeds *Wisdome*, *Wisdome* is mother to *Honour*, *Honour* to *Riches*, *Riches* to *Heart-ease*" (*Jests*, 63). On a more practical level, it was of course just such pamphlets and plays that enabled writers like Dekker to generate the cash they needed to satisfy their creditors and obtain release from prison.

In the epistle to his reader, Dekker begins *Jests to make you merie* (1607) by characterizing his pamphlet as a "bubbling up of wit," or a "tricke," by which he may provide "the heat of laughter" and the "scourge of villainy" (1). Dekker's narrator is a stageplayer, who, having failed to escape his creditors who were constantly "at [his] elbowes" (61), now languishes in the Poultry Street Counter. He begins his testimony by "call[ing] for pen and inke" (60), and with "the instruments of Learning being set before him" (60), he goes on to describe his unjust apprehension and mistreatment in prison. Making literal the metaphoric poison pen, he describes his writing instrument as "cut out of *Indian* cane after the heads of them were poysoned," and the paper he uses as "made of the filthy linen rages that had beene wrapt about the infected and vicerous bodye of beggers that had dyed in a death of the pestilence" (61). He then goes on to imagine his pen as a "pistol" with which he will issue "paper-bullet shots" at his creditors and keepers (62).

The educative benefits of time spent in the Counter are expounded by those who advance the notion of Counter time as akin to a term enrolled at one of the universities.[41] While the Hole remains "a grave to bury men alive," it is also imagined as the "place that will learn a young man."[42] This conceit is advanced by William Fennor, who describes himself as having "matriculated in one of these city universities" (sig. B2). In keeping with the sentiments of prose literature like Fennor's, one of Dekker and Middleton's gallants in the *Roaring Girl* advises another to "send [his] son to Wood Street College," since "a gentleman can nowhere get more knowledge":

> men pay more dear
> There for their wit than anywhere; a Counter,
> Why 'tis an university, who not sees?
> As scholars there, so here men take degrees,
> And follow the same studies all alike.
> Scholars learn first logic and rhetoric.
> So does a prisoner; with fine honey'd speech
> At's first coming in he doth persuade, beseech
> He may be lodged with one that is not itchy,
> To lie in a clean chamber, in sheets not lousy;
> But when he has no money, then does he try
> By subtle logic and quaint sophistry
> To make the keepers trust him

Those who do not "graduate," but remain "freshm[e]n," are expelled from the pay wards and end up in "th' Hole," where "money being the theme," they are compelled to earn a Master of Arts in disputation "with [their] hard creditors' hearts" (3.3.79–102). The idea that the Counter provided the grist for the mill of wit and even endowed those who had exhausted their credit with the veneer of authenticity or "street cred" is advanced by Thomas Nashe: "Hear what I say, a Gentleman is never thoroughly entered into credit till he hath beene there; & that Poet or novice, be he what will, ought to suspect his wit, and remain half in doubt that it is not authentical, till it hath been seen and allowed in unthrifts consistory."[43] As an improvisatory response that enables the debtor to manipulate his world, wit is envisioned in these writings as born of the pit to which it serves as an antidote. Yet, in Middleton's dramatic literature, as I discuss below, even as wit serves as a kind of currency, like actual coins or credit, it too needs to be secured and can be easily spent. Here the exigencies of the bond haunt wit as characters and audience alike are reminded that witty performances can never completely break free of the material conditions underwriting them.

Wit

As his name suggests, Middleton's Witgood is good at "wit," and throughout *A Trick* he embodies a cultural practice successfully executed by those who regard themselves as existing in a privileged relation to their environment. What makes wit a unique form of trickery is its obfuscatory function. The élan of the witty rests upon the practitioner's ability to mystify the very spaces, social relations, and material exchanges that afford him the leisure to exercise wit in the first place. The witty scheme that drives this play enables Witgood to project a notion of worth determined not by the value of what he owns but rather by what he owes—as made evident by the inordinate number of creditors seeking to possess him. The bond thus functions as an instrument that endows him with the means to mystify the link between credit as reputation and credit as fiscal holding. As Ian Munro reminds us, "In the second half of the sixteenth century, the idea of 'wit' went through a remarkable transformation. As the word became increasingly (though never exclusively) associated with the comic and fanciful, its primary meaning shifted from an inherent faculty towards a social performance, less something one is than something one does. In other words, wit became material rather than potential, a change that produced somewhat paradoxical social effects."[44] Through the medium of print, the mechanics of wit, once the essential attribute of the courtly gentleman, were disseminated to a broader audience. In this play, the bond functions as a promiscuous form of writing that indiscriminately bestows wit on the desperate debtor.

The play begins with the problem of Witgood's overdue bonds, placing this character in the same situation as others discussed in this book, such as

Shakespeare's Timon and Antonio and Middleton's Easy. Aptly summarized by one character, Witgood is an "undone man, imperfect in both fame and in estate, his debts wealthier than he, and executions [warrants for seizure of his person] in wait for his due body" (3.1.165–68). Witgood's exclamation "All's gone!" opens the play, as he envisions his lands as "sunk into that little pitte Lechery" (1.1.1–4), a gaping hole, which through its association with the "brothel[s] that [have] consume[d] him" (1.1.7) is imagined as a voracious mouth or vagina. Witgood imagines his own mouth in juxtaposition to the mouth of lechery when he characterizes himself as consuming only what it needs to survive, musing that a "gallant pay[s] but two shillings for his ordinary that nourishes him, and twenty times two for his brothel that consumes him" (1.1.5–7). The projection of his own appetency onto the consuming brothel echoes the debtor's image of prison itself as "the jawes of miserie that are stretched wide open to swallow [the debtor] up alive."[45]

For Witgood his financial predicament is the ultimate affront to his manhood, and, linking the consumptive effects of indebtedness to castration, he accuses his mistress of having been "the secret consumption of my purse" (1.1.30–31). Here the word "purse" echoes person. Suggesting that his debts have left him shamefully exposed, Witgood bemoans he that has "nere a hole to put his head in" (1.2.52), a phrase whose bawdy resonance summons the image of a man left unduly exposed as he stands with his genitals hanging out. Later he amplifies his perception of himself as impotent by comparing himself to a "gelding" (1.2.5).

The solution to the problem of anxious masculinity presents itself when Witgood's fear of imminent imprisonment serves as the impetus for an inventive scheme to restore his credit. Utilizing what he describes as his "last means" (1.1.29), his wit, Witgood summons the potency to "breed" a trick (1.1.61) with his mistress Jane, which Witgood claims as his "embryo" alone (1.1.57). Jane plots to carefully craft her "behavior, discourse [and] fashion," and "artfully disguise [her] wants" (1.1.78–79), allowing her to perfect her guise as a country widow, so as not to "discredit" Witgood (1.1.79). For his part, Witgood depends on neither masquerade nor disguise but rather on rhetoric. Verbal prolixity allows him to mount an offensive against the pit through the use of another hole—his mouth. Aggressively filling others' ears with verbiage proves an effective strategy in the face of the threat of becoming engulfed by debt and its attendant discredit.

Once Witgood's plan is set in motion, his person accrues value in the eyes of his avaricious uncle and unpaid creditors who erroneously believe that he is poised to marry into wealth. His mistress, the courtesan Jane, who poses as a widow worth "four hundred pounds," is also able to rework the otherwise constricting circumstances of mercenary marriage to advance her own interests. Early on, the pit, whether imagined as the unfathomable vortex of debauchery or the actual Hole, is recognized as at once treacherous and as a site of potential. In this respect, the Hole's association with improvisation invokes the playhouse itself, exemplified by the cockpit of *Henry V*'s prologue, a space out of which infinite riches may be conjured. As Witgood confesses, "there's nothing conjures up wit sooner than poverty" (3.1.87), and his accomplishments attest to the potency of the tongue as a crucial instrument by which to stave off the inevitable. Performative speech, exemplified by rumor and report, offers Witgood a riposte to the indignities of legal rectitude, and he aptly characterizes his trick as "out of the compass of law" (1.1.27–28). Becoming in effect like one of Dekker's imprisoned debtors, described as such able perpetrators of tricks that "no one can record the shifts, legerdemains, conveniences, reaches, fetches, ambushes, traines, and close under-minings of a Bankrout," the potential of Witgood's wit seems limitless.[46]

Witgood convinces a tavern host to pose as his servant and provide him with a train of horses and ready cash. He enlists the man's assistance on the mere power of his words, which he uses with "the best art and most profitable form," as he "pour[s] the sweet circumstance into his [the host's] ear, which shall have the gift to turn all the wax to honey" (1.1.104–6). Witgood even goes so far as to brag to the unsuspecting host that he won the supposed wealthy widow with the powers of his "fine little voluble tongue" (1.2.31). Witgood brings his trick to its next phase on the authority of a "report" that the widow and her riches (1.2.20) are lodged nearby in "a house of credit (1.4.1–2). All of this affirms Witgood's powers as "a conjurer" (1.2.13) who can lead men to "leap and sing and dance," as well as ante up great sums of money (1.2.21). After Witgood's uncle hears that his dissolute nephew is engaged to a wealthy widow, he is swayed by the prospect of even greater riches and returns his nephew's lands so as to ameliorate his reputation as a spendthrift, the "report" of which he himself advanced (2.1.90). Even Witgood's creditors who receive "intelligence" that he is to be married delay apprehending him in order to grant him more time to "raise a little money in the city . . . for his own credit" (3.1.30–31). Banking on a specious calculation, they invest further in the already credit-compromised Witgood with a speculative eye toward enhanced profit whether he makes or breaks his bonds.

Yet as the play progresses we see that tricks fail once their performative energy becomes used up and "mischief's spent" (4.3.160). At such moments, wit must be supplemented by more substantial materials, referred to at several junctures as "writings" (1.4.3; 2.1.37). Despite the propulsive power of report, Witgood is ultimately compelled to furnish documents to buttress his and Jane's social performance. The courtesan's presumed wealth needs to be confirmed by the presentation of papers (2.1.37), revisiting the tension between tricks and the law that we see earlier when two suitors competing for the same woman look to the courts as the means by which to restore reputation. When one rival strikes the other, an action that would normally initiate a duel, the offended party resolves not to meet his opponent in an open field with dagger drawn but to bring suit against him (1.3.79–80). In response to the assault, he proclaims, "I am not such a coward to strike again, I warrant you. My ear has the law on her side, for it burns horribly. I will teach him to strike a naked face, the longest day of his life. 'Slid it shall cost me some money, but I'll bring this box into the Chancery" (1.3.76–81). Witgood, too, comes to realize that if he desires to retrieve his actual land and not simply recuperate the posture of landed gentleman, he must return to the compass of the law.

For a moment, it seems that the inexorable force of the law—as embodied by the conditional terms of the debt bond and the city as the staging ground of its penal machinations—prevail. London is described throughout the play as a place of "danger" for Witgood whose "great debts" and "extreme creditors" (2.1.235–36) hold out the threat of imprisonment and death. Indeed, upon arriving in the city, Witgood's creditors demand either "money or [his] carcass" (4.3.51) and herald the "secret delight [they] have amongst us. We that are used to keeping birds in cages have the heart to keep men in prison" (4.3.53–55). Once he is arrested, all of his creditors come forward with bonds in hand. Despite Witgood's pleas for "a little more aid from wits" (4.3.56), the "hole" of which he may now avail himself, as one creditor reminds him, is not that of a "widow of account" (bawdy innuendo implied) but the "hole i'th' counter" (4.3.24).

Rumor first leads Witgood's creditors to him, but when they catch him the second time, they do not mince words. Now his bonds do the talking. As in *Timon of Athens*, the stage directions have one creditor after another "handing him [Witgood] a paper" (s.d., 4.3.30–31), and then "handing another paper" (s.d., 4.3.32), and others "handing another paper" (s.d., 4.3.30–34). Virtually suffocated with bonds, Witgood pleads, "Pray, sirs, you'll give me breath" (4.3.35), as he is no longer able to use his mouth as a means by which to deter the effects of forfeiture by pouring honey in their ears. As one creditor explains, "we know you have too fair a tongue of your own. You overcame us too lately. . . . *Non plus ultra* [no farther]" (4.3.40–44).

Despite the play's acknowledgment of the force of the bond and its authority as a form of monetary writing, in the end *A Trick* turns on its head the trope of prison literature whereby the debtor is "caught" by the proverbial sergeant's clap on the shoulder. Witgood escapes the "old one," a generalized conceit for all creditors particularized in Witgood's avaricious uncle and the Satanic Dampit. This escape is achieved, however, not by Witgood's reformation whereby he disavows wit. Instead, we witness a dispersal of witty tricks among the characters. As the play demonstrates Witgood is not the only character to rely upon the disarticulation of credibility and fiscal holding. As much is suggested when the courtesan admonishes Witgood's uncle as someone who has "been ever full of golden speech, if words were lands, your nephew would be rich" (4.1.67–68). We later witness Witgood "catching" his uncle in his attempt to blur reputation and remuneration when Hoard promises to restore his nephew's credit. In this instance, Witgood recognizes his own witty maneuver as he tries to make his uncle accountable for his promise: "My credit? Nay, my countenance . . . I know, uncle, you would have wrought it so by your wit. You would have made her [the widow] believe in time the whole house had been mine" (2.1.243–46).

In the final act, the indebted Witgood, now in the prison warden's custody, assumes the prerogative of a wronged creditor when he sends his servant to announce to his adversaries that "he [Witgood] will have utmost satisfaction. The law shall give him recompense" (4.3.108–9). Realizing that the elasticity of the law itself offers a full menu of tricks, Witgood claims that he has "litigiously . . . fasten[ed]" onto the courtesan and that he would "rather bind himself to all inconveniences than rot in prison" (4.3.134–35). A deal is struck whereby Jane's new husband, Witgood's uncle's rival, agrees to discharge Witgood of his debts when he "sets his hand" to a quitclaim releasing his former mistress of any prior claim (4.3.138). Credit as reputation and credit as fiscal surety are reunited as the restoration of the former is clearly dependent on the recovery of the latter.

The exchange between Witgood and the courtesan's husband serves as the play's denouement. Jane's husband agrees to "release [Witgood] of his debts" on condition that Witgood "release . . . her of her words" (4.4.198–99), in this case her putative pledge to marry Witgood. Lucre attempts to convince Witgood that he is getting the better end of the deal, as he avers, "are not debts better than words?" (4.4.202). His rhetorical question goes to the heart of the matter since the problem driving the play, and as it turns out the source of its comic solution, is Witgood's steadfast refusal to acknowledge the relation between these two modes of promise. Witgood's reply, "Are not words promises, and are not promises debts?" (4.4.204), betrays his conviction that rumor and report, like debt bonds, may circulate indefinitely in the unsubstantial realm of speculation. The dictates of economic contract, though, as Middleton shows, constrain the expansive possibilities of social performance by threatening to render persons things that may be legitimately claimed or used by another.

The Stench of Debt

While Middleton's play allows Witgood to exploit the elasticity of verbal promise, and later the ambiguities of debt law, it displaces the rigidity of forfeiture onto the character of Dampit. As the play's economic unconscious, Dampit's negative course maps an alternative trajectory of speculation and notoriety. He, too, at first seems to embody the ascendant possibilities of the city's credit economy. Dampit's creditworthiness is constituted solely by what others have "heard" of his success (1.3.8). His credibility, moreover, depends upon his listener's following his directive to "report it." Notably, he and then others insistently narrate his rags-to-riches story of having come to "town but with ten shillings in his purse," only to become "credibly worth ten thousand pound!" (1.3.24–26). Dampit, as one character explains, makes such a point of circulating his narrative that "he that has lost both his ears may hear of him" (1.3.10). Having made himself into a veritable urban legend, akin to Dick Whittington, the Horatio Alger of early modern London, Dampit boasts of having achieved prosperity through a preposterously profitable dogfight (1.3.43).

Dampit's success is based on the activities associated with the pit from which the theater itself evolved, having made his fortune "stealing a Mastiff Dog from a Farmer's house," which he then staked against a noble's dog (1.4.14–15). Dog fighting, along with bear and cock fighting, was the original business of the open part of the amphitheater directly in front of the stage. By reminding his audience that the theatrical performance and animal baiting were "culturally isomorphic events," Middleton invokes one of the key pleasures of the spectacle of animal baiting, the revelation of the mettle of the dog.[47] As Jason Warren-Scott reminds us, the English mastiff was a particularly large and ferocious animal, one for which the English were famous dating back to Roman times.[48] A visitor to London in 1592, Duke Frederick of Württemberg reports on watching a dog fight in the pit, which brought out "the breed and mettle of the dogs" that "do not give in."[49] The Swiss visitor Thomas Platter made note in 1599 of "the excellence and fine temper of [great English] mastiffs," which although "much struck and mauled by the bear . . . did not give in."[50] Reporting that "by great fortune his dog had the day" (1.4.23), Dampit associates himself with the fortitude of the mastiff to affirm his own ability to withstand adversity, including the trials of the Hole.

If Witgood's existence is threatened by the Hole, Dampit's is justified by it. His private chamber transforms into a veritable "Prodigal's Purgatory," overrun by "stinking, noisome [and] unsavory smells."[51] Here Dampit is denied "the very meat that feeds him" and "the very pillow that eases him" (4.5.62–63). In the third, final, and longest of the play's three Dampit scenes, the character languishes in a state of starvation and alcohol-induced delirium surrounded by visitors disgusted by the stench emanating from this "noisome dunghill" of a man (4.5.60). The expiring moneylender embodies the culmination of a life founded on manipulation of credit, one that offers the opportunity for great profit but that also carries the risk of ejection from commercial and social networks and the loss of one's civic standing and even one's manhood.[52]

The full transformation of Dampit's chamber into the Hole is signaled by a visitor's description that mimics the language used by those who describe the Hole as a place where men "dye in the worser state of Slavery" than a slave.[53] Dampit's visitor states: "Note but the misery of this usuring slave, here he lies like a noisesome dunghill, full of poison of his drunken blasphemies, and they to whom he bequeathes all, grudge him the very meat that feeds him, the very pillow that eases him, here may a usurer behold his end" (4.5.63–65). Throughout the play the stink of debt is insinuated by the recurring image of debt as a "horrible plague" (1.1.21), a metaphor evoking Thomas Dekker's notion of imprisonment for debt as akin to contracting the "city gout."[54] The ravages of debt, which inevitably result in untold human waste, haunt Witgood in the ghostly form of Dampit, whose excesses have devolved into an epic case of self-consumption. In Dampit we get a "compressed moral allegory of the life of Urban Man," and, more particularly, a window onto Witgood's potential trajectory in the event that all his tricks had failed.[55] Not long after Witgood vows to forswear "lying a-bed" and consuming "muscadine and eggs at midnight" (3.1.77), we are shown the drunken Dampit confessing to his servant, "I am very weak, truly. I have not eaten so much as the bulk of an egg these three days" (3.3.18–20). The scene ends with his falling silent, overwhelmed by an inexplicable stench, the cause of which, as editors have noted, has never been adequately explained.[56] Dampit expends his waning energy to proclaim: "Fie upon't! What a choice of stinks here is. . . . Fie upon't. Here's a choice of stinks indeed," and then "Foh! I think they burn horns in Barnard's Inn. If ever I smelt such an abominable stink, usury, forsake me!" (3.3.68–70;73–75).

Stench had an abiding symbolic association with criminality itself. Nathan Bailey in *An Universal Etymological English Dictionary* (London, 1773) understands a criminal conviction as a "taint," meaning "a Spot or Blemish in Reputation." He also, though, associates the taint of moral corruption with the stench of corrupted or rank meat. Thus, he concludes, those convicted of a crime are marked by stench, or "having an ill smell."[57] On a more pedestrian level, prisoners did stink and what ultimately marked the Hole as a site of unparalleled inhumane treatment was its unbearable stench. Hygiene was primitive, at best, and in debtor's prison virtually nonexistent. One early modern commentator describes the Wood Street Counter as having "grown so nasty that no man (by his good will) will thrust his nose in any of the grates. Nay, [he] will rather goe a mile about then come near it."[58] As historian Thomas Freeman reminds us, the smell in prisons was so noxious that it was customary to air the prisons before assizes and to sprinkle vinegar in the courtrooms to prevent the judge and jury from becoming ill during the trials.[59] One petition complains bitterly that prisoners are "circumscribed to [this] filthy stinking place," and, according to Fennor, "the Hole . . . stinks many men to death."[60] Thomas Dekker includes the "stench" among his list of the tortures inflicted by the Hole, along with "hunger, cold, and thirst."[61] An exchange between the imprisoned spendthrift Spendall and his warden in *Tu Quoque* stresses the fetid conditions of the Hole by means of reference to the stinking fish offered for food:

> Hold: If you have no monie, you're best remove into some cheaper Ward,
> Spendall: What Ward shall I remove in?
> Hold: Why to the Two-pennie Ward, is likeliest to hold out with your meanes: Or if you will, you may goe into the Holl, and there you may feed for nothing.
> Spend: I, out of the Almes-basket, where Charitie appears in the

> likenesse of a peece of stinking Fish, Such as they beat Bawdes with when they are Carted.[62]

One debtor's testimony laments the "horrible stinks and noisome vermine" infesting the "loathsome den."[63] Geoffrey Mynshul, imprisoned in the King's Bench, attests to the overpowering noxious odor within the Hole and he reports that "it stinckes more than the Lord Mayor's dogge-house or paris-garden in August."[64] Teltroth, the narrator of the anonymously authored *Wonderfull Strange newes from Woodstreet Counter*, decries the "damnable, nasty, stinking Hole . . . a very pit of earthly perdition."[65]

In large part due to its noxious fumes, the Hole was likened to hell on earth. One writer describes it as the "very suburbs of Hell."[66] As Mynshul explains, "as soone as thou comest before the gate of Prison, doe but thinke thou are entering into Hell . . . for thou shalt be sure not onely to finde Hell, but fiends and ugly monsters."[67] The author of *Wonderfull Strange newes from Woodstreet Counter* confirms that "the Woodstreet Counter is an Earthy Hell."[68] Those seeking prison reform mobilized descriptions of the Hole as a living hell established by authors of seriocomic prose pamphlets. In *An Apology* (1614), Richard Vennar, who would go on to petition James I to establish a commission for imprisoned debtors, imagines King David visiting contemporaneous London and touring the prisons, where he discovers "the true parallel of hell, where the wretched onely feele misery, and those that want helpe are most loaden with cruelty" (46). Referring specifically to those incarcerated for debt, Vennar decries the fact that "no nation in the world holds men for debt in such bondage" (47). Walter Ashton, another debtor in the King's Bench, in his *A Prisoner's Plaint* (1622) describes debtor's prison as a "house of tears" (2). In an anonymous petition submitted to the monarch and Parliament later in the century (1646), the authors claim that debtors are regularly "beaten, put into iron bolts, . . . thrust into dungeons, starved, and . . . lamed by Iron Fetters."[69] One petition points out the number of suicides committed by debtors no longer able to "maintain themselves in prison."[70] In *Jests to make you merie* (1607), Dekker describes the plight of those doomed to the Hole: "It stands not next doore to Hell, but it is Hell itselfe: . . . it is a man's grave, wherein he walks alive . . . an unsalable gulfe . . . a feadomelesse wherlepit . . . hell itselfe; for soules lye languishing and cannot dye" (47).

Critics have noted that Dampit, a self-described "trampler of time," personifies a city that is home to diabolic trickery, itself marked by an improvisational energy that treads over or violates a conventional reverence for history and normative expectations of progress (1.4.43). Just as Damp/pit's name evokes the pit of hell, so does his sidekick's, aptly named Gulf, and at various points Dampit is explicitly associated with the devil.[71] Yet Dampit is by no means an exceptional denizen of London, even as he signals the disruption of its established order. Rather, he epitomizes the ubiquity of debt, in which the ever-present possibility of incarceration has made the entire city a sink hole for some. As a "trampler of time," Dampit represents what Jonathan Gil Harris describes as a "distinctive capitalist conception of time," which is anathema to the secular, monumental temporality that promoted continuity.[72] This traditional ideal of temporal alignment, in which past, present, and future demonstrate a perdurance, was most insistently materialized in the early modern period in the language of patrilineal reproduction. Debt bonds, however, interrupted this linear narrative by promising a radical break from the past and transforming the present into the realm of the speculative future.

If the horrors of incarceration cannot be directly depicted in Middleton's play, nonetheless, debt—like a pervasive stench, like a capitalist conception of time—is an intrusion that always signals a rupture. London, described as a "hell mouth" (4.5.1–4) and a pit, devours time in form of patrimonies. As Dampit's servant acknowledges, "there's pits enough to damn anyone before they come to hell. In Holborn some, in Fleet Street some," since "where'er he come, there's some" (4.4.2–5). Similarly, Witgood describes the Counter as hell and his creditors as its devils (4.367–68), echoing the sentiments of Thomas Dekker who explains that once the debtor has "spent his coyne and credit," he is "in Hell" (*Jests*, 47). The notion of spending here invokes the idea of wasting time and money, both in terms of excessive consumption and dissipation.

In the end, it is not the debtor but rather the "old one," the character that embodies the damp pit, that is caught. By imagining the destructive potential of debt as a series of somatic traumas caused by inhabiting a particular noxious place, Middleton's play both expresses and contains the destructive potential of debt bondage to trample upon the present. Using his wits to exploit the loopholes within early modern contract law, Witgood is able to marry off his mistress to his uncle's wealthy rival, satisfy his creditor, and avoid prison. Yet the play's resolution is ambivalent. Much rests upon Witgood's dubious rhetorical performance, whereby he forswears his riotous ways. Critics have noted Witgood's assumption of culpability for his past indiscretions seems insincere in light of the enduring problem of credibility that has been central to the play. The real difficulty with comic closure lies, however, with the fact that the play has convincingly demonstrated wit and the pit to be codependent. The "old" one has really been new all along.

Debt, this play suggests, is generative insofar as it produces the stuff of city-comedy, which, despite an abiding preoccupation with bodily experiences such as erotic satisfaction and status transformation, manages to suppress the physical depredations of incarceration. Yet even in this play, which privileges pecuniary over romantic pursuits, debt always threatens to undermine the conventions of the genre it enables. The fantasy of fiscal freedom inevitably founders on the reality of bondage. The enslaving power the bond had over gallants (and playwrights) no doubt inspired reactive portrayals of the horrors of indebtedness. It would not be for another twenty years, however, that the complete mystification of debt could be achieved. While at the moment of Middleton's play, the imbrication of wit and the pit allowed the debtor some room to maneuver, over the next two decades creditworthiness and fiscal solvency would become effectively divorced, so much so that a new aristocratic ethos would blunt the difference between being good at wit and being consigned to a damp pit. This ethos would offer in its stead a subtler but nonetheless crucial delineation between being someone well born and someone who overreaches one's place.

Enduring Bonds

Massinger's *A New Way to Pay Old Debts*, a play set in the country that borrows liberally from Middleton's Jacobean city comedy, revisits the hostile dependency between debtor and creditor, which by the early Caroline period has transformed into a generalized "reciprocal contempt" among members of the aristocracy, which now includes the titled moneylender who has overcome his city origins.[73] Despite the shared sensibility among the characters in *A New Way*, there is, as Theodore Leinwand has noted, a "remarkably bitter tone" that colors their interactions.[74] This tone creates a problem for those disturbed by what one reader describes as a "grim comedy" presenting "the spectacle of the loathsome pursuing the contemptible."[75] The tonal ambivalence that mars Massinger's play bears more than a passing resemblance to the structural confusion born of the moral ambiguities plaguing Middleton's. While *A New Way* bears the stamp of its era, it offers more than a window onto Caroline class anxiety, exemplified by the staging of an embattled elite attempting to suppress the upwardly mobile.[76] Rather, like Middleton, Massinger offers a case study of a social order riven, rather than conjoined, by the dense web of economic obligations tying each person to the other. Yet even as *A New Way* acknowledges antipathy between debtor and creditor, it achieves, unlike Middleton's play, a near complete mystification of the most troubling aspects of indebtedness by all but expunging its hazards from the world of the play. The debtor confronts neither the horrors nor the productive potential of the Hole but remains at liberty so long as the material forces that underwrite gentility are effaced. Indeed, debt has become so naturalized that social ties themselves are imagined and experienced as a form of bondage, creating a situation in which the constraints one associates with debtor's prison now contour normative society.

Here the play anticipates the "control society" that Gilles Deleuze describes as the postmodern progeny of Foucault's disciplinary societies of the eighteenth and nineteenth centuries.[77] In a control society, there is no imposition of discipline as one would experience at a school, hospital, or in prison, all places within which one is held and from which one is eventually redeemed. Instead of disciplinary sites, the control society offers its citizens metastasizing systems. In this culture, people are neither confined nor refashioned but rather encouraged to be continuously engaged in proliferating networks that allow varying degrees of access to revolving forms of currency, such as money and information. Massinger's play traces the dispersive and perpetual nature of debt—a continuous, mutating arrangement that enables various forms of social constraint.

The motility and ubiquity of debt bondage is exemplified by the play's understanding of time. The temporal distinction between "old" and "new" around which Massinger's play is organized understands debt, and the concomitant threat of forfeiture, not as signaling a violent break in time, exemplified by the sudden clap of the sergeant's hand on the hapless debtor's shoulder. The "old one," which in *A Trick* refers generally to the quasi-Satanic Dampit and more particularly to Witgood's avaricious uncle, could not be extinguished but could be caught or temporarily waylaid circa 1607. However, once debt is imagined as a perpetual condition, the bond becomes a species of not simply a capitalist conception of time but a *finance* capitalist conception of time. In this instance the bond, which I have argued throughout is associated with a speculative logic, also betrays a spectral logic insofar as its value is haunted by its own epistemological conditions.[78] Thus we may interpret the play's title as a nostalgic move: a quaint attempt to reintroduce a temporal logic that no longer holds sway. Just as the debt bond bears the ghostly traces of its formative influences, so too this play is distinguished by the kind of sedimentation to which Jameson refers when he writes of emergent forms as reappropriated or refashioned immanent forms in a different social and cultural context.[79] The play's representation of the abstract states of liberty and abjection, embodied by the two creditor figures Lord Lovell and Giles Overreach, are haunted by the concrete disparate experiences of magical riches, on the one hand, and degrading imprisonment, on the other, that shape Middleton's play.

As Massinger's characters depend on bonds to maintain themselves, such fiscal dependency fosters resentment toward the person with the most capital. At the beginning of this play, every single character is in arrears to the much-despised Sir Giles Overreach who, even though he is fully integrated into aristocratic society, assumes "moral responsibility for genteel indebtedness."[80] A self-made man like Dampit, whose "industry" consists of shady financial and legal transactions, Overreach has secured a place for himself in Nottinghamshire by marrying the sister of Sir John Welborne and now plans to marry his daughter to Lord Lovell to ensure that his grandson will become a "young lord."[81] Like Dampit, Overreach's successes have been enabled by the profligate habits of gentle younger sons who now fear and hate him. He has provided his spendthrift nephew Welborne, who in one fell swoop depleted an inheritance worth £1,200 annually, with untold "mortgages, statutes, and bonds" (1.1.50) and, within the course of the play, furnishes him with yet another bond of a "thousand pounds" (4.2.115–16). Welborne's contemporary, the gentle-born Alworth, is reduced to serving as a Lord's page because of his father's prodigality, which puts his son in debt to Overreach (1.3.100; 4.11.205–6). Even the late husband of the wealthy Lady Alworth was weighed down by "wants, debts and quarrels [that] lay heavy" on his conscience and arguably contributed to his death (1.3.101).

For much of the play Overreach serves as the scapegoat for the recklessness of his betters whose lavish living, based on credit, has driven them into debt. Yet upon closer inspection, it is not Overreach but the prodigal Welborne who most closely echoes Middleton's Dampit. Critics have cited Welborne's aggressive tactics as a weakness of the play, and he is associated with a string of bitter tirades and immoral intrigues.[82] The engine that drives the plot is his manipulation of Lady Alworth when he capitalizes on his past generosity to her deceased husband. Before Welborne is even able to affirm his gentle nature, what stands out about this destitute debtor is his general physical degradation signaled by the overpowering stench emanating from him. He admits to having been "vomited out of an Alehouse" (1.1.178) and is described by another as a "piggestire" (1.3.48). When he seeks suit of the wealthy widow, to whom he later pretends to be betrothed, her ladies register their disgust, complaining bitterly of the "smell here," and deem him "a creature made out of the privie" (1.3.53–54). Lady Alworth is herself unable to address him without first recoiling and can then only entertain this "eye sore" (1.3.84) by putting her glove to her nose and repeatedly requesting her perfumes.

While it would seem that Massinger is acknowledging the stench of debt, and by association the horrors of the Hole, despite the fact that Welborne does not don a new suit of clothes until the third act, his noxious odor magically dissipates once his pedigree is confirmed. This is achieved when he nobly chooses to honor his social bonds over and above satisfying his legal ones. Despite early descriptions of this "common borrower" (1.1.54), his refusal of cash from Lord Lovell's page and Lady Alworth points to his privileging of reputation over fiscal solvency. Welborne's preference for credit as an obfuscatory mode over and above material accumulation testifies to an aristocratic sensibility founded not only on the disavowal of the legal authority of the bond but also the very real needs for satisfaction of hunger and hygiene that desperate debt generates. Welborne's high-minded, and arguably delusional, perspective culminates at the play's end when he volunteers to serve under Lord Lovell's military command in the hope that such an expression of loyalty will sufficiently "redeem" the reputation he lost "in [his] loose course" (5.1.389).

Here it seems that Massinger takes seriously Middleton's premise that debts are promises constituted by words, which in turn may be performatively deployed to defer performance. Welborne, like Witgood, trades on the fictive premise of his engagement to Lady Alworth, which compels Overreach to loan his dissolute nephew even more money. Yet, while he is clever, unlike Witgood, Welborne does not seem to derive any pleasure from his ingenuity. Rather we see him readily abandon witty tricks for the efficacy of violence and then magic, both of which are founded on the brazen violation of notions of fair play underpinning civil and legal conduct. Early in the play, Welborne moves quickly from verbal threats to physical brutality when he is provoked into beating the tavern owner who reminds him of his debts. Later when he is confronted with his overdue bonds, Welborne's defense is to insist that Overreach restore his lands or stand indebted himself for £10,000, the amount he received for sale of his inherited estate. Welborne's outrageous refusal to acknowledge his part in relinquishing his inheritance and boldface lie that the land lay in "trust" to his uncle (5.1.167) leads to the maddening resolution in which a "quaint means" is discovered "to raze out the conveyance" (5.1.328).

Described by the scrivener as "mysteries / Not to be spoke in public" (5.1.329–30), it seems that the mineral components of the ink with which Welborne's bonds have been sealed have dissolved and thus effaced the signatures, rendering them null and void.

This ultimate act of negation points to the "new way" to pay debts, which is nothing more than a perverse culmination of an old way based on unscrupulous improvisation whereby one can successfully avoid satisfying one's bonds. In Massinger's world, the savage elements of the credit economy, as so aptly portrayed by Middleton, are tamed now, as perpetual debt offers a structuring principle of a civic order in which threats of incarceration and the inconvenience of repayment are erased. Yet even as the play presents a powerful example of elimination, it also acknowledges that the social fabric is woven with the threads of debt and criticizes the magical thinking of the elite.[83] Massinger subverts the nobles' high-minded opinion of themselves not through the character of Overreach, but by staging the means to which they resort to expel him, whereby his property is divested and redistributed, along with its attendant obligations, without the sanctioning authority of written contract.

Overreach's ambitions to assert his will exemplifies the pitfalls of a culture of credit in which any one person with a surplus of capital can assume an inordinately powerful position. True to his name, Overreach envisions himself as an Ur-Creditor when he expresses his aim to become the grand encloser, seeking to privatize all common lands and have all men sellers and he the only purchaser (2.1.32–33). Intending to expose the fine lineaments of debt that tie all members of society to him, he desires that his daughter be served by the decayed wives of his debtors, whom have become his "bond slaves" (2.1.81–89). Overreach's turn to realism inspires only rebellion, and in the end, his daughter and servant revolt, producing in Overreach a sudden and inexplicable apoplectic rage that results in his being carted off to the madhouse.

Because of his penchant for brutish candor, Overreach represents a villain who challenges not a social order based on the continuation of outstanding debt but rather that order's insistent substructure of denial. For Overreach "words are no substances" (3.2.128), and here Massinger presents us with an individual unwilling to properly mystify the components of credit as made evident through his execution of his paternal role as one based on legal duties and not affective bonds. As Michael Neill points out, the downgrading of kinship bonds results in an autocratic household in which children and servants are regarded as contracted agents of the master's will.[84] As bound to fail as such an approach to household management is, it is also, though, as Massinger suggests, productive.

Overreach's staunch rejection of the ethos of negation that contours the surrounding social order allows him to live large without incurring the penalty of waste. As one servant admits:

> To have a usurer that starves himself,
> And wears a cloak of one-and-twenty years
> On a suit of fourteen groats, bought of the hangman,
> To grow rich, and then purchase, is too common:
> But this Sir Giles feeds high, keeps many servants,
> Who must at his command do any outrage;
> Rich in his habit; vast in his expenses;
> Yet he to admiration still increases
> In wealth and lordships. (2.2.106–14)

We see the beneficial result of reverence to the law in the other figure in the play whose trajectory follows an alternative route other than that afforded by patronage. Tapwell, Welborne's former under-butler, who having acquired "a little stock" through frugality, has set himself up as an alehouse keeper and is now his own man. When the insolvent Welborne tries to humble Tapwell and force him to continue to serve him although he has outspent his credit, Tapwell reminds him of the powers of "the great prince" of the realm:

> There dwells, and within call, if it please your worship,
> A potent monarch, call'd the constable,
> That does command a citadel, call'd the stocks;
> Whose guards are certain files of rusty billmen. (1.1.12–15)

The defeat of Overreach and the commercial pragmatism that he stands for does not signal the end of a culture of debt but the instantiation of its logic of erasure as rival perceptions of the character of economic obligation are at last settled. As Overreach is dragged off the stage, he expresses his despair:

> Why, is not the whole world
> Included in my self? To what use then
> Are friends, and servants? Say there were a squadron

Of pikes, lin'd through with shot, when I am mounted,
Upon my injuries, shall I fear to charge 'em? (5.1.355–71)

Eerily echoing Timon's speech made decades earlier on friends as musical instruments that are worthless unless played, Overreach expresses a utilitarian understanding of obligation. At base, allies are essentially forms of capital that may be cashed in when needed. This dehumanizing perspective certainly informs the relations among members of the elite, but indebtedness, the play suggests, serves as the spur to civic virtue when economic obligation is properly disguised as genteel patronage. The eventual migration of debtors over from Overreach to Lord Lovell allows for economic necessity to become properly embedded in the ideologies of service and gratitude. This shift thus ensures that otherwise autocratic creditors and recalcitrant beneficiaries never lose sight of the obligatory power of the loan.

Massinger is, nevertheless, not simply asserting a conservative, albeit nostalgic, preference for the primacy of communal bonds over legal ones and social obligation over commercial ties. He is also critiquing this gentler, kinder, extralegal form of bondage and the culture of deference it engenders. Overreach's daughter Margaret is spared her virginity when Lord Lovell gallantly rejects her father's attempt to pawn her off. His refusal of her charms, and her father's additional offer of an earldom, however, is not merely evidence of his noble character but also strategic, since it prevents him from becoming indebted to Overreach (4.1.144). Moreover, his refusal makes Overreach's daughter dependent on him, as evidenced by her vow of indebtedness (4.3.6–7). Despite Lovell's claim that he does not "use" "all such as follow 'em . . . like slaves" (3.1.25), he accepts Margaret's declaration that his honorable behavior "binds" her and Alworth to him, making them his "slaves for ever" (3.2.222–23). Lord Lovell's decision to marry Lady Alworth is similarly sensible not only because, as he notes, their "years . . . states, . . . and births are not unequal," but also because marriage to the Lord offers this bourgeois widow a status promotion, one that she duly acknowledges as a "great favor" (5.1.45). Lovell's page becomes eternally indebted to him when he assists him in marrying Margaret Overreach, whose estate he turns over to Lovell in gratitude (5.1.387). In the end Welborne's debt is not cancelled but transferred over to Lovell, as he is no longer required to satisfy the balance due to Overreach but seeks only to restore his credit by serving in Lovell's regiment.

Conclusion

The dramatic energy of Massinger's *A New Way*, as with Middleton's *A Trick*, derives from its exploration of the ideology of denial underpinning social and marital bonds based on debt. Even though *A Trick* presents a cruder economy of ascension and penalty through the juxtaposition of Witgood and Dampit, the "mood of social decline" marking *A New Way* bespeaks an order whose spurious values stand on the shaky foundation of outstanding loans (Leonard, 179). While imprisonment for debt and even the threat of indiscriminate bondage embodied by the tyrannical patriarch Sir Overreach can be circumvented, what remains in their stead is a culture of discriminate bondage. Reports of prison life in early seventeenth-century London that characterize the penitentiary as "a little commonwealth . . . a famous City wherein are all trades practiced" (Mynshul, 7) suggest that existence within the Counter was an extension of life outside. By the first third of the seventeenth century, the rules of civil coexistence beyond the prison walls were subtended by the penal codes of debt bondage. The social uncertainty of Massinger's world, as I have been arguing, is tied to the enduring dubious implications of the bond and the unscrupulous lengths characters go to displace them. This uncertainty is expressed by the formal disjunction of a play that offers the vexing admixture of romance sans redemption and satire sans justice. The moral ambiguity of protagonist and antagonist alike destabilizes comic form, leaving us with a work that stands as the culmination of so-called problem comedies like *The Merchant of Venice*, as well as hybrid plays like *Timon of Athens*, *The Custom of the Country*, and *Michaelmas Term*. The result is the long-in-the-making arrival of what is arguably the most appropriate dramatic form for a play about debt—the revenge comedy.

Epilogue
The Debtor and the Slave

In its earliest stages, *Of Bondage* was a book about slavery. Working with the presumption that the slave was a human being that came to be categorized as a form of property, my initial aim was to historicize the conceptual conditions that would allow early modern men and women to construe certain persons as things. I soon discovered, however, that even as slaves were referred to as property, no legal code in either England or colonial America had ever denied that the slave was a person. Like villeins on feudal estates, servants who lived-in, and indentured workers, slaves were not considered property in the same way as land or fungibles. Indeed, the moral and political problems of slavery, arguably, grew out of the contradictions born of an economic and social order that insistently acknowledged the slave's humanity.

It was, it turned out, not the slave's status as property but his "liminal incorporation" into his host culture that connected him to the insolvent debtor, whom I soon came to recognize as a symbolic and legal precursor.[1] In my ongoing investigation of the conceptual and legal origins of "priced" people in early modern England, case law emerged as the most efficacious means of determining social customs and rituals of exclusion that resulted in certain persons becoming deprived of their civil rights.[2] It increasingly became clear that any inquiry into the history of priced persons had to begin with the unique set of circumstances within sixteenth-century common law by which personhood, due to changing economic circumstances and an array of legal maneuvers, became increasingly subjected to the domain of property. My book about slavery had transformed into a genealogy of bondage, one that began and remained with the figure of the debtor for the course of its argument.

As I have emphasized throughout, the law in this period borrowed liberally from extralegal domains that over time came to haunt its precepts. Thus one of the core concerns of this book has been to demonstrate how certain forms of law were not derived from the stability of their object of scrutiny—the bond—but were contoured by sundry social, theological, and political forms that variously engaged their own modes and conventions. For instance, debt bondage was realized through and against labor relations, marriage contracts, primogeniture, and even scriptural belief, all of which advanced their own peculiar logic. The collusion of debt law with these other domains at times necessitated an intervention, if not radical innovation, on the part of judges and lawyers. As I discussed in Chapter 2, for example, a moral dilemma arises when the debtor used that which was understood to be God's original nontransferable property, the human body, as a form of collateral. In *The Merchant of Venice*, the solution is to identify the debtor's blood as a form of corporate property. On stage and off, debt bondage understood blood as a metaphor that defined the debtor's natural humanity ("if you prick us, do we not bleed") but also as an abstraction, which like the debtor's "body, land, and goods" could upon forfeiture portend the law's right to divest the insolvent of his civic identity, while preserving his life.

Perhaps, most important, as I have stressed, the singular innovation of debt bondage was its unleashing of the law's ability to transform the human body into a new species of money. In this respect, debt bonds created the conceptual conditions for realizing the body as a form of property whose value was endowed by a speculative logic. As Ian Baucom reminds us, the slave trade was as much a trade in credit as it was a trade in commodities. Investors at various ports drew up bonds, which would not be redeemed for anywhere from three months to three years after the cargo had reached its destination and been sold. These arrangements, protracted over time and space, depended on mutual agreement in the legal fiction that profit was grounded in the physical body of the slave. As vehicles of investment slaves were in effect bonds/men:

> They [the business partners of the ship's owners, the local factor, the purchaser of the slave] were not just selling slaves on the far side of the Atlantic, they were lending money across the Atlantic. And, as significantly, they were lending money they did not yet possess or only possessed in the form of slaves. The slaves were thus treated not only as a type of commodity but as a type of interest-bearing money. They functioned in this system simultaneously as commodities for sale and as the reserve deposits of a loosely organized, decentered, but vast trans-Atlantic banking system: deposits made at the moment of sale and instantly reconverted into short-term bonds.[3]

Such global transactions could not have occurred without there already existing a form of value that secured the credibility of the system itself. This form of value, I have argued, was born of debt bonds in collusion with the period's drama—each of which served as the other's dialectical condition of possibility. The genre of the bond offered a particular type of speculative economy, which was collectively articulated in the dramatic literature's imagination of forfeiture. Both bonds and plays went beyond recognizing human beings as nonfungible property by identifying them initially as collateral against the payment of debt and then as reserve deposits for a network of interested parties.

The drama of the late sixteenth and early seventeenth centuries, I have also argued, anticipated the writings of Hobbes and Locke that put the bond at the center of civic belonging and political obligation and in so doing, construed social relations as akin to credit relations. Hobbes saw the distinction between servant and slave as resting on a notion of liberty as freedom from external impediments and, for Hobbes, bonds facilitated various conditions of subjugation that were legitimate. Coerced consent was foundational to the establishment of political authority. The vanquished, for instance, are forced into a covenant but they are not technically slaves; even though they are bound, they maintain corporal liberty.[4] Locke's social contract theory deployed an expanded notion of liberty, which included the idea of remaining free from the will of another. For Locke, citizenship rests on the exclusion of slaves, who are defined as persons who have forfeited their liberties "as a substitute for death."[5] Hobbes's absolutist theory of obligation, which regards all citizens as willing to subject themselves, put undue authority in the bond. Locke built on Hobbes by theorizing slavery as a condition of those who had broken their bond, whether by means of war or defying the law, and thus as having forfeited their natural right to liberty.[6]

Plays about debt did not speak in the language of political philosophy but were invested in expounding the meaning of self-ownership. By mobilizing various cultural forms—satiric invective, romance, and revenge-tragedy—they offer critical perspective on economic agency and its limits. Writers engaged formal devices particular to drama, such as extended analogy, embodied metaphor, and characterization, to name a few, in order to pry open the internal logic of possessive individualism as they showcased how bonds, like stage plays, were forms of writing that troubled ideas of consent and coercion and the continuity of self-identity. As plays about debt elaborated the problem of defining value as enmeshed in the definition of persons, they left in perpetuity a scandal whose legacy abides in our imagination of freedom as a function of possession.

Notes

PREFACE

1. Alain Sherter, *CBS MoneyWatch*, April 23, 2012, 1.
2. Sherter, *CBS MoneyWatch*, 1.
3. Quoted in Sherter, *CBS MoneyWatch*, 1.
4. David Graeber, *Debt: The First 5,000 Years* (New York: Melville House, 2011), 19

INTRODUCTION

Note to epigraph: Margaret Atwood, *Payback: Debt and the Shadow Side of Wealth* (Toronto: Anansi Press, 2008), 10.

1. Marc Norman and Tom Stoppard, *Shakespeare in Love: A Screenplay* (New York: Hyperion, 1998), 1–2.

2. John Locke, *Second Treatise of Government* (1690), ed. C. B. Macpherson (Indianapolis: University of Indiana Press, 1980), sec. 27, p. 19.

3. Craig Muldrew, "Credit and the Courts: Debt Litigation in a Seventeenth-Century Urban Community," *Economic History Review* 46 (1993): 30. By Muldrew's estimation, the number of debt cases brought before the Central Courts of King's Bench and Common Pleas rose from 10,556 in 1560 to 57,468 by 1640; see *The Economy of Obligation: The Culture of Credit and Social Relations in Early Modern England* (New York: Palgrave, 1998), 240, table 8.7. 5.

4. Having consulted thousands of inventories and court cases from late sixteenth and early seventeenth centuries, Muldrew has single-handedly revised our long-standing assumptions about everyday economic life in early modern England. Among his many crucial discoveries is that most participants in exchange relations were at once both creditors and debtors. C. W. Brooks also revised our presumptions about the social class of those who pursued debt litigation. His findings show that between 1560 and 1640 among those who came before King's Bench and Common Pleas, 75 percent of those who ended up incarcerated for debt included yeomen, husbandmen, commercial artisans, clergymen, lawyers, and widows, while peers, knights, esquires, and gentlemen accounted for at least 25 percent; Appendix I of *Pettyfoggers and Vipers of the Commonwealth: The "Lower Branch" of the Legal*

Profession in Early Modern England (Cambridge: Cambridge University Press, 1986) as analyzed and as cited in William Sherman, "Patents and Prisons: Simon Sturtevant and the Death of the Renaissance Inventor," *Huntington Library Quarterly* 72 (June 2009): 252.

5. Ian Baucom, *Specters of the Atlantic: Finance Capital, Slavery, and the Philosophy of History* (Durham, N.C.: Duke University Press, 2005), 7.

6. Muldrew, *Economy of Obligation*, 195.

7. On the etymology of the word "free," see David Graeber, *Debt: The First 5,000 Years* (New York: Melville House, 2011), 203.

8. C. B. Macpherson, *The Political Theory of Possessive Individualism: Hobbes to Locke* (Oxford: Oxford University Press, 1962), 3.

9. See George Caffentzis, *Clipped Coins, Abused Words, and Civil Government: John Locke's Philosophy of Money* (New York: Autonomedia, 1989).

10. Richard Byrne, *Prisons and Punishments of London* (London: Harrup Press, 1989), 110.

11. See Muldrew, *The Economy of Obligation*, 2. The influence of social history on economic history may be traced to earlier works such as Joyce Appleby, *Economic Thought and Ideology in Seventeenth Century England* (Princeton, N.J.: Princeton University Press, 1978), Joan Thirsk, *Economic Policy and Projects: The Development of a Consumer Society in Early Modern England* (London: Clarendon Press, 1978), Richard Grassby, *The Business Community of Seventeenth-Century England* (Cambridge: Cambridge University Press, 1995), and more recently, Deborah Valenze, *The Social Life of Money in the English Past* (Cambridge: Cambridge University Press, 2006), and Carl Wennerlind, *Casualties of Credit: The English Financial Revolution, 1620–1720* (Cambridge, Mass.: Harvard University Press, 2011).

12. According to J. H. Baker, in the first half of the fifteenth century, the Court of Common Pleas was adjudicating between 1,000 and 2,000 cases of debt annually. By 1640, this court alone was processing over 20,000 debt cases a year. "The Superior Courts in England, 1450–1800," in *Oberste Gerichtsbarkeit und Zentrale Gewalt im Europa der Frühen Neuzeit*, ed. Bernhard Diestelkamp (Cologne: Böhlau, 1996), 83.

13. As in Raymond Anselment, "*The Confinement*: The Plight of the Imprisoned English Debtor in the Seventeenth Century," *Restoration* 15 (1991): 3.

14. See William Ingram, *The Business of Playing* (Ithaca, N.Y.: Cornell University Press, 1988), and Natasha Korda, *Labors Lost: Women's Work and the Early Modern Stage* (Philadelphia: University of Pennsylvania Press, 2011).

15. Clifford Dobb, "London's Prisons," *Shakespeare Survey* 17 (1964): 93, and Jean Howard, "Credit, Incarceration, and Performance: Staging London's Debtors Prisons," in *Theater of a City: The Places of London Comedy, 1598–1642* (Philadelphia: University of Pennsylvania Press, 2007), 73.

16. Sample bond from the legal manual, also known as precedent book, *Carta Feodi* (London, 1510) as in A. W. B. Simpson, "The Penal Bond with Conditional Defeasance," *Law Quarterly Review* 82 (1966): 393–34. The Latin word *obligo* is related to *ligature*, which means "to tie up." The word *solvenda* could also mean "to be paid," but literally meant "to release or untie." Bob Hasenfratz, professor of English at the University of Connecticut, generously provided a translation of the Latin for me.

17. As legal historian Morris Arnold points out, in early modern French law the word "duty" was translated as the English word "debt," in "Towards an Ideology of the Early English Law of Obligations," *Law and History Review* 5 (Sept. 1987): 512.

18. Allan Farnsworth, "The Past of Promise: An Historical Introduction to Contract," *Columbia Law Review* 69 (April 1969): 584.

19. Frederick Pollock and William Maitland, *The History of English Law Before the Time of Edward I*, 2nd ed. (Cambridge: Cambridge University Press, 1968), 2:186.

20. According to Ralph Pugh, the penal sum was called a "security," in "Some Mediaeval Moneylenders," *Speculum* 43 (April 1968): 279. Simpson emphasizes that the general lawfulness of the debt bond was taken for granted. He notes that there are only two existing cases, both dating from the reign of Henry VIII, where the defendant who forfeited his bond attempted to avoid imprisonment by claiming that his creditor had usurious intent; "The Penal Bond," 413.

21. The distinction between the debt bond and the usurious transaction hinged on the difference between the creditor's seeking *interesse* as opposed to being awarded *damnum emergens* or *lucrum cessans*, both phrases for compensation for the potential loss a creditor suffered when his debtor did not repay his loan on time. See Simpson, "The Penal Bond," 412–13.

22. As in Simpson, "The Penal Bond," 415.

23. Thomas Grantham, *A Motion Against Imprisonment* (London, 1642), 8.

24. Muldrew, *Economy of Obligation*, 275. In cases of forfeiture, the medieval writ of *levari facias* allowed the sergeant-in-arms to seize the borrower's "goods and chattels," while the writ of *fieri facias* allowed for the seizure of half the profits of the borrower's freehold property. See Ian P. H. Duffy, "English Bankrupts, 1571–1861," *American Journal of Legal History* 24 (1980): 285, and John C. Fox, "Process of Imprisonment at Common Law," *Law Quarterly Review* 39 (1923): 48–49. By the late thirteenth century, the procedure of *elegit* granted the creditor rights to the borrower's chattels or land; A. W. B. Simpson, *A History of the Common Law of Contract: The Rise of the Action of Assumpsit* (Oxford: Clarendon Press, 1975), 587–88. Within this same period, the more severe Statute of Acton Burnell (1283) and Statute of Merchants (1285) were passed, allowing the creditor to seize the debtor's body on a writ of *capias ad satisfacienndum*. See Abraham L. Freedman, "Imprisonment for Debt," *Tempe Law Quarterly* 2 (1927–1928): 335n25. The writ of *capias ad satisfaciendum* remained part of English law until 1869. See Richard Ford, "Imprisonment for Debt," *Michigan Law Review* 25, no. 1 (1926–1927): 24–49.

25. Blackstone as in Simpson, *A History of the Common Law of Contract*, 587.

26. Bacon asserted "no person could be arrested for debt according to the constitution," and Coke added, "the King, by Magna Charta, is debarred from imprisoning his debtor," as in anonymous, "Legality of illegality of imprisonment for debt? Section II. The case of prisoners reconsidered," *Knowsley Pamphlet Collection* (London, 1837), 26.

27. Richard Bowers, "From Rolls to Riches: King's Clerks and Moneylending in Thirteenth Century England," *Speculum* 58 (January 1983): 62. The written bond also prevented the possibility of the wager of law, in which the borrower could escape liability if he could bring before a judge twelve oath-takers willing to swear to his integrity.

28. Richard Grassby, *The Business Community of Seventeenth-Century England*, 177, and Margaret Hunt, *The Middling Sort: Commerce, Gender, and the Family in England, 1680–1780* (Berkeley: University of California Press, 1996).

29. Graeber, *Debt: The First 5,000 Years*, 332.

30. John Bouvier's *A Law Dictionary* (1856) as in Joan Dayan, *The Law Is a White Dog: How Legal Rituals Make and Unmake Persons* (Princeton, N.J.: Princeton University Press, 2011), 269, n. 9.

31. Beginning with Roman law and extending into Germanic and through Anglo-Saxon law, slavery was the normal fate of the insolvent; see William H. Loyd, "Executions at Common Law," *University of Pennsylvania Law Review* and *American Law Register* 62 (March 1914): 355. On the links between civil and social death and slavery, see Orlando Patterson, *Slavery and Social Death: A Comparative Study* (Cambridge, Mass.: Harvard University Press, 1982), 21–27.

32. William Shakespeare, *Timon of Athens*, in David Bevington, ed., *The Complete Works of Shakespeare*, 6th ed. (New York: Longman, 2008), 3.4.91–93.

33. Thomas Middleton, *Michaelmas Term*, ed. Gail Kern Paster (Manchester: Manchester University Press, 2000), 2.3.367.

34. William Shakespeare, *The Merchant of Venice: Texts and Contexts*, ed. Lindsay Kaplan (Boston: Bedford St. Martin's, 2002), 4.1.92. Hereafter cited in the text.

35. Muldrew, *The Economy of Obligation*, 109.

36. As in Norman Jones, *God and the Moneylenders: Usury and Law in Early Modern England* (Oxford: Basil Blackwell, 1989), 131.

37. Anonymous, *A Godlie Treatice Concerning the Lawfull use of Ritches* (London, 1578), 8.

38. Peter F. Grav, *Shakespeare and the Economic Imperative: "'What's aught but as 'tis valued?"* (New York: Routledge: 2008), and David Hawkes, *The Culture of Usury in Renaissance England* (New York: Palgrave, 2010), offer insightful readings of early modern plays that feature credit arrangements, yet each exemplifies an approach that conflates debt and usury.

39. Carl Wennerlind, *Casualties of Credit: The English Financial Revolution, 1620–1720* (Cambridge, Mass.: Harvard University Press, 2011), 18. Wennerlind estimates that in the first half of the seventeenth century, the ratio of personal credit to coin transaction was 11:1 (18).

40. Actions of debt based on penal bonds underwent a fivefold increase from 1560 to 1605 and an eightfold increase by 1640, at which point debt suits accounted for 88 percent of the cases brought before the Court of Common Pleas and 80 percent of the cases brought before the Court of King's Bench. See table 4.5, C. W. Brooks, *Pettyfoggers and Vipers of the Commonwealth*, 69. In 1560, 5,278 debt cases were brought before the courts of Common Pleas and King's Bench. By 1606, there were 23,147, and by 1640, 28,734 debt cases were in advanced stages of litigation. See Brooks, table 4.1, p. 51, and table 4.3, p. 56 in *Pettyfoggers*.

41. *A Petition to the Kings Majestie; the Lords and Commons of the Parliament from Prisoners for Debt* (London, 1622), C4r.

42. As in Hugh Barty-King, *The Worst Poverty: A History of Debt and Debtors* (London: Alan Sutton, 1991), 3.

43. Jean-Christophe Agnew, *Worlds Apart: The Market and the Theater in Anglo-American Thought, 1550–1750* (Cambridge: Cambridge University Press, 1986), 12.

44. Antedating Agnew, Marc Shell in his seminal *The Economy of Literature* (Baltimore: Johns Hopkins University Press, 1978) describes economic literary criticism as seeking to "understand the relation between such literary exchanges and the exchanges that constitute the political economy" (7). For an overview of the New Economic Criticism post-Agnew, see *The New Economic Criticism: Studies at the Intersection of Literature and Economics*, ed. Martha Woodmansee and Mark Osteen (New York: Routledge, 1999), and Linda Woodbridge, *Money and the Age of Shakespeare: Essays in New Economic Criticism* (New York: Palgrave, 2003).

45. Two compelling studies that engage this approach are Jonathan Gil Harris, *Sick Economies: Drama, Mercantilism, and Disease in Shakespeare's England* (Philadelphia: University of Pennsylvania Press, 2004), and Valerie Forman, *Tragicomic Redemptions: Global Economics and the Early Modern English Stage* (Philadelphia: University of Pennsylvania Press, 2008).

46. Mary Poovey, *Genres of the Credit Economy: Mediating Value in Eighteenth- and Nineteenth-Century Britain* (Chicago: University of Chicago Press, 2008), 3.

47. I am referring here to early economic writings of Thomas Mun and Gerard de Malynes, among others, that scholars like Gil Harris and Valerie Forman have brilliantly explicated in their work. On the methodological limits of selective attention to the four "M"s: Gerard de Malynes, Thomas Milles, Edward Misselden, and Thomas Mun, in thinking about economic issues in the early modern period, see Julian Hoppit, "The Contexts and Contours of British Economic Literature, 1660–1760," *Historical Journal* 49 (2006): 79–80.

48. See for instance, Poovey, *Genres of the Credit Economy*, and David Landreth, *The Face of Mammon: The Matter of Money in English Renaissance Literature* (Oxford: Oxford University Press, 2012).

49. For an extended discussion of historical formalism and its (vexed) relationship to new formalism, see the introduction to *Formal Matters: Reading the Forms of Early Modern Texts*, ed. Allison Deutermann and András Kiséry (Manchester: Manchester University Press, 2013).

50. My thinking on form has been influenced by Ellen Rooney, "Form and Contentment," *Modern Language Quarterly* 61 (March 2000): 17–40; Caroline Levine, "Strategic Formalism: Toward a New Method in Cultural Studies," *Victorian Studies* 48 (Summer 2006): 625–57; Marjorie Levinson, "What Is New Formalism?" *PMLA* 122 (2008): 558–69; Susan Wolfson and Marshall Brown, *Reading for Form* (Seattle: University of Washington Press, 2006); and Mark David Rasmussen, *Renaissance Literature and Its Formal Engagements* (New York: Palgrave, 2002).

51. Graeber, *Debt: The First 5,000 Years*, 75. On the immateriality of early modern coins, see Landreth, *The Face of Mammon.*

52. On the agency of form, see Stephen Best, *The Fugitive's Properties: Law and the Poetics of Possession* (Chicago: University of Chicago Press, 2004), 21–25.

53. Baucom, *Specters of the Atlantic*, 7.

54. Baucom, *Specters of the Atlantic*, 139.

55. Karl Polanyi, *The Great Transformation: The Political and Economic Origins of Our Time*, 2nd ed., foreword by Joseph E. Stiglitz and introduction by Fred Block (1944; Boston: Beacon Press, 2001), 72.

56. On property as a "set of legal norms," see Jennifer Nedelsky, "Law, Boundaries, and the Bounded Self," *Representations* 30 (Spring 1990): 177.

57. *Topica* in *The Basic Works of Aristotle*, ed. Richard McKeon (New York: Random House, 1941), book 1, chapter 4, 19–23.

58. Best, *The Fugitive's Properties*, 157.

59. As in Nedelsky, "Law, Boundaries, and the Bounded Self," 163.

60. Best, *The Fugitive's Properties*, 37, emphasis mine.

61. John Hawkyns writes in 1562 of amassing "300. Negros at the least, besides other merchandises which that countrey yeeldeth," as in Richard Hakluyt, *The Principal Navigations Voyages Traffiques & Discoveries of the English Nation*, 12 vols. (London, 1589) facsimile reprint (Glasgow: James MacLehose & Sons, 1904), 10:8. In 1566, Captain John Lovell reports of leaving ashore "ninety-two pieces of Blacks," as in Kenneth R. Andrews, *Trade, Plunder, and Settlement: Maritime Enterprise and the Genesis of the British Empire, 1480–1630* (Cambridge: Cambridge University Press, 1984), 125.

62. As in Robert J. Steinfeld, *The Invention of Free Labor: The Employment Relation in English and American Law and Culture, 1350–1870* (Chapel Hill: University of North Carolina Press, 1991), 222 n. 115.

63. Steinfeld, *Invention of Free Labor*, 222 n. 115.

CHAPTER 1. *TIMON OF ATHENS*, FORMS OF PAYBACK, AND THE GENRE OF DEBT

Note to epigraph: Simone Weil as in John Kerrigan, *Revenge Tragedy: Aeschylus to Armageddon* (Oxford: Clarendon Press, 1996), 10.

1. Muriel Bradbrook, *The Tragic Pageant of Timon of Athens* (Cambridge: Cambridge University Press, 1966), quoted in Coppelia Kahn, "'Magic of Bounty': *Timon of Athens*, Jacobean Patronage, and Maternal Power," *Shakespeare Quarterly* 38 (Spring 1987): 35 n. 3. For an overview of *Timon*'s production history and critical reception, see Francelia Butler, *The Strange Critical Fortunes of Shakespeare's Timon of Athens* (Ames: Iowa State University Press, 1966), and A. D. Nuttall, Introduction to *Timon of Athens* (Boston: Twayne Publishers, 1989). On the play's aesthetic failings, see Una Ellis-Fermor, "*Timon of Athens*: An Unfinished Play," *Research in English Studies* 18 (1942): 270–83, and on *Timon*'s relationship to *Lear*, see Ruth Levitsky, "*Timon*: Shakespeare's *Magnyfycence* and an Embryonic *Lear*," *Shakespeare Studies* 11 (1978): 107–22.

2. Sharon O'Dair, "Introduction to *The Life of Tymon of Athens*," in *Thomas Middleton: The Collected Works*, ed. Gary Taylor and John Lavagnino (Oxford: Clarendon Press, 2007), 476.

3. For recent discussions of *Timon* that focus on credit, see Michael Chorost, "Biological Finance in Shakespeare's *Timon of Athens*," *English Literary Renaissance* 21 (Autumn 1991): 349–70; Derek Cohen, "The Politics of Wealth: *Timon of Athens*," *Neophilologus* 77 (January 1993): 149–60; Sandra K. Fischer, "'Cut My Heart in Sums': Shakespeare's Economics and *Timon of Athens*," in *Money: Lure, Lore, and Literature*, ed. John Louis DiGaetani (Westport, Conn.: Greenwood, 1994), 187–97; Luke Wilson, "Promissory Performances," *Renaissance Drama* 25 (1994): 59–89; Theodore B. Leinwand, *Theatre, Finance, and Society in Early Modern England* (Cambridge: Cambridge University Press, 1999), 32–40; and John Jowett, "Middleton and Debt in *Timon of Athens*," in *Money and the Age of Shakespeare: Essays in New Economic Criticism*, ed. Linda Woodbridge (New York: Palgrave, 2003), 219–37.

4. Leinwand, *Theatre, Finance, and Society*, 35.

5. Jowett, "Middleton and Debt in *Timon of Athens*," 230.

6. Cuthbert Burbage as in William Ingram, *The Business of Playing: The Beginnings of the Adult Professional Theater in Elizabethan London* (Ithaca, N.Y.: Cornell University Press, 1992), 42.

7. Clifford Dobb, "London's Prisons," *Shakespeare Survey* 17 (1964): 93, and Jean Howard, "Credit, Incarceration, and Performance: Staging London's Debtors Prisons," in *Theater of a City: The Places of London Comedy, 1598–1642* (Philadelphia: University of Pennsylvania Press, 2007), 73.

8. In *Labors Lost: Women's Work and the Early Modern English Stage* (Philadelphia: University of Pennsylvania Press, 2011) Natasha Korda reminds us that "the professional playing companies were . . . transitional economic formations that in certain respects retained the residual structure of guilds while at the same time assuming the emergent form of innovative capital ventures. Situated on the cusp of the formal and informal economies, they enjoyed a hybrid status that allowed them to take opportunistic advantage of both" (25).

9. See, for instance, Norman Nathan, "Is Shylock Philip Henslowe?" *Notes and Queries* 193 (1948): 163–65, and Murray Bromberg, "The Reputation of Philip Henslowe," *Shakespeare Quarterly* 1.3 (July 1950): 135–39. Joseph Donohue writes, "From Philip Henslowe to David Merrick, the producer or theatre manager has generally been seen as a combination of Shylock and Simon Legree, usurer and slavedriver," as in Joseph W. Donohue, Jr., ed., *The Theatrical Manager in England and America: Player of a Perilous Game* (Princeton, N.J.: Princeton University Press, 1971), foreword, v.

10. Walter W. Greg, *Henslowe's Diary*, 2 vols. (London: A. H. Bullen, 1904–1908), 2:144.

11. Deborah Valenze, *The Social Life of Money in the English Past* (Cambridge: Cambridge University Press, 2006), 2.

12. Peter Holland discusses *Timon* in "*The Merchant of Venice* and the Value of Money," *Cahiers Elisabethians* 60 (2001): 13.

13. *The Lawfull Use of Ritches*, as in Ceri Sullivan, *The Rhetoric of Credit: Merchants in Early Modern Writing* (London: Associated University, 2002), 82. For an overview of the devaluation crisis of the 1590s, see Jesse M. Lander, "'Crack'd Crowns' and Counterfeit Sovereigns: The Crisis of Value in *1 Henry IV*," *Shakespeare Studies* 30 (2002): 138–43.

14. Sir Frederick Pollock and Frederic William Maitland, *The History of English Law*

Before the Time of Edward I, 2nd ed., 2 vols. (Cambridge: Cambridge University Press, 1968), 2:226.

15. Francis Bacon as in J. H. Baker, "New Light on *Slade's Case,*" *Cambridge Law Review* 29 (1971): 60.

16. Allan Farnsworth, "The Past of Promise: An Historical Introduction to Contract," *Columbia Law Review* 69 (April 1969): 584.

17. Pollock and Maitland, *The History of English Law,* 2:186.

18. Blackstone as in A. W. B. Simpson, *A History of the Common Law of Contract: The Rise of the Action of Assumpsit* (Oxford: Clarendon Press, 1975), 587. Muldrew notes that by the early seventeenth century, "most attachments" were made "against a defendant's person rather than goods;" *The Economy of Obligation: The Culture of Credit and Social Relations in Early Modern England* (New York: Palgrave, 1998), 275.

19. George P. Costigan, Jr., "Trust Which Are Miscalled 'Spendthrift Trusts'," in *Legal Essays in Tribute to Orrin Kip McMurray*, ed. Max Radin and A. M. Kidd (Berkeley: University of California Press, 1935), 90.

20. Incarcerated debtors were charged for room and board, and as a result there were, in the words of one contemporary, "as many men, very neere, that [were] condemned to perpetuall imprisonment for their fees as suffer that misery for their debts." The destitute relied on charity and eventually ended up in the infamous "Hole," where they died of starvation or so-called gaol-fever. See Samuel Cotesford, *A Very Soveraigne Oyle to restore Debtors; being rightly and seasonably used* (London, 1622), sig. A3-A3. Hereafter cited in the text.

21. See Phillip Shaw, "The Position of Thomas Dekker in Jacobean Prison Literature," *PMLA* 62.2 (June 1947): 379.

22. Thomas Dekker, *English Villainies Discovered* in *Thomas Dekker*, ed. E. D. Pendry (Cambridge, Mass.: Harvard University Press, 1968), 262.

23. Richard Vennar. *An Apology* (London, 1616), sig. A.

24. William Miller discusses the historical relation between the ideas of paying back and paying for in *An Eye for an Eye* (Cambridge: Cambridge University Press, 2006), 68.

25. Aristotle juxtaposes distributive and rectificatory forms of justice in *The Nicomachean Ethics*, 2nd ed., translated and introduced by Terence Irwin (Indianapolis: Hackett, 1999), "Justice in Exchange," book 5, chapter 5, 74–76.

26. Frederick Gard Fleay, *A Chronicle History of the London Stage, 1559–1642* (New York: Burt Franklin, 1890), 117–18.

27. Introduction to *Documents of the Rose Playhouse*, edited and introduced by Carol Chillington Rutter (Manchester: Manchester University Press, 1984; rev. ed., 1999), 44.

28. William Ingram, *A London Life in the Brazen Age: Francis Langley, 1548–1602* (Cambridge, Mass.: Harvard University Press, 1978), 155. On the popularity of the debt bond in a wide range of business transactions, see A. W. B. Simpson, "The Penal Bond with Conditional Defeasance," *Law Quarterly Review* 82 (1966): 412. For a general overview of the so-called burgeoning age of contract and its significance to a range of commercial endeavors in the early modern period, see P. S. Atiyah, *The Rise and Fall of Freedom of Contract* (Oxford: Clarendon Press, 1979).

29. Felix Schelling (1928), as in Bromberg, "The Reputation of Philip Henslowe," 139; E. K. Chambers, *The Elizabethan Stage*, 4 vols. (Oxford: Clarendon Press, 1923): 2:368.

30. Blurb on frontispiece of Neil Carson, A *Companion to Henslowe's Diary* (Cambridge: Cambridge University Press, 1988); *A Companion*, 32. Hereafter cited in the text by page number.

31. This is especially true of Craig Muldrew who emphasizes throughout *Economy of Obligation* that bonds created reciprocal obligations of neighborliness that cast the lending of money in altruistic terms.

32. Lynn Johnson, "Friendship, Coercion, and Interest: Debating the Foundations of Justice in Early Modern England," *Journal of Early Modern History* 8 (2004): 46–64. Hereafter cited in the text.

33. Coke as in A. W. B. Simpson, *A History of the Common Law of Contract*, 123–24.

34. For theatrical managers' investments in their players see Robert Barrie, "Elizabethan Play-Boys in the Adult London Companies," *Studies in English Literature* 48 (Spring 2008): 237–57, and David Kathman, "Grocers, Goldsmiths, and Drapers: Freemen and Apprentices in the Elizabethan Theater," *Shakespeare Quarterly* 55 (Spring 2004): 15.

35. As in Rutter, *Documents of the Rose Playhouse*, 58.

36. This applied to the player Robert Dawes. For the language of 1614 bond between Robert Dawes and Philip Henslowe, see William Ingram, et al., *English Professional Theatre, 1530–1660* (Cambridge: Cambridge University Press, 2000), 282–284.

37. Simpson, "The Penal Bond with Conditional Defeasance," 411.

38. "Articles of Oppression," as in Walter W. Greg, ed., *Henslowe Papers: Being Documents Supplement to Henslowe's Diary* (London: A. H. Bullen, 1907), 86–90. Hereafter cited in the text as *HP*.

39. According to Rutter the total disputed amount added up to £567.

40. Korda, *Labors Lost*, 65–66.

41. Derived from the Latin *quietum clamare*, "quit claim" literally meant "to cry quits" (*OED*).

42. As in R. A. Foakes, *Henslowe's Diary*, fol. 39; fol. 42. Hereafter cited in the text as *HD* and by folio entry.

43. For a discussion of the early modern neo-Aristotelian proto-political economists, see Carl Wennerlind, *Casualties of Credit: The English Financial Revolution, 1620–1720* (Cambridge, Mass.: Harvard University Press, 2011), 30–43.

44. William Shakespeare, *The Life of Tymon of Athens*, edited and annotated by John Jowett in *Thomas Middleton: The Collected Works*, ed. Gary Taylor and John Lavagnino (Oxford: Clarendon Press, 2007), 1.1.14. I have used the version of the play divided into five separate acts, as in David Bevington, *The Complete Works of Shakespeare*, 6th ed. (New York: Longman, 2008). All subsequent quotations in the text are from the Bevington edition.

45. This is the Folio rendition of these lines, which subsequent editors, including Bevington and Jowett, emend as: "a gum which ozzes / From whence 'tis nourished" (1.2.23–4). I learned of this discrepancy in Hugh Grady, "*Timon of Athens*: The Dialectic of Usury, Nihilism, and Art," in *A Companion to Shakespeare's Works, Volume I: The Tragedies*, ed. Richard Dutton and Jean E. Howard (Oxford: Blackwell, 2003), 437.

46. On the theme of appetency in *Timon*, see Daniel W. Ross, "What Number of Men Eats Timon," *Iowa State Journal of Research* 59.3 (1985): 273–84. On cannibalism and patronage, see Jody Greene, "You Must Eat Men: The Sodomitic Economy of Renaissance Patronage," *GLQ: A Journal of Lesbian and Gay Studies* 1 (1994): 163–97.

47. William Shakespeare, *The Merchant of Venice: Texts and Contexts*, ed. M. Lindsay Kaplan (New York: New Bedford Press, 2002), 3.2.259–61.

48. Karen Newman, "Rereading Shakespeare's *Timon of Athens* at the Fin de Siècle," in *Shakespeare and the Twentieth Century: The Selected Proceedings of the International Shakespeare Association World Congress, Los Angeles, 1996*, ed. Jonathan Bate, et al. (Newark: University of Delaware Press, 1998), 379. For a discussion of the terms "magic" and "bounty," see Kahn, "'Magic of Bounty'," 34–57.

49. Critics often invoke anthropologist Marcel Mauss's exposition of "*potlatching*," a competitive form of gift-exchange in which the giver attempts to outdo a rival by giving everything away to the point of self-destruction in order to establish superiority by preventing reciprocity. See, e.g., Lewis Walker, "Fortune and Friendship in *Timon of Athens*," *Texas Studies in Literature and Language* 18 (Winter 1977): 577–600; Lewis Walker, "Money in *Timon of Athens*," *Philological Quarterly* 57 (1978): 269–71; Cohen; Kahn; and Chorost. Julia Reinhardt Lupton, however, up ends this trend by suggesting that in refusing parity, Timon attempts to remove himself from the social fabric of friendship that serves as the basis of the classical ideal of citizenship. Thus his misanthropy is set in motion long before the second half of the play insofar as his extravagant philanthropy enacts the same principal of separation; see her "Job of Athens, Timon of Uz," in *Thinking with Shakespeare: Essays on Politics and Life* (Chicago: University of Chicago Press, 2011), 145–46.

50. Leinwand, *Theatre, Finance, and Society*, 35.

51. Kahn, "'Magic of Bounty'," 36.

52. One could also interpret the "sovereign lady" Fortune as a female creditor, which, as Korda shows, was an increasingly familiar figure associated with debt litigation in the period, in general, and with the playhouse managers' financial lawsuits, in particular; *Labors Lost*, 59.

53. On the all-male world of the play, see Kenneth Burke, *Language as Symbolic Action: Essays on Life Literature and Method* (Berkeley: University of California Press, 1966), 118.

54. Thomas Middleton, *The Revenger's Tragedy*, ed. R. A. Foakes, Revels Student Editions (Manchester: Manchester University Press, 1996), 1.1.39.

55. This scene is not in Plutarch and is original to Shakespeare and Middleton's play.

56. Rabelais as in Graeber, *Debt: The First 5,000 Years*.

57. Henry Peacham "Worth of Penny," as in Wennerlind, *Casualties of Credit*, 42.

58. As in Graeber, *Debt*: *The First 5,000 Years*, 60.

59. In his introduction to the Arden edition of the play, H. J. Oliver argues that Alcibiades, like Fortinbras, represents a man of action and functions as a foil to the more contemplative Timon. William Shakespeare, *Timon of Athens*, ed. H. J. Oliver (London: Methuen, 1959). Others see Alcibiades as a figure of heroic virtue. See, for instance, David Cook, "*Timon of Athens*," *Shakespeare Studies* 16 (1963): 83–94.

60. Karl Marx, *Early Writings*, trans. Rodney Livingstone and Gregor Benton, introduction by Lucio Colletti (New York: Vintage Books, 1975), 377.

61. Aristotle, *Niomachean Ethics*, trans. Martin Ostwald (New York: Macmillan, 1962), 124–25.

62. Ibid., 127.

63. William W. E. Slights, "*Genera Mixta* and *Timon of Athens*," *Studies in Philology* 74 (1977): 40. Although he maintains that in the final analysis *Timon* is a tragedy, G. Wilson Knight has written extensively on *Timon* as a problem play in *The Wheel of Fire: Interpretations of Shakespearian Tragedy with Three New Essays*, 4th ed. (London: Methuen, 1949), 207–39. On *Timon* as satire, see Robert E. Morsberger, "*Timon of Athens*: Tragedy or Satire?" in *Shakespeare in the Southwest: Some New Directions* (El Paso: Texas Western Press,, 1969), 56–70. On the conventions of revenge in the period, see Fredson Bowers, *Elizabethan Revenge Tragedy, 1587–1642* (Princeton, N.J.: Princeton University Press, 1940), and Ronald Broude, "Revenge and Revenge Tragedy in Renaissance England," *Renaissance Quarterly* 28.1 (Spring 1975): 38–58.

CHAPTER 2. SHYLOCK AND THE SLAVES

Note to epigraph: William Shakespeare, *The Merchant of Venice: Texts and Contexts*, ed. M. Lindsay Kaplan (New York: Bedford St. Martin's Press, 2002), 3.2.18–20. Hereafter cited in the text.

1. Walter Cohen, "*The Merchant of Venice* and the Possibilities of Historical Criticism," *English Literary History* 49 (1982): 769.

2. Cohen, "*The Merchant of Venice* and the Possibilities of Historical Criticism," 769. For Lars Engle, the bond is "as unbusinesslike proposition as one could find," see "'Thrift Is Blessing': Exchange and Explanation in *The Merchant of Venice*," *Shakespeare Quarterly* 37 (1986): 27. According to William O. Scott, Shylock rejects "rational choice economics"; see "Conditional Bonds, Forfeitures, and Vows in *The Merchant of Venice*," *English Literary Renaissance* 34 (November 2004): 290.

3. On the early modern culture of credit, see Craig Muldrew, *The Economy of Obligation: The Culture of Credit and Social Relations in Early Modern England* (New York: Palgrave, 1998), and Deborah Valenze, *The Social Life of Money in the English Past* (Cambridge: Cambridge University Press, 2006).

4. Analyses of the play that emphasize legal and affective bonds, which have greatly influenced my thinking, fail to address the play's engagement with the social and moral implications of forfeiture. See, for instance, Maxine MacKay, "*The Merchant of Venice*: A Reflection of the Early Conflict Between Courts of Law and Courts of Equity," *Shakespeare Quarterly* 15.4 (Autumn 1964): 371–75; E. F. J. Tucker, "The Letter of the Law in *The Merchant of Venice*," *Shakespeare Survey* 29 (1976): 93–101; Jan Lawson Hinely, "Bond Priorities in *The Merchant of Venice*," *Studies in English Literature* 20 (1980): 217–39; William Chester

Jordan, "Approaches to the Court Scene in the Bond Story: Equity and Mercy or Reason and Nature," *Shakespeare Quarterly* 33.1 (Spring 1982): 49–59; Charles Spinosa, "Shylock and Debt and Contract in *The Merchant of Venice*," *Cardozo Studies in Law and Literature* 5.1 (Spring 1993): 65–85, and Spinosa, "The Transformation of Intentionality: Debt and Contract in *The Merchant of Venice*," *English Literary Renaissance* 24.2 (1994): 370–409. More recently, Tim Stretton has addressed these themes in "Contract, Debt Litigation, and Shakespeare's *The Merchant of Venice*," *Adelaide Law Review* 31 (2010): 111–25.

5. Confusingly, Shylock refers to the bond as a "single bond," one that has no condition attached, although he and Antonio clearly devise a conditional bond. Critics have suggested that Shylock intends to downplay the condition and thus make it seem like "merry sport"; see M. M. Mahood, "Introduction," in William Shakespeare, *The Merchant of Venice*, ed. M. M. Mahood, New Cambridge edition (Cambridge: Cambridge University Press, 2003).

6. Muldrew, *Economy of Obligation*, 109.

7. Table 4.5, C. W. Brooks, *Pettyfoggers and Vipers of the Commonwealth: The "Lower Branch" of the Legal Profession in Early Modern England* (Cambridge: Cambridge University Press, 1986). In 1560, 5,278 debt cases were brought before the courts of Common Pleas and King's Bench. By 1606, there were 23,147, and by 1640, 28,734 debt cases were in advanced stages of litigation. See Brooks, table 4.1, p. 51 and table 4.3, p. 56 in *Pettyfoggers*.

8. Debtors remained the largest numerical group of imprisoned in the seventeenth century and unlike those facing criminal charges, were without hope of release for a trial, transport, pardon, or even execution. See Christopher Harding et al., *Imprisonments in England and Wales: A Concise History* (London: Croom Helm, 1985), 56. As one historian reminds us, from the fourteenth to the nineteenth centuries, "at least as many Londoners were locked up for debt as for crime" and these debtors "spent longer behind bars than the most serious offenders"; Richard Byrne, *Prisons and Punishments of London* (London: Harrap Press, 1989), 110.

9. Muldrew, *Economy of Obligation*, 275. Before the thirteenth century, there was no process by which a borrower could pledge his person as collateral. The year 1285 marked the instantiation of *elegit*, a procedure that granted the creditor rights to the borrower's chattels or land. See A. W. B. Simpson, *A History of the Common Law of Contract: The Rise of the Action of Assumpsit* (Oxford: Clarendon Press, 1975), 587–88. Within the same period, the even more severe Statute of Acton Burnell (1283) and Statute of Merchants (1285) were passed, allowing the creditor to seize the debtor's body on a writ of *capias ad satisfacienndum*. See Abraham L. Freedman, "Imprisonment for Debt," *Tempe Law Quarterly* 2 (1927–28): 335 n. 25. In accordance with a series of fourteenth-century statutes, the purview for recoverable action was gradually expanded from king to manor lord to merchant; by the mid-sixteenth century, all creditors could initiate the apprehension and incarceration of their debtors without the benefit of a jury trial. See John C. Fox, "Process of Imprisonment at Common Law," *Law Quarterly Review* 39 (1923): 48–49. The writ of *capias ad satisfaciendum* remained part of English law until 1869; see Richard Ford, "Imprisonment for Debt," *Michigan Law Review* 25.1 (1926–27): 24–49.

10. Francis Bacon, "Of Usury," in *The Works of Francis Bacon*, ed. James Spedding, Robert L. Ellis, and Douglas D. Heath (Boston: Brown and Taggard, 1861), 12:220.

11. Phillip Stubbes, *Anatomy of the Abuses in England* (London, 1583), ed. Frederick J. Furnivall (London: New Shakespeare Society, 1877–79), 127.

12. *Dive v. Manningham* (1551) determined that every prisoner would finance his own living expenses; nonsensically, this applied to the defaulted debtor as well (Simpson, *Common Law* of *Contract*, 591). Imprisoned debtors were lodged according to their means: the two-penny ward charged that much for a bed and a pair of sheets, the knights ward charged eight pence, and the third-pay ward, or the Master's side, charged ten pence or more, depending on the prisoners' needs. There was no charge for the "Hole," where the destitute were fed from the almsbasket. See William Fennor, *The Compter's Commonwealth* (London, 1617), 475–76, and John H. Langbein, "The Historical Origins of the Sanction of Imprisonment for Serious Crime," *Journal of Legal Studies* 35 (1976): 38.

13. On the scarcity of cash in the period see Craig Muldrew, "'Hard Food for Midas': Cash and Its Social Value in Early Modern England," *Past and Present* 170 (February 2001): 78–120.

14. The influence of Aquinas on the distinction between usurious and nonusurious lending in English common law is discussed in John T. Noonan, *The Scholastic Analysis of Usury* (Cambridge, Mass.: Harvard University Press, 1957).

15. 11 Henry VII c. 8, sec. 1, as in Jones, *God and the Moneylenders*, 119.

16. William Blackstone, *Commentaries on the Laws of England: A Facsimile of the First Edition of 1765–1769*, ed. Stanley N. Katz, 4 vols. (Chicago: University of Chicago Press, 1979), 2:2. Legal scholars have demonstrated that Blackstone never convincingly reconciled his notion of "absolute property" with feudal landholding; see Robert P. Burns, "Blackstone's Theory of the 'Absolute' Rights of Property," *University of Cincinnati Law Review* 54 (1985): 79–82.

17. Blackstone, *Commentaries*, 3:14. In Book 2, Blackstone defines waste as the owner's right to spoil or destroy "houses, gardens, trees or other corporeal hereditaments," and in Book 3, he explains the owner's right to waste "estate, either in houses, woods, or lands; by demolishing not the temporary profits only, but the very substance of the thing," as in Edward J. McCaffery, "Must We Have the Right to Waste?" in *New Essays in the Legal and Political Theory of Property*, ed. Stephen Munzer (Cambridge: Cambridge University Press, 2001), 85.

18. David J. Seipp, "The Concept of Property in the Early Common Law," *Law and History Review* 12.1 (Spring 1994): 33.

19. For C. B. Macpherson, Hobbes and Locke share a conception of the individual as "essentially the proprietor of his own person or capacities"; *The Political Theory of Possessive Individualism Hobbes to Locke* (London: Oxford University Press, 1962), 3.

20. John Locke, *Two Treatises of Government*, ed. Peter Laslett (Cambridge: Cambridge University Press, 1988), I.85–86. I am building on Jeffrey Paul and Ellen Frankel Paul's discussion of qualified ownership and self-ownership in "Locke's Usufructuary Theory of Self-Ownership," *Pacific Philosophical Quarterly* 61 (1980): 384–95.

21. Locke, *Two Treatises*, I.85–86. The idea of trust even poses limits on the notion of self-ownership; Locke II.6 stresses, "For Men being all the Workmanship of one Omnipotent, and infinitely wise Maker . . . they are his Property, whose Workmanship they are, made to last during his, not one another's Pleasure."

22. Seipp, "The Concept of Property," 51.

23. As Pollock and Maitland explain, in the case of debt, the lender receives security because in the eyes of the law the lender has entrusted his property to another. This is why the creditor "shall not receive any certain sum for the use of his money" but is entitled to "damages when he has only proved that the debt was not paid when it was due." Frederick Pollock and Frederic William Maitland, *The History of English Law before the Time of Edward I*, 2nd ed., 2 vols. (Cambridge: Cambridge University Press, 1968), 2:216.

24. See, for example, Engle, "'Thrift Is Blessing,'" 31, and Marc Shell, *Money, Language, and Thought: Literary and Philosophic Economies from the Medieval to the Modern Era* (Baltimore: Johns Hopkins University Press, 1982), 50.

25. Seipp, "The Concept of Property," 34.

26. Plowden as in Seipp, "The Concept of Property," 65.

27. For an example of the creation myth of property, see Edward Coke, *Commentary on Littleton* (London, 1628), 116.

28. Seipp, "The Concept of Property," 62; Mark Edwin Andrews, *Law versus Equity in the Merchant of Venice* (Boulder: University of Colorado Press, 1965), 65.

29. While some argue that Shylock brings Tubal into the equation as a contrivance, others, myself included, regard him as integral to the play's depiction of embedded credit relations. See Mahood, "Introduction."

30. A. J. McClean, "The Common Law Life of Estate and the Civil Law Usufruct: A Comparative Study," *International and Comparative Law Quarterly* 12 (April 1963): 650.

31. Seipp, "The Concept of Property," 46.

32. Francis Bacon, *The Use of the Law Provided for the Preservation of Our Persons, Goods, and Good Names* (London, 1635), sig. A1 (emphasis mine).

33. Simpson, *Common Law of Contract*, 124.

34. David Graeber, *Debt: The First 5,000 Years* (New York: Melville House, 2011), 59.

35. Alexander Silvayn, "Of a Jew, who would for his debt have a pound of the flesh of a Christian," declamation 95, in Alexander Silvayn, *The Orator*, trans. Lazarus Piot (London, 1596).

36. Henry Wilkinson, *The Debt Book* (London, 1625), 5.

37. On slavery as an evocative concept, see Igor Kopytoff, "Slavery," *Annual Review of Anthropology* 11 (1982): 221.

38. Susan Dyer Amussen, *Caribbean Exchanges: Slavery and the Transformation of English Society, 1640–1700* (Chapel Hill: University of North Carolina Press, 2007), 219.

39. Paul Vinogradoff, *Villeinage*, 151, as in W. S. Holdsworth, *A History of English Law*, 7 vols., 3rd ed. (Boston: Little Brown, 1923), 3:495.

40. Blackstone, *Commentaries on the Laws of England*, 1:411. On the history of slavery in sixteenth-century England, see I. S. Leadam, "The Last Days of Bondage in England,"

Law Quarterly Review 9 (1893): 348–65, and C. S. L. Davies, "Slavery and Protector Somerset: The Vagrancy Act of 1547," *Economic History Review* 19.3 (1966): 533–49.

41. E. F. J. Tucker and William J. Jones have shown that interpretations that engage this premise exaggerate the extent of the conflict between the courts of equity and courts of common law in this period. See E. F. J. Tucker, "The Letter of the Law in *The Merchant of Venice*," *Shakespeare Survey* 29 (1976): 93–101, and William J. Jones, "Conflict or Collaboration? Chancery Attitudes in the Reign of Elizabeth I," *American Journal of Legal History* 5 (1961): 12–54.

42. Pollock and Maitland, *History of English Law*, 2:186.

43. See J. M. Price, "What Did Merchants Do?" *Journal of Economic History* 69 (1989): 267–84.

44. Andre Gunder Frank, *ReOrient: Global Economy in the Asian Age* (Berkeley: University of California Press, 1998), 150. For this reason, English merchants were regarded as extravagant men who indulged in "costly building, costly diet, and costly apparel." The idea that merchants used up or wasted their wealth was "a common attitude of the time." See W. J. Jones, "The Foundations of English Bankruptcy: Statutes and Commissions in the Early Modern Period," *Transactions of the American Philosophical Society* 69.3 (1979): 53.

45. Thomas Middleton, *Michaelmas Terme*, *Thomas Middleton: The Collected Works*, ed. Gary Taylor and John Lavagnino (Oxford: Clarendon Press, 2007), 2.3.228–29.

46. *Michaelmas Terme*, 2.3.379–80.

47. William Shakespeare and Thomas Middleton, *The Life of Tymon of Athens*, in *Thomas Middleton: The Collected Works*, Scene 4, l.37–38; Scene 8, l.86; 88; 92; 94.

48. Thomas Middleton, *The Phoenix*, in *Thomas Middleton: The Collected Works*, 12. 120; 125–26.

49. Bonds were referred to as "letters obligatory." On the link between bonds and letters, see Alan Stewart, *Shakespeare's Letters* (Oxford: Oxford University Press, 2008).

50. For a discussion of the "*in terrorem*" aspects of debt bonds, see Simpson, *History of the Common Law of Contract*, 123–24.

51. Blackstone, *Commentaries*, 4:395.

52. Anthony Munday as in William Chester Jordan, "Approaches to the Court Scene in The Bond Story: Equity and Mercy or Reason and Nature," *Shakespeare Quarterly* 33.1 (Spring 1982): 56.

53. Benjamin Nelson and Joshua Starr as quoted in Theodore Leinwand, *The Theater, Finance, and Society in Early Modern England* (Cambridge: Cambridge University Press, 1999), 172 n. 74.

54. St. Ambrose, as in Leinwand, 172 n. 74. For an extended discussion of the play's "Pauline coordinates," see Julia Reinhard Lupton, *Citizen-Saints: Shakespeare and Political Theology* (Chicago: University of Chicago Press, 2005), 90; 75–103.

55. On the concept of institutionalized marginality, see Orlando Patterson, *Slavery and Social Death*, 46. For Lupton, while Shylock's forced conversion is not inherently tragic, it is an example of "death into citizenship," whereby his civic membership is predicated on a renunciation of previous modes of affiliation that gave his life meaning (Lupton, *Citizen-Saints*, 101).

56. See Amy Louise Erickson, *Women and Property in Early Modern England* (New York: Routledge, 1993), and B. J. Sokol and Mary Sokol, *Shakespeare, Law, and Marriage* (Cambridge: Cambridge University Press, 2003).

57. John Dod and Robert Cleaver, *A Godly Forme of Household Government* (London, 1630); see Michael Neill, *Putting History to the Question: Power, Politics, and Society in English Renaissance Drama* (New York: Columbia University Press, 2000), 94.

58. Ibid.

59. Seipp, "The Concept of Property," 53–54. See also Susan Staves, *Married Women's Separate Property in England, 1660–1833* (Cambridge, Mass.: Harvard University Press, 1990), 29, 35 (quoting Peter Earle, *The Making of the English Middle Class: Business, Society, and Family Life in London 1660–1730* [London: Methuen, 1989], 159).

60. Natasha Korda, "Dame Usury: Gender, Credit and (Ac)counting in the Sonnets and *The Merchant of Venice*," *Shakespeare Quarterly* 60.2 (Summer 2009): 138.

61. Korda, "Dame Usury," 141.

62. See Carol Leventen, "Patrimony and Patriarchy in *The Merchant of Venice*," in *The Matter of Difference: Materialist Feminist Criticism of Shakespeare*, ed. Valerie Wayne (Ithaca, N.Y.: Cornell University Press, 1991), 59–81.

63. Lynda E. Boose, "The Comic Contract and Portia's Golden Ring," *Shakespeare Studies* 20 (1987): 241.

CHAPTER 3. *MICHAELMAS TERM* AND THE PROBLEM OF SATISFACTION

Note to epigraphs: 2 *Henry VI*, 4.2.75–80, in *The Complete Works of Shakespeare*, ed. David Bevington, 6th ed. (New York: Longman, 2008). Judith Butler, *The Psychic Life of Power: Theories in Subjection* (Stanford: Stanford University Press, 1997), 78.

1. Thomas Middleton, *Michaelmas Term*, *The Revels Plays*, ed. Gail Kern Paster (Manchester: Manchester University Press, 2000), 5.1.57–61. Hereafter cited in the text.

2. Ruby Chatterji, "Unity and Disparity: *Michaelmas Term*," *Studies in English Literature* 8 (1968): 359.

3. Paul Yachnin, "Social Competition in Middleton's *Michaelmas Term*," *Explorations in Renaissance Culture* 13 (1987): 91.

4. Richard Levin, Introduction to *Michaelmas Term*, *Regents Renaissance Drama* (Lincoln: University of Nebraska Press, 1966), p. xviii. Anthony Covatta agrees that Easy is a strange choice for a protagonist, since "it is difficult to summon much sympathy for him in the first two-thirds of the play," in *Thomas Middleton's City Comedies* (Lewisburg, Penn.: Bucknell University Press, 1973), 91.

5. Theodore B. Leinwand, "Redeeming Beggary/Buggery in *Michaelmas Term*," *English Literary History* 61 (1994): 54. W. Nicholas Knight also addresses the overlay of sexual and monetary manipulation in the play in "Sex and Law Language in Middleton's

Michaelmas Term," in Kenneth Friedenrich, ed., "*Accompanying the Players": Essays Celebrating Thomas Middleton, 1580–1980* (New York: AMS, 1983), 89–108.

6. Here I understand genre not only in terms of iterable conventions but also function, insofar as there is a finite range of uses to which any given text may be subjected. On monies as forms of writing, see Mary Poovey, *Genres of the Credit Economy: Mediating Value in Eighteenth- and Nineteenth-Century Britain* (Chicago: University of Chicago Press, 2008).

7. For the phrase "putting one's hand," see the sample bond in William West, *The First Part of Simboleography* (London, 1615), sig. H6v. West's *Simboleography* went through 7 editions between 1590 and 1598, and 6 more over the next 30 years. For a rich discussion of contractual agency and the hand in the early modern period, see Katherine Rowe, *Dead Hands: Fictions of Agency, Renaissance to Modern* (Stanford, Calif.: Stanford University Press, 1999), esp. "Introduction: Essentialism, Agency, and the Exemplary Hand," 1–24.

8. On the "fugitive" as a historical form of crisis involving the legal subjection of personhood to property, see Stephen Best, *The Fugitive's Properties: Law and the Poetics of Possession* (Chicago: University of Chicago Press, 2004), esp. the introduction, 1–21. On the seal as adjunct to the signature and its "fugitive character," see Joseph Loewenstein, "Forms in Wax: Shakespeare and the Personality of the Seal," in Bella Mirabella, ed., *Ornamentalism: The Art of Renaissance Accessories* (Ann Arbor: University of Michigan Press, 2011), 205.

9. George E. Rowe, Jr., "Prodigal Sons, New Comedy, and Middleton's *Michaelmas Term*," *English Literary Renaissance* 7 (1977): 102–3.

10. In 1663, England's Lord Chancellor wrote, "In every contract there is mutual *assent* of their [the bargainers'] minds . . . but a *feme covert* cannot give a mutual assent of her mind . . . for her will and mind, as also herself, is under and subject to the will or mind of her husband," as in Craig Muldrew, "'A Mutual Assent of her Mind?': Women, Debt Litigation and Contract in Early Modern England," *History Workshop Journal* 55 (2003): 48. On women's agency and contract law, see Kathryn Schwartz, *What You Will: Gender, Contract, and Shakespearean Social Space* (Philadelphia: University of Pennsylvania Press, 2011).

11. Subha Mukherji, "Middleton and the Law," in Suzanne Gossett, ed., *Thomas Middleton in Context* (Cambridge: Cambridge University Press, 2011), 109. On the lawyers' objections that writs could be obtained by any one who could pay the fee, see Edward Jenks, "The Prerogative Writs in English Law," *Yale Law Journal* 32 (1923): 523–34 (523).

12. Bradin Cormack, "Shakespeare Possessed: Legal Affect and the Time of Holding," in Paul Raffield and Gary Watt, eds., *Shakespeare and the Law* (Portland, Ore.: Hart Publishing, 2008), 84.

13. Marjorie K. McIntosh, "Money Lending on the Periphery of London, 1300–1600," *Albion: A Quarterly Concerned with British Studies* 20 (1988): 568.

14. Columbia RBML SMITH, DE Documents 1589 Walcott, Th.

15. Robin Mundill, "Christian and Jewish Lending Patterns and Financial Dealings," in *Credit and Debt in Medieval England, c. 1180–c. 1350*, ed. P. R. Schofield and N. J. Mayhew (Oxford: Oxford University Press, 2002), 61.

16. Blackstone as in A. W. B. Simpson, *A History of the Common Law of Contract: The Rise of the Action of Assumpsit* (Oxford: Clarendon Press, 1975), 587. Common law recognized the debtor who forfeited on his bond as guilty of the criminal offense of wrongfully detaining another's property and therefore as eligible for imprisonment. See John C. Fox, "Process of Imprisonment at Common Law," *Law Quarterly Review* 39 (1923): 48–49; Craig Muldrew, *The Economy of Obligation: The Culture of Credit and Social Relations in Early Modern England* (New York: St. Martin's Press, 1998), 275.

17. Karl Polanyi, *The Great Transformation: The Political and Economic Origins of Our Time*, 2nd ed., foreword by Joseph E. Stiglitz and introduction by Fred Block (1944; 1957; Boston: Beacon Press, 2001), 72.

18. West, *The First Part of Simboleography*, sig. B4r.

19. Charles Donahue, Jr., Introduction to the Exhibit Catalogue, "History in Deed: Medieval Society and the Law in England, 1100–1600," October 13, 1993, Harvard Law School.

20. On early modern writing manuals and their construal of the hand see Jonathan Goldberg, *Shakespeare's Hand* (Minneapolis: University of Minnesota Press, 2003).

21. Rather than regard the fiction of consent as false consciousness, Elaine Scarry understands the fiction of consent as a narrative that imparts meaning to the structures it influences. Thus the signature may be seen as an "artifactual response at a moment when the will is in danger of being impaired. That is, an actual recreation of one's relation to one's external circumstances comes about. . . . thus the generation of the artifact by those in a position of passivity at a moment of great polarization from the active (the surgeon, the governors) equalizes the relation." See Scarry, "Consent and the Body: Injury, Departure and Desire," *New Literary History* 21 (1990): 882.

22. Randy E. Barnett, "A Consent Theory of Contract," *Columbia Law Review* 86 (1986): 273.

23. William Fulbecke, *A Paralellle or Conference of the Civil Law* (London, 1618), sig. A.

24. In 1595, John Slade sold wheat and rye to Humphrey Morley on credit, but after the grains were delivered Morley refused to pay. Slade sought recompense through the recovery of debt, the usual action the plaintiff would take under the circumstances. Without a written contract, Slade, however, had no way of proving that Morley had agreed to pay him. But, by trying the case as breach of promise—a legal innovation—the court could argue that the delivery of the grains automatically implied that Morley, the recipient, was obligated to pay for what he had received.

25. For an overview of significance of the 1602 decision on *Slade's Case* see H. K. Lücke, "*Slade's Case* and the Origins of the Common Counts," *Law Quarterly Review* 81 (1965): 422–561; J. H. Baker, "New Light on *Slade's Case*," *Cambridge Law Journal* 29 (1971): 51–67; David Ibbetson, "Assumpsit and Debt in the Early Sixteenth Century: The Origins of the Indebitatus Count," *Cambridge Law Journal* 41 (1982): 142–61, and Ibbetson, "Sixteenth Century Contract Law: *Slade's Case* in Context," *Oxford Journal of Legal Studies* 4 (1984): 295–317.

26. As in Ibbetson, "Sixteenth Century Contract Law: *Slade's Case* in Context," 317. See also J. H. Baker, "New Light on *Slade's Case*," 61.

27. Luke Wilson, *Theaters of Intention: Drama and Law in Early Modern England* (Stanford, Calif.: Stanford University Press, 2000), 79.

28. For the political-theological implications of ownership and self-ownership in the case of forfeiture, see Amanda Bailey, "Shylock and the Slaves: Owing and Owning in *The Merchant of Venice*," *Shakespeare Quarterly* 62 (2011): 1–24.

29. The private theaters were known for their repertory of satirical comedies about law and their legal audience; see Jayne Elisabeth Archer, Elizabeth Goldring, and Sarah Knight, eds., *The Intellectual and Cultural World of the Inns of Court* (Manchester: Manchester University Press, 2011).

30. Richard Levin cites the early modern lawyer John Hayward's observation that *Michaelmas Term* held particular interest to Inns of Court students in "Introduction," *Michaelmas Term*, xii–xiii. The speculation that Middleton was enrolled at Gray's Inn (see, for instance, W. Nicholas Knight, "Sex and Law Language in Middleton's *Michaelmas Term*," 89) has been overturned; see Mukherji, "Middleton and the Law," 106–15.

31. On the play's locutions involving anality, see Leinwand.

32. *Oxford English Dictionary* (OED), 2nd ed. (Oxford: Oxford University Press, 1989), s.v. "fathom," online version, November 2010; http://www.oed.com (accessed 17 January 2011).

33. *Oxford English Dictionary* (OED), 2nd ed. (Oxford: Oxford University Press, 1989), s.v. "fresh," online version, November 2010; http://www.oed.com (accessed 17 January 2011).

34. On the process of initiation as making up "the heart of the play," see Covatta, *Thomas Middleton's City Comedies*, 85, and Paster, "Introduction," 17–25.

35. As in Mukherji, "Middleton and the Law," 107.

36. In the so-called commodity game, the lender offers to loan the borrower overpriced merchandise to garner him a profit equal to the amount of money he seeks to borrow. After the bond is sealed, however, the commodity can only be sold at a lower rate, if it can be sold at all. The borrower then defaults on his loan, awarding his creditor the collateral he put up at the beginning. For a discussion of the commodity game and other schemes detailed in late sixteenth-century rogue literature, see George R. Price, "Introduction," in *Michaelmas Term and A Trick to Catch the Old One*, ed. Price (The Hague: Mouton, 1976), 15. On Middleton's familiarity with rogue literature, see Paster, "Introduction," in *Michaelmas Term*, 13.

37. Thomas Middleton, *A Trick to Catch the Old One*, 3.1.39–40.

38. Grace Ioppolo, "Early Modern Handwriting," in *A New Companion to English Renaissance Literature and Culture*, ed. Michael Hattaway, 2 vols. (Oxford: Blackwell, 2000), 1:178.

39. Ioppolo, "Early Modern Handwriting," 179.

40. For a fascinating discussion of ideas in the period about textual production as

parthenogenesis, see Stephen Guy-Bray, *Against Reproduction: Where Renaissance Texts Come From* (Toronto: University of Toronto Press, 2009), esp. "Introduction: The Work of Art in the Age of Human Reproduction," 3–44.

41. David Graeber, *Debt: The First 5,000 Years* (New York: Melville House, 2011), 192.

42. Upon his realization that he is "encounter'd / with [the] clamorous demands of debt [and] broken bonds," Timon understands his overdue bonds as threatening to "knock [him] down" and "cleave [him] to the girdle!" He regards the rising piles of bonds carried on stage by the handful as akin to knives that will "cut [his] heart in sums," let his blood "five thousand drops," and "tear . . . and take" his flesh (3.4.90–95). William Shakespeare and Thomas Middleton, *The Life of Tymon of Athens* in *Thomas Middleton: The Collected Works*, ed. Gary Taylor and John Lavagnino (Oxford: Oxford University Press, 2007).

43. While satisfaction was a key term within doctrines of repentance and expiation, in which *satisfacere* (meaning to do or make enough) described the nature and scope of human and divine atonement, the earliest recorded use of the word in English related to debt repayment. See William Ian Miller, *Eye for an Eye* (Cambridge: Cambridge University Press, 2006), 140. On the economic and theological registers of satisfaction, see Heather Hirschfeld, "'And He Hath Enough': The Penitential Economies of *The Merchant of Venice*," *Journal of Medieval and Early Modern Studies* 40 (2010): 89–117.

44. Mukherji, "Middleton and the Law," 109.

CHAPTER 4. FREEDOM, BONDAGE, AND REDEMPTION IN *THE CUSTOM OF THE COUNTRY*

Note to epigraph: *A Petition Entitled Liberty Vindicated Against Slavery* (London, 1646), 24.

1. *Custom* was entered into the Stationers' Register February 22, 1619, and first performed by the King's Men circa 1619–20. For a performance history of the play, see G. E. Bentley, *The Jacobean and Caroline Stage*, 7 vols. (Oxford: Clarendon Press, 1941–68), 3:324–38. For eighteenth- and nineteenth-century responses to the play, see Lawrence B. Wallis, *Fletcher, Beaumont & Company, Entertainers to the Jacobean Gentry* (New York: Kings Crown Press, 1947), 21–22, 83, 118, and 175.

2. On *Custom* as in keeping with the chastity play tradition, see Nancy C. Pearse, *John Fletcher's Chastity Plays: Mirrors of Modesty* (Lewisburg, Pa.: Bucknell University Press, 1973), 210–17.

3. Carolyn Prager, "The Problem of Slavery in *The Custom of the Country*," *Studies in English Literature* 28.2 (Spring 1988): 301–17. On Lisbon as epicenter of human traffic, see Ferdinand Braudel, *The Mediterranean and the Mediterranean World in the Age of Philip II*, 2 vols., trans. Sian Reynolds, rev. 2nd ed. (New York: Harper, 1975), 2:865–91. On the play's use of Cervantes, see W. D. Howarth, "Cervantes and Fletcher: A Theme with Variations," *Modern Language Review* 56.4 (October 1961): 563–66, and T. L. Darby, "Resistance to

Rape in *Persiles y Sigismunda* and *The Custom of the Country*," *Modern Language Review* 90.2 (April 1995): 273–84.

4. On the Mediterranean as a popular topic for the London stage, see Daniel Vitkus, "Turks and Jews in *The Jew of Malta*," in *Early Modern English Drama: A Critical Companion*, ed. Andrew Hadfield et al. (New York: Oxford University Press, 2006), 63.

5. James Horn and Philip D. Morgan, "Settlers and Slaves: European and African Migrations to Early Modern British America," in *The Creation of the British Atlantic World*, ed. Elizabeth Mancke and Carole Shammas (Baltimore: Johns Hopkins University Press, 2005), 36.

6. Mark Netzloff notes that the Virginia Company's early promotional literature emphasized the interdependence of investors and laborers, but by 1611 investors and laborers were clearly distinguished as two separate categories of persons; *England's Internal Colonies: Class, Capital, and the Literature of Early Modern English Colonialism* (New York: Palgrave, 2003), 95.

7. Over the course of the seventeenth century, merchants and their so-called *Spirits* kidnapped and shipped over 200,000 young Englishmen to America. Slang terms that came into existence during the 1640s reflect this phenomenon, such as to "nab," or to take into custody; to "kidnap," which was to seize a child; to "spirit," which was to abduct and carry someone overseas, to "barbados," which was to abduct someone and ship him/her to Barbados; and to "trepan," which was to entrap or ensnare someone into labor. See Peter Linebaugh and Marcus Rediker, *The Many-Headed Hydra: Sailors, Slaves, Commoners, and the Hidden History of the Revolutionary Atlantic* (Boston: Beacon Press, 2000), 110. On the forced migration of colonial laborers, see Mark Netzloff, "Venting Trinculos: *The Tempest* and Discourses of Colonial Labor," in *England's Internal Colonies*, 91–127; Stanley L. Engerman, "Servants to Slaves to Servants: Contract Labour and European Expansion," in *Colonialism and Migration: Indentured Labour Before and After Slavery*, ed. P. C. Emmer (Dordrecht: Martinus Nijhoff Publishers, 1986), 269; and Robert C. Johnson, "The Transportation of Vagrant Children from London to Virginia, 1618–1622," in *Early Stuart Studies: Essays in Honor of David Harris Wilson*, ed. Howard S. Reinmuth, Jr. (Minneapolis: University of Minnesota Press, 1970), 137–51.

8. Ian Baucom stresses that the Atlantic slave trade could not have occurred without a functioning system of credit already in place in England. The slave trade, he argues, was "as much a trade in credit as a trade in commodities," since the global investors at various ports relied on promissory notes, which would be redeemed with interest at a future point once the slaves had been sold; *Specters of the Atlantic: Finance Capital, Slavery, and the Philosophy of History* (Durham, N.C.: Duke University Press, 2005), 15.

9. David W. Galenson, *White Servitude in Colonial America: An Economic Analysis* (Cambridge: Cambridge University Press, 1981), 8. On juridical rulings on property in person in the period, see Sir William Blackstone, *Commentaries on the Laws of England*, 4 vols. (Oxford: Oxford University Press, 1765–69), 1:412–17, 2:440–54, and 3:142; and Duncan Kennedy, "The Structure of Blackstone's *Commentaries*," *Buffalo Law Review* 28 (1979): 205–382.

10. Galenson, *White Servitude in Colonial America*, 8.

11. Frederick Pollock and Frederic William Maitland, *The History of English Law Before the Time of Edward I*, 2 vols., 2nd ed. (Cambridge: Cambridge University Press, 1968), 2:186.

12. Indenture served as a contract as well as a covenant because it provided a legal means by which to pass property that was actionable by writ of debt. See A. W. B. Simpson, *The History of the Common Law of Contract: The Rise of the Action of Assumpsit* (Oxford: Clarendon Press, 1975), 187.

13. Abbot Emerson Smith, *Colonists in Bondage: White Servitude and Convict Labor in America, 1607–1776* (Chapel Hill: University of North Carolina Press, 1947), 227.

14. Lorena S. Walsh, "Servitude and Opportunity in Charles County, Maryland, 1658–1705," in *Law, Society, and Politics in Early Maryland*, ed. Aubrey C. Land et al. (Baltimore: Johns Hopkins University Press, 1977), 112; 129; 131. See also Abbot Emerson Smith, *Colonists*, chapter 11, "Custom of the Country," in *Colonists in Bondage*, 226–52.

15. See, for example, the 1683 Indenture bond in Galenson, *White Servitude*, 41.

16. See E. P. Thompson, *Custom in Common: Studies in Traditional Popular Culture* (London: Merlin Press, 1991), esp. chapter 3, 97–185; and D. R. Kelley, "'Second Nature': The Idea of Custom in European Law, Society, and Culture," in *The Transmission of Culture in Early Modern Europe*, ed. A. Grafton and A. Blair (Philadelphia: University of Pennsylvania Press, 1990), 131–72.

17. Abbot Emerson Smith, *Colonists in Bondage*, 227.

18. Ibid, *Colonists in Bondage*, 227.

19. Susan Myra Kingsbury, ed., *The Records of the Virginia Company of London, 1607–1626*, 4 vols. (Washington, D.C.: United States Government Printing Office, 1906–35), 3:71. Hereafter cited in text as *RVC* by volume and page number.

20. As in Edmund S. Morgan, *American Slavery, American Slavery, American Freedom: The Ordeal of Colonial Virginia* (New York: W. W. Norton, 1975), 121.

21. *A Brief Declaration of the Plantation of Virginia* (London, 1624), in Alison Games, *The Web of Empire: English Cosmopolitans in an Age of Expansion, 1560–1660* (Oxford: Oxford University Press, 2008), 145.

22. Kasey Evans, "How Temperance Becomes 'Blood Guiltie' in the *Faerie Queene*," *Studies in English Literature* 49 (Winter 2009): 38. The idea that an individual's achievement of moderation was essential to the well-being of the commonwealth was advanced within the translated works of Cicero and Seneca that explicated the ancient concepts of *moderatio*, *frugalitas*, *modestio*, and *temperantia.*

23. Francis Bacon, "Of Plantations," in *The Genesis of the United States*, 2 vols, ed. Alexander Brown (New York: Russell & Russell, 1964), 2:801.

24. Games, *Web of Empire*, 145.

25. William Barret and the Councell of Virginia, *A True Declaration of the Estate of the Colonie in Virginia with a Confutation of Such Scandalous Reports as have Tended to Disgrace so Worthy an Enterprise* (London, 1610), 11.

26. Ibid., 12.

27. On the putatively regenerative effects of Virginia's environment, see Jean Feerick, *Strangers in Blood: Relocating Race in the Renaissance* (Toronto: University of Toronto Press, 2010), 80.

28. On language of temperance taking on new force in period's tragicomedy, see Feerick, *Strangers in Blood*, 120–22.

29. See Valerie Forman, *Tragicomic Redemptions: Global Economies and the Early Modern English Stage* (Philadelphia: University of Pennsylvania Press, 2008), and Zachery Lesser, "Tragical-Comical-Pastoral-Colonial: Economic Sovereignty, Globalization, and the Form of Tragicomedy," *ELH* 74 (2007): 881–908.

30. See James J. Yoch, "The Renaissance Dramatization of Temperance: The Italian Revival of Tragicomedy and *The Faithful Shepherdess*," in *Renaissance Tragedy: Explorations in Genre and Politics*, ed. Nancy McGuire (New York: AMS Press, 1987), 117.

31. For a discussion of the economic logic of temperance, see Evans, "How Temperance Becomes 'Blood Guiltie'," 50. On temperance as a crucial concept in English Renaissance New World propaganda, see Casey Evans, *Colonial Virtue: The Mobility of Temperance in Renaissance England* (Toronto: University of Toronto Press, 2012).

32. Craig Muldrew, *The Economy of Obligation: The Culture of Credit and Social Relations in Early Modern England* (New York: Palgrave, 1998), 10.

33. On the role of the passions in forging political obligation, see Victoria Kahn, "'The Duty to Love': Passion and Obligation in Early Modern Political Theory," *Representations* 68 (Autumn 1999): 84–107.

34. Edmund S. Morgan, *American Slavery, American Freedom*, 296. Revisionist scholarship on the relation between indentured service and slavery includes Leonie Archer, ed., *Slavery and Other Forms of Unfree Labour* (New York: Routledge, 1988); James Walvin, *Questioning Slavery* (New York: Routledge, 1996); Robin Blackburn, *The Making of New World Slavery: From the Baroque to the Modern, 1492–1800* (London: Verso, 1998); Tommy L. Lott, ed., *Subjugation and Bondage: Critical Essays on Slavery and Social Philosophy* (Boulder, Colo.: Rowman and Littlefield, 1998); Ira Berlin, *Many Thousands Gone: The First Two Centuries of Slavery in North America* (Cambridge, Mass.: Harvard University Press, 1998); David Turley, *Slavery* (Oxford: Blackwell, 2000); Kevin Bales, *Understanding Global Slavery: A Reader* (Berkeley: University of California Press, 2005); and Susan Dwyer Amussen, *Caribbean Exchanges: Slavery and the Transformation of English Society, 1640–1700* (Chapel Hill: University of North Carolina Press, 2007).

35. Hilary McD. Beckles, "The Concept of 'White Slavery' in the English Caribbean During the Early Seventeenth Century," in *Early Modern Conceptions of Property*, ed. John Brewer and Susan Staves (New York: Routledge, 1996), 575.

36. Abbot Emerson Smith, *Colonists in Bondage*, 233.

37. Beckles, "The Concept of 'White Slavery'," 576.

38. Henry Peacham, *The Art of Living in London* (London, 1642), sig. A1.

39. T. F., *Pictures of Passions, Fancies, and Affections Poetically Deciphered in Variety of Characters* (London, 1641), sig. D3; William Fennor, title page of *The Compters Commonwealth* (London, 1617).

40. John Fletcher and Philip Massinger, *The Custom of the Country* (New York: Routledge Theatre Arts Books, 1999), 12. Hereafter cited in the text by page number only.

41. See W. D. Howarth, "'Droit du Seigneur': Fact or Fantasy," *Journal of European Studies* 1 (1971): 300.

42. Winthrop D. Jordan, *White over Black: American Attitudes Towards the Negro, 1550–1812* (Chapel Hill: University of North Carolina Press, 1968), 50.

43. Howarth, "'Droit du Seigneur': Fact or Fantasy," 296.

44. Aristotle, *Nicomachean Ethics*, 2nd ed., translated and introduced by Terence Irwin (Indianapolis: Hackett, 1999), "Justice in Exchange," book 5, chapter 5, 74–76. On the implications of Aristotle's ideas about justice for economic theory, see Scott Meikle, *Aristotle's Economic Thought* (Oxford: Oxford University Press, 1995).

45. Aristotle, *Nicomachean Ethics*, book 5, chapter 5, 74.

46. Constance Jordan, "'Eating the Mother': Property and Propriety in *Pericles*," in *Creative Imitation: New Essays on Renaissance Literature in Honor of Thomas M. Green*, ed. David Quint et al. (Binghamton, N.Y.: Medieval and Renaissance Texts & Studies, 1992), 336.

47. On the analogy between rape and tyranny, see Melissa Sanchez, "'Accessory Yieldings': Consent Without Agency in *The Rape of Lucrece* and *Pericles*," in *Erotic Subjects: The Sexuality of Politics in Early Modern English Literature* (Oxford: Oxford University Press, 2011), 87–115.

48. Malynes, *England's Treasure by Forraign Trade*, 180, as in Carl Wennerlind, *Casualties of Credit: The English Financial Revolution, 1620–1720* (Cambridge, Mass.: Harvard University Press, 2011), 38.

49. Bernard Davanzati, *A Discourse upon Coins* (1588), as in Wennerlind, *Casualties of Credit*, 39.

50. Wennerlind, *Casualities of Credit*, 39.

51. Casey Evans, *Colonial Virtue*, 164.

52. My discussion of the transformation of disruptive passion into something constructive, namely interest in monetary gain, is indebted to Albert O. Hirschmann, *The Passions and the Interests: Political Arguments for Capitalism Before Its Triumph* (Princeton, N.J.: Princeton University Press, 1977).

53. Jocelyn O. Dunlop, *English Apprenticeship and Child Labour: A History* (New York: Macmillan, 1912), 57–58; 128–29.

54. Morgan, *American Slavery*, 129.

55. *Minutes of the Council*, 82.

56. *Minutes of the Council*, 82.

57. As in Morgan, *American Slavery*, 175.

58. John Smith, *Travels and Works*, 2:542, as in Morgan, *American Slavery*, 128.

59. Perkins, as in Prager, 309; Henry Fitzherbert as in C. S. L. Davies, "Slavery and Protector Somerset: The Vagrancy Act of 1574," *Economic History Review* 19, no. 3 (1966): 547.

60. Thomas Smyth, *De Republica Anglorum* (London, 1583), 110.

61. William Gouge, *Of Domesticall Duties*, 1st ed. (London, 1622), 593.

62. Some have argued that New World servants were taken on as agricultural laborers and, in this respect, may be rightly compared not to English apprentices but to farm workers. Yet this comparison serves only to highlight the extent to which colonial planters broke with English legal precedent. Agricultural workers in early modern England were classified in accordance with a number of discrete statuses, each with its own legal implication. Despite the diverse forms service took, in the eyes of the law, compensation in one form or another defined the master-servant relation. Most significantly, farmers who hired agricultural workers were bound by the provisions of the 1562–63 *Statute of Artificers*, an extension of the mid-fourteenth-century *Ordinance and Statute of Laborers* (1350–51), which regulated wage rates, terms of labor, and conditions of enforcement. On the legal evolution of the *Statute of Artificers*, see S. T. Bindoff, "The Making of the Statute of Artificers," in *Elizabethan Government and Society: Essays Presented to Sir John Neale*, ed. S. T. Bindoff et al. (London: Athlone Press, 1961), 56–95, and Donald Woodward, "The Background to the Statute of Artificers: The Genesis of Labour Policy, 1558–63," *Economic History Review*, 2nd ser., 33.1 (February 1980): 32–44. By 1705, we can see signs of the effort to resolve the fraught issue of the English prerogative to indenture other Christian men, as made evident by additions to the Virginia Council's policies explicitly distinguishing between servants and slaves; see Jordan, "'Eating the Mother': Property and Propriety in *Pericles*," 94.

63. Aristotle, *Nicomachean Ethics*, book 9, chapter 2, 139.

64. Meikle in *Aristotle's Economic Thought* makes a convincing case for proportionate reciprocity, exchange premised on *inequity*, as a distinct kind of justice rather than a species of either corrective or distributive justice, 129–46.

65. Jordan, *White Over Black*, 44.

66. See Robin Blackburn, "The Old World Background to European Colonial Slavery," *William and Mary Quarterly*, 3rd ser., 54.1 (January 1997): 65–102, and John Michael Archer, *Old Worlds: Egypt, Southwest Asia, India, and Russia in Early Modern English Writing* (Stanford, Calif.: Stanford University Press, 2001), esp. chapter 3, "Slave-Born Muscovites: Sidney, Shakespeare, Fletcher and the Geography of Servitude," 101–39.

67. David Harris Sacks and Michael Lynch, "Ports, 1540–1700," in *The Cambridge Urban History of Britain, Vol. 2, 1540–1840*, ed. Peter Clark (Cambridge University Press, 2000), 390–91.

68. Josef W. Konvitz, *Cities of the Sea: Port Planning in Early Modern Europe* (Baltimore: Johns Hopkins University Press, 1978), 13.

69. See Douglas Bruster, "Local *Tempest*: Shakespeare and the Work of the Early Modern Playhouse," *Journal of Medieval and Renaissance Studies* 25.1: 33–53, and Daniel Vitkus, "'Meaner Ministers': Mastery, Bondage, and Theatrical Labor in *The Tempest*," in *A Companion to Shakespeare's Works*, vol. 4, ed. Richard Dutton and Jean Howard (Oxford: Blackwell, 2003), 408–26. For a discussion of bound stage players, see Chapter 1, "*Timon of Athens*, Forms of Payback, and the Genre of Debt."

70. For instance, commercial playhouses were risky investments that could go under as the result of an outbreak of the plague or at the whim of authorities; see Vitkus, "'Meaner Ministers,'" 419.

CHAPTER 5, PRISON PROSE, THE PIT, AND THE END OF TRICKS

Note to epigraphs: Gilles Deleuze, "Postscript on Control Societies," in *Negotiations, 1972–1990*, trans. Marin Joughin (New York: Columbia University Press, 1995), 181; Francis Mussell, *The Prisoner's Observation by Way of Complaint* (London, 1645), as in Raymond Anselment, "The Confinement: The Plight of the Imprisoned English Debtor in the Seventeenth Century," *Restoration: Studies in English Literary Culture, 1660–1700* 15.1 (1991): 7.

1. *The Prisoner's Plaint, A Petition Submitted by a Prisoner in the King's Bench for Debt* (London, 1622), 2.

2. Valerie Forman, *Tragicomic Redemptions: Global Economies and the Early Modern English Stage* (Philadelphia: University of Pennsylvania Press, 2008), 6.

3. Mark Benbow, "Thomas Dekker and Some Cures for the 'City Gout'," *Yearbook of English Studies* 5 (1975): 54.

4. William Fennor, *The Compter's Common-wealth* (London, 1617), sig. A; *To the most honourable assembly of the Commons House of Parliament . . . the humble petition of the distressed prisoners in the King's Bench and Fleete* (1624), 1; *Petition to the right, Honourable Sir Thomas Fairfax* (London, 1647), sig. B.

5. C. W. Brooks, *Pettyfoggers and Vipers of the Commonwealth: The "Lower Branch" of the Legal Profession in Early Modern England* (Cambridge: Cambridge University Press, 1986), Table 4.1, p. 51.

6. *Acts of the Privy Council*, as in Benbow, "Thomas Dekker and Some Cures," 55.

7. The legal category of consideration was complex, and while it involved, in certain instances, examining the circumstances leading up to the credit transaction, consideration had not yet fully developed into an account of the parties' motives. On the early history of consideration, see J. H. Baker, "Origins of the 'Doctrine' of Consideration, 1535–1585," in *On the Laws and Customs of England: Essays in Honor of Samuel E. Throne*, ed. Morris S. Arnold et al. (Chapel Hill: University of North Carolina Press, 1981), 336–58, and John L. Barton, "The Early History of Consideration," *Law Quarterly Review* 85 (July 1969): 372–91.

8. Petition as in Christopher Harding et al., *Imprisonment in England and Wales: A Concise History* (London: Croom Helm, 1985), 80. The Elizabethan administration made various attempts to provide relief for insolvent debtors, such as the Acts of 1572 and 1597, which had little effect. The Privy Council established the Commission for Poor Prisoners in 1576, which attempted to offer mediation between creditor and debtor, but the commission lapsed on Elizabeth's death and was not revived until 1618. In 1649, there was an act passed allowing for the release of those incarcerated who owned less of £5 of property, and the passage of this statute resulted in the release of only 300 debtors from King's Bench due to the courts' inefficency in administrating this new policy. None of these initiatives, however, made any meaningful impact on securing the release of prisoners or controlling the profiteering of jailers. These details are discussed by Harding et al. in *Imprisonment in England and Wales*, 81.

9. The two-penny ward charged the inmate two pence daily for a bed and linens. The Knight's ward charged eight pence. The third pay ward on the Master's side was more costly than both of these. Humphrey Giffard, Warden of Poultry Counter, *A Second account of what progress hath been hitherto made* (London, 1670) as in Clifford Dobb, "London's Prisons," *Shakespeare Survey* 17 (1964): 96. Apparently, in some instances, wardens rented out overnight accommodations to prostitutes and their clients; see Bruce Watson, "The Compter's Prisons of London," *London Archaeologists* 7 (1993): 115–21.

10. As in Phillip Shaw, "The Position of Thomas Dekker in Jacobean Prison Literature," *PMLA* 62 (June 1947): 373.

11. *A Petition entitled, The Humble Remonstrance and Complaint of Many Thousands of poore, distressed Prisoners* (London, 1643), A3.

12. The writers of *The Humble Remonstrance and Complaint* point out that "in all other Nations debtors are held only for a yeare and a day and then discharged," whereas in England, "debtors are imprisoned past hope of release" (A2–A3).

13. Debtors who were not housed at King's Bench were kept at either the Wood Street or Poultry Street Counter within the city walls, and there is some evidence suggesting that there was a third Counter in Southwark; see E. D. Pendry, *Elizabethan Prisons and Prison Scenes*. 2 vols. (Salzburg, Austria: Institute for English Language and Literature, 1974), 1:54–100.

14. Thomas Dekker, *English Villainies*, sig. I4r. For descriptions of prisoners living large in the Fleet and King's Bench, see sig. H4v–J1.

15. Dekker as in Shaw, "The Position of Thomas Dekker," 367 n. 5.

16. For descriptions of the Hole, see Alexander Harris, *The Oeconomy of the Fleete* (London, 1621), ed. Augustus Jessop (London: Camden Society, 1879), introduction, xvi.

17. Luke Hutton, *The Black Dog of Newgate* (London, 1596) as in Dobb, "London's Prisons," 95.

18. Thomas S. Freeman, "The Rise of Prison Literature," *Huntington Library Quarterly* 72 (June 2009): 133. Carceral writings, according to Shaw, attained a "flood tide" from 1614 to 1618; "The Position of Thomas Dekker," 391. See also Raymond Anselment, "Confinement," 1.

19. Christopher Harding et al., *Imprisonments in England and Wales: A Concise History* (London: Croom Helm, 1985), 56.

20. Jean Howard, *Theater of a City: The Places of London Comedy, 1598–1642* (Philadelphia: University of Pennsylvania Press, 2007), 113.

21. Thomas Dekker, *A Strange Horse-Race* (London, 1613), Cr.

22. See Dobb, "London's Prisons," 98.

23. John Cooke, *Greene's Tu Quoque, or The Cittie Gallant*, ed. Alan J. Berman (New York: Garland, 1984), Scene 15, pp. 77–78.

24. Howard, *Theater of a City*, 73.

25. On Middleton's own dealings with debt litigation with John Knapp in 1600 and Robert Keysar, manager of the Children of the Revels, in 1609, see Subha Mukherji, "Middleton and the Law," in, *Thomas Middleton in Context*, ed. Suzanne Gossett (Cambridge:

Cambridge University Press, 2011), 108, and P. G. Phiales, "Middleton's Early Contact with the Law," *Studies in Philology* 52 (1955): 186–94.

26. In 1886, Swinburne deemed *A Trick* "by far . . . one of the best he [Middleton] ever wrote," and in 1927, T. S. Eliot cited the play as distinguishing Middleton as a "great" dramatist; see Valerie Wayne, Introduction to *A Trick to Catch the Old One*, in *Thomas Middleton: The Collected Works*, ed. Gary Taylor and John Lavagnino (Oxford: Clarendon Press, 2007), 373.

27. Thomas Middleton, *A Trick to Catch the Old One*, in *Thomas Middleton: The Collected Works*, ed. Gary Taylor and John Lavagnino, 1.3.27. Hereafter cited in the text.

28. The exceptions are Richard Levin, "The Dampit Scenes in *A Trick to Catch the Old One*," *Modern Language Quarterly* 25 (June 1964): 140–52, and Scott Cutler Shershow, "The Pit of Wit: Subplot and Unity in Middleton's *A Trick to Catch the Old One*," *Studies in Philology* 88.3 (Summer 1991): 363–81.

29. For the phrase "Hogarthian 'Usurers Progress'," see Levin, "The Dampit Scenes in *A Trick to Catch the Old One*," 144. On character sketches in Dekker's debtor's prison writings, see Shaw, "The Position of Thomas Dekker," 366. Some scholars have justified these scenes as set pieces Middleton interpolated to accommodate a particular actor. See, for instance, P. K. Ayers, "Plot, Subplot, and the Uses of Dramatic Discord in *A Mad World, My Masters* and *A Trick to Catch the Old One*," *Modern Language Quarterly* 47 (1986): 10, and Levin, "The Dampit Scenes," 141.

30. For this phrase, see Jonathan Gil Harris, "Simon Eyre's Oath and the Temporal Economies of *The Shoemaker's Holiday*," *Huntington Library Quarterly* 71 (March 2008): 28.

31. Thomas Dekker, *Jests to make you merie* (London, 1607), 1.

32. Shaw, "The Position of Thomas Dekker," 376 n. 58.

33. Adam Zucker defines "the social logic of wit" as reliant upon "both an exposure to and an erasure of . . . the economic relations that allow it to exist in the first place," in *The Places of Wit in Early Modern English Comedy* (Cambridge: Cambridge University Press, 2011), 19.

34. Shershow, "The Pit of Wit," 30 n. 377.

35. For this formulation, see Richard Halpern, *Shakespeare Among the Moderns* (Ithaca, N.Y.: Cornell University Press, 1997), 13.

36. Geoffrey Mynshul, *Certaine Characters and Essayes of Prison and Prisoners* (London, 1618), Epilogue, 4.

37. Jerome de Groot, "Prison Writing, Writing Prison in the 1640s and 1650s," *Huntington Library Quarterly* 72 (June 2009): 203.

38. William Bagwell, *The Distressed Merchant and the Prisoner's Comfort in Distresse* (London, 1645), Epistle.

39. Dekker, *Jests to make you merie*, 46.

40. "A Paradox in Praise of Sergiants, and of A Prison," in Dekker, *Jests to make you merie*, 61.

41. For several examples of this trope, see Pendry, *Elizabethan Prisons and Prison Scenes*, 2:270–78.

42. Mynshul, *Certaine Characters*, 6. Molly Murray discusses the innumerable desperate debtors who describe themselves as benefiting from the "Muses habitation" of the Counter (Murray, 149). As Murray urges, we need to attend to the prison as a site of significant textual and literary production, alongside the court and the university, as well as the experimental nature of the early modern carceral imagination in regard to both the thematic conventions and literary forms it produced. Molly Murray, "Measured Sentences: Forming Literature in the Early Modern Prison," *Huntington Library Quarterly* 72.2 (2009): 149.

43. Thomas Nashe, *Strange News* (London, 1592), as in Howard, *Theater of a City*, 232 n. 14.

44. Ian Munro, "Shakespeare's Jestbook: Wit, Print, Performance," *ELH* 71 (2004): 98.

45. Thomas Dekker, "A Prayer for a Prisoner," in *Foure Birds of Noah's Ark* (London, 1609), "The Dove," 53–54.

46. Thomas Dekker, *A Strange Horse-Race* (London, 1613), G1.

47. Jason Scott-Warren, "When the Theaters Were Bear-Gardens; or, What's at Stake in the Comedy of Humors," *Shakespeare Quarterly* 54 (2003): 72.

48. Scott-Warren, "When the Theaters Were Bear-Gardens," 72.

49. As in Stephen Dickey, "Shakespeare's Mastiff Comedy," *Shakespeare Quarterly* 42 (1991): 255.

50. As in Scott-Warren, "When the Theaters Were Bear-Gardens," 71.

51. Fennor, *Compter's Common-wealth*, sig. C.

52. See Alexandra Shepard, *Meanings of Manhood in Early Modern England* (Oxford: Oxford University Press, 2003), 186–95.

53. Dekker, *Jests*, 46.

54. Dekker as in Benbow, "Thomas Dekker and Some Cures for the 'City Gout'," 52.

55. Ayers, "Plot, Subplot, and the Uses of Dramatic Discord," 12.

56. See 397 n. 73 in Middleton, *A Trick to Catch the Old One*, ed. Taylor and Lavagnino.

57. Nathan Bailey as in Dayan, *The Law is a White Dog: How Legal Rituals Make and Unmake Persons* (Princeton, N.J.: Princeton University Press, 2011), 269 n. 16.

58. Robert Speed, *The Counter-Scuffle* (London, 1635) as in Freeman, "The Rise of Prison Literature," *Huntington Library Quarterly* 72 (June 2009): 44.

59. Freeman, "The Rise of Prison Literature." 44.

60. *The Humble Remonstrance*, A3; Fennor, *Compter's Common-wealth*, sig. L4.

61. Thomas Dekker, *English Villianies Discovered* in *Thomas Dekker*, ed. E. D. Pendry (Cambridge, Mass.: Harvard University Press, 1968), 257.

62. *Greene's Tu Quoque*, Scene 15, p. 75.

63. Henry Thornton, *The Prisoner's Remonstrance* (London, 1649), A1.

64. Geoffrey Mynshul, *Certaine Characters*, 7.

65. Anon., *Wonderfull Strange newes from Woodstreet Counter* (London, 1642), sig. A2.

66. William Cornwallis, *Essayes of Certaine Paradoxes* (London, 1616), F3.

67. Mynshul, *Certaine Characters*, 21.

68. Anon., *Wonderfull Strange newes from Woodstreet Counter*, sig. Iv.

69. *Liberty Vindicated Against Slavery* (London, 1646), 8.

70. *A Petition to the Kings Majestie, the Lords and Commons of the Parliament from Prisoners for debt*, 1622, 19; 19–22 describes the plight of those who committed suicide.

71. Levin, "The Dampit Scenes," 143. According to Levin, "the old one" was a common euphemism for the devil, 150. On the diabolical associations of Dampit, see also Shershow, "The Pit of Wit," 369.

72. Harris, "Simon Eyre's Oath and the Temporal Economies of *The Shoemaker's Holiday*," 23.

73. Leinwand, *Theater, Finance and Society*, 86. On Massinger's familiarity with Middleton's comedies, see the introduction to *A New Way to Pay Old Debts* in *The Plays and Poems of Philip Massinger*, ed. Philip Edward and Colin Gibson, 5 vols. (Oxford: Clarendon Press, 1977). 4:3. *A New Way* was first published in 1633 and performed by the Queen's Men at a private theater, the Phoenix, sometime between 1623 and 1625.

74. Leinwand, *Theater, Finance and Society*, 84.

75. See Nancy S. Leonard, "Overrreach at Bay: Massinger's *A New Way to Pay Old Debts*," in *Philip Massinger: A Critical Reassessment*, ed. Douglas Howard (Cambridge: Cambridge University Press, 1985), 171.

76. As a play exemplifying Caroline class anxiety see, for instance, Patricia Thompson, "The Old Way and the New Way in Dekker and Massinger," *Modern Language Review* 51.2 (April 1956): 168–78, and Michael Neill, "Massinger's Patriarchy: The Social Vision of *A New Way to Pay Old Debts*," *Renaissance Drama* 10 (1979): 185–213. L. C. Knights characterizes this play as a portrait of the landed gentry under siege by the financial and social ambitions of a rising commercial class in *Drama and Society in the Age of Jonson* (1936; London; George W. Stewart, 1951), 270–92. On a reading that challenges the standard interpretation of the play as an attack on a class enemy embodied by Overreach, see Martin Butler, "The Outsider as Insider," in *The Theatrical City: Culture, Theatre and Politics in London, 1576-1649*, ed. David L. Smith et al. (Cambridge: Cambridge University Press, 1995), 193–209, and Butler, "Massinger's Grim Comedy," *English Comedy*, ed. Michael Cordner et al. (Cambridge: Cambridge University Press, 1994), 119–37.

77. Deleuze, "Postscript on Control Societies," in *Negotiations, 1972–1990*, trans. Marin Joughin (New York: Columbia University Press, 1995), 179.

78. On the spectral logic of finance capital, see Ian Baucom, *Specters of the Atlantic: Finance Capital, Slavery, and the Philosophy of History* (Durham, N.C.: Duke University Press, 2005), 113–41.

79. Frederic Jameson, *The Political Unconscious: Narrative as A Socially Symbolic Act* (Ithaca, N.Y.: Cornell University Press, 1981), 141.

80. Martin Butler, "Massinger's Grim Comedy," *English Comedy*, 120.

81. Philip Massinger, *A New Way to Pay Old Debts*, ed. T. W. Craik (London: A. & C. Black, 1999), 4.1.102. Hereafter cited in the text.

82. Alexander Leggatt, *Citizen Comedy in the Age of Shakespeare* (Toronto: University of Toronto Press, 1973), 66–69.

83. On the striking gap between rhetoric and action among the aristocracy, see Leonard, "Overreach at Bay," 171–72.

84. Michael Neill, "Massinger's Patriarchy: The Social Vision of *A New Way to Pay Old Debts*," 193.

EPILOGUE

1. See Orlando Patterson, *Slavery and Social Death: A Comparative Study* (Cambridge, Mass.: Harvard University Press, 1982), 50.

2. Deborah Valenze, *The Social Life of Money in the English Past* (Cambridge: Cambridge University Press, 2006), 6.

3. Ian Baucom, *Specters of the Atlantic: Finance Capital, Slavery, and the Philosophy of History* (Durham, N.C.: Duke University Press, 2005), 61.

4. Thomas Hobbes, *Leviathan*, ed. Richard Tuck (Cambridge: Cambridge University Press, 1991), 20.10:141.

5. John Locke, *Two Treatises of Government*, ed. Peter Laslett (New York: New American Library, 1965), 2.22:324.

6. Locke, *Two Treatises*, 2.23:325.

Works Cited

Agnew, Jean-Christophe. *Worlds Apart: The Market and the Theater in Anglo-American Thought, 1550–1750*. Cambridge: Cambridge University Press, 1986.

Amussen, Susan D. *Caribbean Exchanges: Slavery and the Transformation of English Society, 1640–1700*. Chapel Hill: University of North Carolina Press, 2007.

Andrews, Kenneth R. *Trade, Plunder, and Settlement: Maritime Enterprise and the Genesis of the British Empire, 1480–1630*. Cambridge: Cambridge University Press, 1984.

Andrews, Mark Edwin. *Law Versus Equity in The Merchant of Venice*. Boulder: University of Colorado Press, 1965.

Anselment, Raymond. "The Confinement: The Plight of the Imprisoned English Debtor in the Seventeenth Century." *Restoration: Studies in English Literary Culture 1660–1700* 15 (1991): 1–16.

Appleby, Joyce Oldham. *Economic Thought and Ideology in Seventeenth-Century England*. Princeton, N.J.: Princeton University Press, 1978.

Archer, Jayne, et al., eds. *The Intellectual and Cultural World of the Inns of Court*. Manchester: Manchester University Press, 2011.

Archer, John Michael. *Old Worlds: Egypt, Southwest Asia, India, and Russia in Early Modern English Writing*. Stanford, Calif.: Stanford University Press, 2001.

Archer, Leonie, ed. *Slavery and Other Forms of Unfree Labour*. New York: Routledge, 1988.

Aristotle. *The Basic Works of Aristotle*. Ed. Richard McKeon. New York: Random House, 1941.

——. *Nicomachean Ethics*. Trans. Martin Ostwald. New York: Macmillan, 1962.

Arnold, Morris. "Towards an Ideology of the Early English Law of Obligation." *Law and History Review* 5 (September 1987): 505–21.

Atiyah, P. S. *The Rise and Fall of Freedom of Contract*. Oxford: Clarendon Press, 1979.

Atwood, Margaret. "Debtor's Prism." *Wall Street Journal*, 20 September 2008.

——. *Payback: Debt and the Shadow Side of Wealth*. Toronto: Anansi Press, 2008.

Ayers, P. K. "Plot, Subplot, and the Uses of Dramatic Discord in *A Mad World, My Masters* and *A Trick to Catch the Old One*." *Modern Language Quarterly* 47 (1986): 3–18.

Bacon, Francis. "Of Plantations." *The Genesis of the United States*. 2 vols. Ed. Alexander Brown. New York: Russell & Russell, 1964, 799–802.

——. "Of Usury." *The Works of Francis Bacon*. 14 vols. Ed. James Spedding et al. Boston: Brown and Taggard, 1861, 415–21.

———. *The Use of the Law Provided for the Preservation of Our Persons, Goods, and Good Names*. London, 1635.

Bagwell, William. *The Distressed Merchant and the Prisoner's Comfort in Distresse*. London, 1645.

Bailey, Amanda. "Shylock and the Slaves: Owing and Owning in *The Merchant of Venice*." *Shakespeare Quarterly* 62 (2011): 1–24.

Baker, J. H. *An Introduction to English Legal History*. 3rd edition. London: Butterworth, 1990.

———. "New Light on *Slade's Case*." *Cambridge Law Review* 29 (1971): 51–236.

———. "Origins of the 'Doctrine' of Consideration, 1535–1585." In *On the Laws and Customs of England: Essays in Honor of Samuel E. Throne*. Ed. Morris S. Arnold et al. Chapel Hill: University of North Carolina Press, 1981, 336–58.

———. "The Superior Courts in England, 1450–1800." In *Oberste Gerichtsbarkeit und Zentrale Gewalt im Europa der Frühen Neuzeit*. Ed. Bernhard Diestelkamp. Cologne: Böhlau, 1996.

Bales, Kevin. *Understanding Global Slavery: A Reader*. Berkeley: University of California Press, 2005.

Barnett, Randy E. "A Consent Theory of Contract." *Columbia Law Review* 86 (1986): 269–321.

Barret, William, and the Councell of Virginia. *A True Declaration of the Estate of the Colonie in Virginia with a Confutation of Such Scandalous Reports as have Tended to Disgrace so Worthy an Enterprise*. London, 1610.

Barrie, Robert. "Elizabethan Play-Boys in the Adult London Companies." *Studies in English Literature* 48 (Spring 2008): 237–57.

Barton, John L. "The Early History of Consideration." *Law Quarterly Review* 85 (1969): 372–91.

Barty-King, Hugh. *The Worst Poverty: A History of Debt and Debtors*. London: Alan Sutton, 1991.

Baucom, Ian. *Specters of the Atlantic: Finance Capital, Slavery, and the Philosophy of History*. Durham, N.C.: Duke University Press, 2005.

Beckles, Hilary McD. "The Concept of 'White Slavery' in the English Caribbean During the Early Seventeenth Century." In *Early Modern Conceptions of Property*. Ed. John Brewer and Susan Staves. New York: Routledge, 1996, 572–85.

Benbow, Mark. "Thomas Dekker and Some Cures for the 'City Gout'." *Yearbook of English Studies* 5 (1975): 52–69.

Bentley, G. E. *The Jacobean and Caroline Stage*. 7 vols. Oxford: Clarendon Press, 1948–61.

Berlin, Ira. *Many Thousands Gone: The First Two Centuries of Slavery in North America*. Cambridge, Mass: Harvard University Press, 1998.

Best, Stephen. *The Fugitive's Properties: Law and the Politics of Possession*. Chicago: University of Chicago Press, 2004.

Bevington, David. *The Complete Works of Shakespeare*. 5th edition. New York: Longman, 2007.

Bindoff, S. T. "The Making of the Statute of Artificers." In *Elizabethan Government and Society: Essays Presented to Sir John Neale*. Ed. S. T. Bindoff et al. London: Athlone Press, 1961, 56–94.

Blackburn, Robin. *The Making of New World Slavery: From the Baroque to the Modern, 1492–1800*. London: Verso, 1998.

——. "The Old World Background to European Colonial Slavery." *William and Mary Quarterly*, 3rd series, 54 (1997): 65–102.

Blackstone, Sir William. *Commentaries on the Laws of England*. 4 vols. Oxford: Oxford University Press, 1765–1769.

——. *A Facsimile of the First Edition of 1765–1769*. Ed. Stanley N. Katz. Chicago: University of Chicago Press, 1979.

Boose, Lynda E. "The Comic Contract and Portia's Golden Ring." *Shakespeare Studies* 20 (1987): 241–54.

Bowers, Fredson. *Elizabethan Revenge Tragedy, 1587–1642*. Princeton, N.J.: Princeton University Press, 1940.

Bowers, Richard. "From Rolls to Riches: King's Clerks and Moneylending in Thirteenth Century England." *Speculum* 58 (January 1983): 60–71.

Braudel, Fernand. *The Mediterranean and the Mediterranean World in the Age of Philip II*. 2 vols. Trans. Sian Reynolds. Revised second edition. New York: Harper, 1975.

Brewer, John, and Susan Staves, eds. *Early Modern Conceptions of Property*. New York: Routledge, 1996.

Bromberg, Murray. "The Reputation of Philip Henslowe." *Shakespeare Quarterly*, 1.3 (1950): 135–39.

Brooks, C. W. *Pettyfoggers and Vipers of the Commonwealth: The "Lower Branch" of the Legal Profession in Early Modern England*. Cambridge: Cambridge University Press, 1986.

Broude, Ronald. "Revenge and Revenge Tragedy in Renaissance England." *Renaissance Quarterly* 28 (1975): 38–58.

Bruster, Douglas. "Local *Tempest*: Shakespeare and the Work of the Early Modern Playhouse." *Journal of Medieval and Renaissance Studies* 25: 33–53.

Burke, Kenneth. *Language as Symbolic Action: Essays on Life Literature and Method*. Berkeley: University of California Press, 1966.

Burns, Robert P. "Blackstone's Theory of the 'Absolute' Rights of Property." *University of Cincinnati Law Review* 54 (1985): 79–82.

Butler, Francelia. *The Strange Critical Fortunes of Shakespeare's Timon of Athens*. Ames: Iowa State University Press, 1966.

Butler, Judith. *The Psychic Life of Power: Theories in Subjection*. Stanford, Calif.: Stanford University Press, 1997.

Butler, Martin. "The Outsider as Insider." In *The Theatrical City: Culture, Theatre and Politics in London, 1576–1649*. Ed. David L. Smith et al. Cambridge: Cambridge University Press, 1995, 193–209.

——. "Massinger's Grim Comedy." In *English Comedy*. Ed. Michael Cordner et al. Cambridge: Cambridge University Press, 1994, 119–37.

Byrne, Richard. *Prisons and Punishments of London*. London: Harrup Press, 1989.

Caffentzis, George. *Clipped Coins, Abused Words, and Civil Government: John Locke's Philosophy of Money*. New York: Automedia, 1989.

Carson, Neil. A *Companion to Henslowe's Diary*. Cambridge: Cambridge University Press, 1988.

Chambers, E. K. *The Elizabethan Stage*. 4 vols. Oxford: Clarendon Press, 1923.

Chatterji, Ruby. "Unity and Disparity: *Michaelmas Term*." *Studies in English Literature* 8 (1968): 349–63.

Chorost, Michael. "Biological Finance in Shakespeare's *Timon of Athens*." *English Literary Renaissance* 21 (1991): 349–70.

Cohen, Derek. "The Politics of Wealth: *Timon of Athens*." *Neophilologus* 77 (1993): 149–60.

Cohen, Jay. "The History of Imprisonment for Debt and Its Relation to the Development of Discharge in Bankruptcy." *Journal of Legal History* 3 (1982): 153–71.

Cohen, Walter. "*The Merchant of Venice* and the Possibilities of Historical Criticism." *English Literary History* 49 (1982): 765–89.

Coke, Edward. *Commentary on Littleton*. London, 1628.

Cook, David. "*Timon of Athens*." *Shakespeare Studies* 16 (1963): 83–94.

Cooke, John. *Greene's Tu Quoque, or The Cittie Gallant*. Ed. Alan J. Berman. New York: Garland Press, 1984.

Cormack, Bradin. "Shakespeare Possessed: Legal Affect and the Time of Holding." In *Shakespeare and the Law*. Ed. Paul Raffield and Gary Watt. Portland, Ore.: Hart Publishing, 2008, 83–100.

Cornwallis, William. *Essayes of Certaine Paradoxes*. London, 1616.

Costigan, Jr., George P. "Those Protective Trusts which Are Miscalled 'Spendthrift Trusts' Reexamined." In *Legal Essays in Tribute to Orrin Kip McMurray*. Ed. Max Radin and A. M. Kidd. Berkeley: University of California Press, 1935, 85–116.

Cotesford, Samuel. *A Very Soveraigne Oyle to restore Debtors; being rightly and seasonably used*. London, 1622.

Covatta, Anthony. *Thomas Middleton's City Comedies*. Lewisburg, Pa.: Bucknell University Press, 1973.

Darby, T. L. "Resistance to Rape in *Persiles y Sigismunda* and *The Custom of the Country*." *Modern Language Review* 90 (1995): 273–84.

Davies, C. S. L. "Slavery and Protector Somerset: The Vagrancy Act of 1574." *Economic History Review* 19 (1966): 533–49.

Dawson, John P. "The Privy Council and Private Law in the Tudor and Stuart Periods: I." *Michigan Law Review* 48 (1950): 393–428.

Dayan, Joan. *The Law Is a White Dog: How Legal Rituals Make and Unmake Persons*. Princeton, N.J.: Princeton University Press, 2011.

———. "Legal Slaves and Civil Bodies. " In *Materializing Democracy: Toward a Revitalized Cultural Politics*. Ed. Russ Castronovo and Dana D. Nelson. Durham, N.C.: Duke University Press, 2002, 53–95.

de Groot, Jermone. "Prison Writing, Writing Prison in the 1640s and 1650s." *Huntington Library Quarterly* 72 (June 2009): 193–215.

de Roover, Raymond. *Business, Banking, and Economic Thought in Late Medieval and Early Modern Europe: Selected Studies of Raymond de Roover*. Ed. Julius Kirshner. Chicago: University of Chicago Press, 1974.

Dekker, Thomas. *English Villainies Discovered*. In *Thomas Dekker*. Ed. E. D. Pendry. Cambridge, Mass.: Harvard University Press, 1968.

——. *Jests to make you Merie*. London, 1607.

——. "A Prayer for a Prisoner." In *Foure Birds of Noah's Ark*. London, 1609.

——. *A Strange Horse-Race*. London, 1613.

Deleuze, Gilles. "Postscript on Control Societies." In *Negotiations, 1972–1990*. Trans. Marin Joughin. New York: Columbia University Press, 1995, 177–82.

Deutermann, Allison, and András Kiséry, eds. *Formal Matters: Reading the Forms of Early Modern Texts*. Manchester: Manchester University Press, 2013.

Dickey, Stephen. "Shakespeare's Mastiff Comedy." *Shakespeare Quarterly* 42 (1991): 255–75.

Dobb, Clifford. "London's Prisons." *Shakespeare Survey* 17 (1964): 87–100.

Dod, John, and Robert Cleaver. *A Godly Forme of Household Government*. London, 1630.

Donohue, Joseph W. Jr., ed. *The Theatrical Manager in England and America: Player of a Perilous Game*. Princeton, N.J.: Princeton University Press, 1971.

Duffy, Ian P. H. "English Bankrupts, 1571–1861." *American Journal of Legal History* 24 (1980): 283–305.

Dunlop, Jocelyn O. *English Apprenticeship and Child Labour: A History*. New York: MacMillan, 1912.

Ellis-Fermor, Una. "*Timon of Athens*: An Unfinished Play." *Research in English Studies* 18 (1942): 270–83.

Engerman, Stanley L. "Servants to Slaves to Servants: Contract Labour and European Expansion." In *Colonialism and Migration: Indentured Labour Before and After Slavery*. Ed. P. C. Emmer. Dordrecht: Martinus Nijhoff, 1986.

Engle, Lars. "'Thrift Is Blessing': Exchange and Explanation in *The Merchant of Venice*." *Shakespeare Quarterly* 37 (1986): 20–37.

Erickson, Amy Louise. *Women and Property in Early Modern England*. New York: Routledge, 1993.

Evans, Kasey. *Colonial Virtue: The Mobility of Temperance in Renaissance England*. Toronto: University of Toronto Press, 2012.

——. "How Temperance Becomes 'Blood Guiltie' in the *Faerie Queene*." *Studies in English Literature* 49 (Winter 2009): 35–66.

Farnsworth, Allan. "The Past of Promise: An Historical Introduction to Contract." *Columbia Law Review* 69, no. 4 (April 1969): 576–607.

Feaveryear, A. E. *The Pound Sterling: A History of English Money*. London: 1931.

Feerick, Jean. *Strangers in Blood: Relocating Race in the Renaissance*. Toronto: University of Toronto Press, 2010.

Fennor, William. *The Compters Common-wealth*. London, 1617.

Finn, Margot C. *The Character of Credit: Personal Debt in English Culture, 1740–1914*. Cambridge: Cambridge University Press, 2003.

Fischer, Sandra K. "'Cut My Heart in Sums': Shakespeare's Economics and *Timon of Athens*." In *Money: Lure, Lore, and Literature*. Ed. John Louis DiGaetani. Westport, Conn.: Greenwood Press, 1994, 187–97.

Fleay, Frederick Gard. *A Chronicle History of the London Stage, 1559–1642*. New York: Burt Franklin, 1890.

Fletcher, John, and Philip Massinger. *The Custom of the Country*. New York: Routledge Theatre Arts Books, 1999.

Foakes, R. A. *Henslowe's Diary*. Second edition. Cambridge: Cambridge University Press, 2002.

Ford, Richard. "Imprisonment for Debt." *Michigan Law Review* 25 (1926–27): 24–49.

Forman, Valerie. *Tragicomic Redemptions: Global Economies and the Early Modern English Stage*. Philadelphia: University of Pennsylvania Press, 2008.

Fox, John C. "Process of Imprisonment at Common Law." *Law Quarterly Review* 39 (1923): 46–59.

Frank, Andre Gunder. *ReOrient: Global Economy in the Asian Age*. Berkeley: University of California Press, 1998.

Freedman, Abraham L. "Imprisonment for Debt." *Tempe Law Quarterly* 2 (1927–28): 330–65.

Freeman, Thomas S. "The Rise of Prison Literature." *Huntington Library Quarterly* 72 (June 2009): 133–47.

Galenson, David W. *White Servitude in Colonial America: An Economic Analysis*. Cambridge: Cambridge University Press, 1981.

Games, Alison. *The Web of Empire: English Cosmopolitans in an Age of Expansion, 1560–1660*. Oxford: Oxford University Press, 2008.

A Godlie Treatice Concerning the Lawfull use of Ritches. London, 1578.

Goldberg, Jonathan. *Shakespeare's Hand*. Minneapolis: University of Minnesota Press, 2003.

Gouge, William. *Of Domesticall Duties*. 1st edition. London, 1622.

Grady, Hugh. "*Timon of Athens*: The Dialectic of Usury, Nihilism, and Art." In *A Companion to Shakespeare's Works, Volume I: The Tragedies*. Ed. Richard Dutton and Jean E. Howard. Oxford: Blackwell, 2003, 430–52.

Graeber, David. *Debt: The First 5,000 Years*. New York: Melville House, 2011.

Grantham, Thomas. *A Motion Against Imprisonment*. London, 1642.

Grassby, Richard. *The Business Community of Seventeenth-Century England*. Cambridge University Press, 1995.

Grav, Peter F. *Shakespeare and the Economic Imperative: 'What's aught but as 'tis valued?"* New York: Routledge: 2008.

Greene, Jody. "You Must Eat Men: The Sodomitic Economy of Renaissance Patronage." *GLQ: A Journal of Lesbian and Gay Studies* 1 (1994): 163–97.

Greg, Walter W. *Henslowe's Diary*. 2 vols. London: A. H. Bullen, 1904–8.

——, ed. *Henslowe Papers: Being Documents Supplement to Henslowe's Diary*. London: A. H. Bullen, 1907.

Guy-Bray, Stephen. *Against Reproduction: Where Renaissance Texts Come From*. Toronto: University of Toronto Press, 2009.

Hakluyt, Richard. *The Principal Navigations Voyages Traffiques & Discoveries of the English Nation*. 12 vols. London, 1589. Facsimile reprint. Glasgow: James MacLehose & Sons, 1904.

Halpern, Richard. *Shakespeare Among the Moderns*. Ithaca, N.Y.: Cornell University Press, 1997.

Harding, Christopher, et al. *Imprisonments in England and Wales: A Concise History*. London: Croom Helm, 1985.

Harris, Alexander. *The Oeconomy of the Fleete*. London, 1621. Ed. Augustus Jessop. London: Camden Society, 1879.

Harris, Jonathan Gil. *Sick Economies: Drama, Mercantilism, and Disease in Shakespeare's England*. Philadelphia: University of Pennsylvania Press, 2004.

——. "Simon Eyre's Oath and the Temporal Economies of *The Shoemaker's Holiday*." *Huntington Library Quarterly* 71 (March 2008): 11–32.

Hawkes, David. *The Culture of Usury in Renaissance England*. New York: Palgrave, 2010.

Henderson, Edith G. "Relief from Bonds in the English Chancery: Mid-Sixteenth Century." *American Journal of Legal History* 18 (1974): 298–306.

Hinely, Jan Lawson. "Bond Priorities in *The Merchant of Venice*." *Studies in English Literature* 20 (1980): 217–39.

Hirschman, Albert O. *The Passions and the Interests: Political Arguments for Capitalism Before Its Triumph*. Princeton, N.J.: Princeton University Press, 1997.

Hirschfeld, Heather. "'And He Hath Enough': The Penitential Economies in *The Merchant of Venice*." *Journal of Medieval and Early Modern Studies* 40 (2010): 89–117.

Hobbes, Thomas. *Leviathan*. Ed. Richard Tuck. Cambridge: Cambridge University Press, 1991.

Holderness, B. A. "The Clergy as Money-Lenders in England, 1550–1700." In *Princes and Paupers in the English Church, 1500–1800*. Ed. Rosemary O'Day and Felicity Heal. Leicester, 1981, 195–209.

——. "Widows in Pre-Industrial Society: An Essay upon Their Economic Functions." In *Land, Kinship, and Life-Cycle*. Ed. R. M. Smith. Cambridge: Cambridge University Press, 1984, 423–42.

Holdsworth, W. S. *A History of English Law*. 7 vols. 3rd edition. Boston: Little Brown, 1923.

Holland, Peter. "*The Merchant of Venice* and the Value of Money." *Cahiers Elisabethians* 60 (2001): 13–30.

Hoppit, Julian. "The Contexts and Contours of British Economic Literature, 1660–1760." *Historical Journal* 49 (2006): 79–110.

Horn, James, and Philip D. Morgan. "Settlers and Slaves: European and African Migrations to Early Modern British America." In *The Creation of the British Atlantic World*. Ed. Elizabeth Mancke and Carole Shammas. Baltimore: Johns Hopkins University Press, 2005, 19–44.

Howard, Jean. *Theater of a City: The Places of London Comedy, 1598–1642.* Philadelphia: University of Pennsylvania Press, 2007.

Howarth, W. D. "Cervantes and Fletcher: A Theme with Variations." *Modern Language Review* 56 (1961): 563–66.

——. "'Droit du Seigneur': Fact or Fantasy." *Journal of European Studies* 1 (1971): 291–312.

Hunt, Margaret. *The Middling Sort: Commerce, Gender, and the Family in England, 1680–1780.* Berkeley: University of California Press, 1996.

Ibbetson, David. "Assumpsit and Debt in the Early Sixteenth Century: The Origins of the Indebitatus Count." *Cambridge Law Journal* 41 (1982): 142–61.

——. "Sixteenth Century Contract Law: *Slade's Case* in Context." *Oxford Journal of Legal Studies* 4 (1984): 295–317.

Ingham, Geoffrey. "On the Underdevelopment of the 'Sociology of Money.'" *Acta Sociologicia: Journal of the Scandinavian Sociological Association* 41 (1998): 9–13.

Ingram, William. *The Business of Playing.* Ithaca, N.Y.: Cornell University Press, 1988.

——. *A London Life in the Brazen Age: Francis Langley, 1548–1602.* Cambridge, Mass.: Harvard University Press, 1978.

——, et al. *English Professional Theatre, 1530–1660.* Cambridge: Cambridge University Press, 2000.

Ioppolo, Grace. "Early Modern Hands." In *A New Companion to English Renaissance Literature and Culture.* Vol 1. Ed. Michael Hattaway. Oxford: Blackwell, 2000, 177–90.

Jameson, Frederic. *The Political Unconscious: Narrative as A Socially Symbolic Act.* Ithaca, N.Y.: Cornell University Press, 1981.

Jenks, Edward. "The Prerogative Writs in English Law." *Yale Law Journal* 32 (1923): 523–34.

Johnson, Lynn. "Friendship, Coercion, and Interest: Debating the Foundations of Justice in Early Modern England." *Journal of Early Modern History* 8 (2004): 46–64.

Johnson, Robert C. "The Transportation of Vagrant Children from London to Virginia, 1618–1622." In *Early Stuart Studies: Essays in Honor of David Harris Wilson.* Ed. Howard S. Reinmuth, Jr. Minneapolis: University of Minnesota Press, 1970, 137–51.

Jones, Malcolm. "The Horn of Suretyship." *Print Quarterly* 16 (1999): 219–28.

Jones, Norman. *God and the Moneylenders: Usury and Law in Early Modern England.* Oxford: Oxford University Press, 1989.

Jones, W. J. "Conflict or Collaboration? Chancery Attitudes in the Reign of Elizabeth I." *American Journal of Legal History* 5 (1961): 12–54.

——. "The Foundations of English Bankruptcy: Statutes and Commissions in the Early Modern Period." *Transactions of the American Philosophical Society* 69 (1979): 1–63.

Jordan, Constance. "'Eating the Mother': Property and Propriety in *Pericles.*" In *Creative Imitation: New Essays on Renaissance Literature in Honor of Thomas M. Green.* Ed. David Quint et al. Binghamton, N.Y.: Medieval and Renaissance Texts & Studies, 1992, 331–53.

Jordan, William Chester. "Approaches to the Court Scene in the Bond Story: Equity and Mercy or Reason and Nature." *Shakespeare Quarterly* 33 (1982): 49–59.

Jordan, Winthrop D. *White over Black: American Attitudes Towards the Negro, 1550–1812.* Chapel Hill: University of North Carolina Press, 1968.

Jowett, John. "Middleton and Debt in *Timon of Athens.*" In *Money and the Age of Shakespeare: Essays in New Economic Criticism*. Ed. Linda Woodbridge. New York: Palgrave, 2003, 219–37.

Kahn, Coppelia. "'Magic of Bounty': *Timon of Athens*, Jacobean Patronage, and Maternal Power." *Shakespeare Quarterly* 38 (1987): 34–57.

Kahn, Victoria. "'The Duty to Love': Passion and Obligation in Early Modern Political Theory." *Representations* 68 (1999): 84–107.

Kathman, David. "Grocers, Goldsmiths, and Drapers: Freemen and Apprentices in the Elizabethan Theater." *Shakespeare Quarterly* 55 (Spring 2004): 1–49.

Kelley, D. R. "'Second Nature': The Idea of Custom in European Law, Society, and Culture." In *The Transmission of Culture in Early Modern Europe*. Ed. A. Grafton and A. Blair. Philadelphia: University of Pennsylvania Press, 1990, 131–72.

Kennedy, Duncan. "The Structure of Blackstone's *Commentaries.*" *Buffalo Law Review* 28 (1979): 205–382.

Kerrigan, John. *Revenge Tragedy: Aeschylus to Armageddon*. Oxford: Clarendon Press, 1996.

Kingsbury, Susan Myra, ed. *The Records of the Virginia Company of London, 1607–1626.* 4 vols. Washington, D.C.: United States Government Printing Office, 1906–35.

Kirshner, Julius, ed. *Business, Banking and Economic Thought in Late Medieval and Early Modern Europe*. Chicago: University of Chicago Press, 1974.

Knight, G. Wilson. *The Wheel of Fire: Interpretations of Shakespearian Tragedy with Three New Essays*. 4th edition. London: Methuen, 1949.

Knight, W. Nicholas. "Sex and Law Language in Middleton's *Michaelmas Term.*" In *'Accompaninge the Players': Essays Celebrating Thomas Middleton, 1580–1980*. Ed. Kenneth Friedenreich. New York: AMS Press, 1983, 89–108.

Knights, L. C. *Drama and Society in the Age of Jonson*. 1936. Reprint. London: George W. Stewart, 1951.

Konvitz, Josef W. *Cities of the Sea: Port Planning in Early Modern Europe*. Baltimore: Johns Hopkins University Press, 1978.

Kopytoff, Igor. "Slavery." *Annual Review of Anthropology* 11 (1982): 207–31.

Korda, Natasha. *Labors Lost: Women's Work and the Early Modern Stage*. Philadelphia: University of Pennsylvania Press, 2011.

——. "Dame Usury: Gender, Credit and (Ac)counting in the Sonnets and *The Merchant of Venice.*" *Shakespeare Quarterly* 60 (2009): 1–26.

Lander, Jesse M. "'Crack'd Crowns' and Counterfeit Sovereigns: The Crisis of Value in *1 Henry IV.*" *Shakespeare Studies* 30 (2002): 138–43.

Landreth, David. *The Face of Mammon: The Matter of Money in English Renaissance Literature*. Oxford: Oxford University Press, 2012.

Langbein, John H. "The Historical Origins of the Sanction of Imprisonment for Serious Crime." *Journal of Legal Studies* 35 (1976): 35–60.

Leadam, I. S. "The Last Days of Bondage in England." *Law Quarterly Review* 9 (1893): 348–65.

Leggatt, Alexander. *Citizen Comedy in the Age of Shakespeare*. Toronto: University of Toronto Press, 1973.

Leinwand, Theodore. "Redeeming Beggary/Buggery in *Michaelmas Term*." *English Literary History* 61 (1994): 53–70.

——. *The Theater, Finance, and Society in Early Modern England*. Cambridge: Cambridge University Press, 1999.

Leonard, Nancy S. "Overrreach at Bay: Massinger's *A New Way to Pay Old Debts*." In *Philip Massinger: A Critical Reassessment*. Ed. Douglas Howard. Cambridge: Cambridge University Press, 1985, 171–93.

Lesser, Zachery. "Tragical-Comical-Pastoral-Colonial: Economic Sovereignty, Globalization, and the Form of Tragicomedy." *ELH* 74 (2007): 881–908.

Leventen, Carol. "Patrimony and Patriarchy in *The Merchant of Venice*." In *The Matter of Difference: Materialist Feminist Criticism of Shakespeare*. Ed. Valerie Wayne. Ithaca, N.Y.: Cornell University Press, 1991, 59–81.

Levin, Richard. "The Dampit Scenes in *A Trick to Catch the Old One*." *Modern Language Quarterly* 25 (1964): 140–52.

Levine, Caroline. "Strategic Formalism: Toward a New Method in Cultural Studies." *Victorian Studies* 48 (Summer 2006): 625–57.

Levinson, Marjorie. "What Is New Formalism?" *PMLA* 122 (2008): 558–69.

Levitsky, Ruth. "*Timon*: Shakespeare's *Magnyfycence* and an Embryonic *Lear*." *Shakespeare Studies* 11 (1978): 107–22.

Linebaugh, Peter, and Marcus Rediker. *The Many-Headed Hydra: Sailors, Slaves, Commoners, and the Hidden History of the Revolutionary Atlantic*. Boston: Beacon Press, 2000.

Locke, John. *Second Treatise of Government*. Ed. C. B. Macpherson. Indianapolis: University of Indiana Press, 1980.

——. *Two Treatises of Government*. Ed. Peter Laslett. New York: New American Library, 1965.

Loewenstein, Jospeh. "Forms in Wax: Shakespeare and the Personality of the Seal." *Ornamentalism: The Art of Renaissance Accessories*. Ed. Bella Mirabella. Ann Arbor: University of Michigan Press, 2011, 202–21.

Lott, Tommy L., ed. *Subjugation and Bondage: Critical Essays on Slavery and Social Philosophy*. Boulder, Colo.: Rowman and Littlefield, 1998.

Loyd, William H. "Executions at Common Law." *University of Pennsylvania Law Review* and *American Law Register* 62 (March 1914): 354–407.

Lücke, H. K. "*Slade's Case* and the Origins of the Common Counts." *Law Quarterly Review* 81 (1965): 422–561.

Lupton, Julia Reinhard. *Citizen-Saints: Shakespeare and Political Theology*. Chicago: University of Chicago Press, 2005.

——. *Thinking with Shakespeare: Essays on Politics and Life*. Chicago: University of Chicago Press, 2011.

MacKay, Maxine. "*The Merchant of Venice*: A Reflection of the Early Conflict Between Courts of Law and Courts of Equity." *Shakespeare Quarterly* 15 (1964): 371–75.

Macpherson, C. B. *The Political Theory of Possessive Individualism: Hobbes to Locke*. Oxford: Oxford University Press, 1962.

Marx, Karl. *Early Writings*. Trans. Rodney Livingstone and Gregor Benton. Introduction by Lucio Colletti. New York: Vintage Books, 1975.

Massinger, Philip. *A New Way to Pay Old Debts*. Ed. T. W. Craik. London: A & C Black, 1999.

——. *A New Way to Pay Old Debts*. In *The Plays and Poems of Philip Massinger*. Ed. Philip Edward and Colin Gibson. 5 vols. Oxford: Clarendon Press, 1977.

McCaffery, Edward J. "Must We Have the Right to Waste?" *New Essays in the Legal and Political Theory of Property*. Ed Stephen Munzer. Cambridge: Cambridge University Press, 2001, 76–106.

McClean, A. J. "The Common Law Life of Estate and the Civil Law Usufruct: A Comparative Study." *International and Comparative Law Quarterly* 12 (1963): 649–67.

McIntosh, Marjorie K. "Money Lending on the Periphery of London, 1300–1600." *Albion* 20 (1988): 557–71.

Meikle, Scott. *Aristotle's Economic Thought*. Oxford: Oxford University Press, 1995.

Meyers, Charles. "Debt in Elizabethan England: The Adventures of Dr. Hector Nunez, Physician and Merchant." *Jewish Historical Studies: Transactions of the Jewish Historical Society of England* 34 (1994): 125–40.

Middleton, Thomas. *Michaelmas Term*. Edited and introduced by Richard Levin. Regents Renaissance Drama Series. Lincoln: University of Nebraska Press, 1966.

——. *Michaelmas Term*. The Revels Plays. Edited with an introduction by Gail Kern Paster. Manchester: Manchester University Press, 2000.

——. *Michaelmas Term and A Trick to Catch the Old One*. Edited and introduced by George R. Price. The Hague: Mouton, 1976.

——. *The Revenger's Tragedy*. Ed. R. A. Foakes. The Revels Student Edition. Manchester: Manchester University Press, 1996.

——. *A Trick to Catch the Old One*. In *Thomas Middleton: The Collected Works*. Ed. Gary Taylor and John Lavagnino. Oxford: Clarendon Press, 2007.

Miller, William. *An Eye for an Eye*. Cambridge: Cambridge University Press, 2006.

Miskimin, H. A. *Cash, Credit, and Crisis in Europe, 1300–1600*. London, 1989.

Morgan, Edmund S. *American Slavery, American Freedom: The Ordeal of Colonial Virginia*. New York: W. W. Norton, 1975.

Morsberger, Robert E. "*Timon of Athens*: Tragedy or Satire?" In *Shakespeare in the Southwest: Some New Directions*. El Paso, Tex., 1969, 56–70.

Mukherji, Subha. "Middleton and the Law." In *Thomas Middleton in Context*. Ed. Suzanne Gossett. Cambridge: Cambridge University Press, 2011, 106–14.

Muldrew, Craig. "Credit and the Courts: Debt Litigation in a Seventeenth-Century Urban Community." *Economic History Review* 46 (1993): 23–38.

——. "The Culture of Reconciliation: Community and the Settlement of Economic Disputes in Early Modern England." *Historical Journal* 39 (1996): 915–42.

——. *The Economy of Obligation: The Culture of Credit and Social Relations in Early Modern England.* New York: St. Martin's Press, 1998.

——. "'Hard Food for Midas': Cash and Its Social Value in Early Modern England." *Past and Present* 170 (2001): 78–120.

——. "Interpreting the Market: The Ethics of Credit and Community Relations in Early Modern England." *Social History* 18 (1993): 163–85.

——. "'A Mutual Assent of Her Mind?': Women, Debt Litigation and Contract in Early Modern England." *History Workshop Journal* 55 (2003): 47–71.

Mundill, Robin. "Christian and Jewish Lending Patterns and Financial Dealings." In *Credit and Debt in Medieval England, c. 1180–c. 1350.* Ed. P. R. Schofield and N. J. Mayhew. Oxford: Oxford University Press, 2002, 42–67.

Munro, Ian. "Shakespeare's Jestbook: Wit, Print, Performance." *ELH* 71 (2004): 89–113.

Murray, Molly. "Measured Sentences: Forming Literature in the Early Modern Prison." *Huntington Library Quarterly* 72 (2009): 147–67.

Mynshul, Geoffrey. *Certaine Characters and Essayes of Prison and Prisoners.* London, 1618.

Nathan, Norman. "Is Shylock Philip Henslowe?" *Notes and Queries* 193 (1948): 163–65.

Nedelsky, Jennifer. "Law, Boundaries and the Bounded Self." *Representations* 30 (Spring 1990): 162–89.

Neill, Michael. "Massinger's Patriarchy: The Social Vision of *A New Way to Pay Old Debts.*" *Renaissance Drama* 10 (1979): 185–213.

——. *Putting History to the Question: Power, Politics, and Society in English Renaissance Drama.* New York: Columbia University Press, 2000.

Netzloff, Mark. *England's Internal Colonies: Class, Capital, and the Literature of Early Modern English Colonialism.* New York: Palgrave, 2003.

Newman, Karen. "Rereading Shakespeare's *Timon of Athens* at the Fin de Siècle." In *Shakespeare and the Twentieth Century: The Selected Proceedings of the International Shakespeare Association World Congress, Los Angeles, 1996.* Ed. Jonathan Bate et al. Newark: University of Delaware Press, 1998, 378–89.

Noonan, John T. *The Scholastic Analysis of Usury.* Cambridge, Mass.: Harvard University Press, 1957.

Norman, Marc, and Tom Stoppard. *Shakespeare in Love: A Screenplay.* New York: Hyperion, 1998.

Nuttall, A. D. *Timon of Athens.* Boston: Twayne, 1989.

Patterson, Orlando. *Slavery and Social Death: A Comparative Study.* Cambridge, Mass.: Harvard University Press, 1982.

Paul, Jeffrey, and Ellen Frankel Paul. "Locke's *Usufructuary* Theory of Self-Ownership." *Pacific Philosophical Quarterly* 61 (1980): 384–95.

Peacham, Henry. *The Art of Living in London.* London, 1641.

Pearse, Nancy C. *John Fletcher's Chastity Plays: Mirrors of Modesty.* Lewisburg, Pa.: Bucknell University Press, 1973.

Pendry, E. D. *Elizabethan Prisons and Prison Scenes.* Salzburg Studies in English Literature 17. 2 vols. Salzburg, Austria: Institute for English Language and Literature, 1974.

A Petition entitled Liberty Vindicated against Slavery. London, 1646.

A Petition entitled, The Humble Remonstrance and Complaint of Many Thousands of poore, distressed Prisoners. London, 1643.

A Petition to the Kings Majestie; the Lords and Commons of the Parliament from Prisoners for Debt. London, 1622.

A Petition to the right, Honourable Sir Thomas Fairfax. London, 1647.

Polanyi, Karl. *The Great Transformation: The Political and Economic Origins of Our Time*. 2nd edition. Foreword by Joseph E. Stiglitz and introduction by Fred Block. 1944; Boston: Beacon Press, 2001.

Pollock, Frederick, and William Maitland. *The History of English Law Before the Time of Edward I*. 2nd edition. Cambridge: Cambridge University Press, 1968.

Ponko, Jr., Vincent. "The Privy Council and the Spirit of Elizabethan Economic Management, 1558–1603." *Transactions of the American Philosophical Society* 58 (1968): 1–63.

Poovey, Mary. *Genres of the Credit Economy: Mediating Value in Eighteenth- and Nineteenth-Century Britain*. Chicago: University of Chicago Press, 2008.

Powell, Thomas. *The Mystery and Misery of Lending and Borrowing*. London, 1636.

Prager, Carolyn. "The Problem of Slavery in *The Custom of the Country*." *Studies in English Literature* 28 (1988): 301–17.

Price, J. M. "What Did Merchants Do?" *Journal of Economic History* 69 (1989): 267–84.

Pugh, Ralph. "Some Medieval Moneylenders." *Speculum* 43 (April 1968): 274–89.

Purchas, Samuel. *Hakluytus Posthumus or Purchas his Pilgrimes*. 20 vols. Glasgow: MacLehose and Sons, 1905–7.

Rasmussen, Mark David. *Renaissance Literature and Its Formal Engagements*. New York: Palgrave, 2002.

Reddy, William. *Money and Liberty in Modern Europe: A Critique of Historical Understanding*. Cambridge: Cambridge University Press, 1987.

Reisbord, John Phillip. "Petitions to Conscience: Imprisonment for Debt and the Pursuit of Justice in Early Modern England, 1560–1625." Ph.D. diss., Northwestern University, 1997.

Rooney, Ellen. "Form and Contentment." *Modern Language Quarterly* 61 (March 2000): 17–40.

Rose, Carol. *Property and Persuasion: Essays on the History, Theory, and Rhetoric of Ownership*. Boulder Colo.: Westview, 1994.

Ross, Daniel W. "What Number of Men Eats Timon." *Iowa State Journal of Research* 59 (1985): 273–84.

Rowe, George E. "Prodigal Sons, New Comedy, and Middleton's *Michaelmas Term*." *English Literary Renaissance* 7 (1977): 90–107.

Rowe, Katherine. *Dead Hands: Fictions of Agency Renaissance to Modern*. Stanford, Calif.: Stanford University Press, 1999.

Rutter, Carol Chillington, ed. *Documents of the Rose Playhouse*. Manchester: Manchester University Press, 1984; rev. ed., 1999.

Sacks, David Harris, and Michael Lynch. "Ports, 1540–1700." In *The Cambridge Urban*

History of Britain, Vol. 2, 1540–1840. Ed. Peter Clark. Cambridge University Press, 2000.

Sanchez, Melissa. *Erotic Subjects: The Sexuality of Politics in Early Modern English Literature.* Oxford: Oxford University Press, 2011.

Scarry, Elaine. "Consent and the Body: Injury, Departure, and Desire." *New Literary History* 21 (1990): 867–96.

Schwartz, Kathryn. *What You Will: Gender, Contract, and Shakespearean Social Space.* Philadelphia: University of Pennsylvania Press, 2011.

Scott, William O. "Conditional Bonds, Forfeitures, and Vows in *The Merchant of Venice.*" *English Literary Renaissance* 34 (November 2004): 286–305.

Scott-Warren, Jason. "When the Theaters Were Bear-Gardens; or, What's at Stake in the Comedy of Humors." *Shakespeare Quarterly* 54 (2003): 63–82.

Searle, G. R. "Selling People Is Wrong: Slavery and Political Economy." In *Morality and the Market in Victorian Britain.* Oxford: Oxford University Press, 1998, 48–76.

Seipp, David J. "The Concept of Property in the Early Common Law." *Law and History Review* 12 (1994): 29–91.

Shakespeare, William. *The Complete Works of Shakespeare.* Ed. David Bevington. 6th edition. New York: Longman, 2008.

——. *The Merchant of Venice: Texts and Contexts.* Ed. M. Lindsay Kaplan. New York: Bedford St. Martin's Press, 2002.

——. *The Merchant of Venice.* Ed. M. M. Mahood. New Cambridge edition. Cambridge: Cambridge University Press, 2003.

——. *Timon of Athens.* Ed. H. J. Oliver. London: Methuen, 1959.

Shaw, Phillip. "The Position of Thomas Dekker in Jacobean Prison Literature." *PMLA* 62 (1947): 366–91.

Shell, Marc. *Money, Language, and Thought: Literary and Philosophic Economies from the Medieval to the Modern Era.* Berkeley: University of California Press, 1982.

Shepard, Alexandra. *Meanings of Manhood in Early Modern England.* Oxford: Oxford University Press, 2003.

Sherman, William. "Patents and Prisons: Simon Sturtevant and the Death of the Renaissance Inventor." *Huntington Library Quarterly* 72 (June 2009): 239–56.

Shershow, Scott Cutler. "The Pit of Wit: Subplot and Unity in Middleton's *A Trick to Catch the Old One.*" *Studies in Philology* 88 (1991): 363–81.

Silvayn, Alexander. *The Orator.* Trans. Lazarus Piot. London, 1596.

Simpson, A. W. B. *The History of the Common Law of Contract: The Rise of the Action of Assumpsit.* Oxford: Clarendon Press, 1975.

——. "The Penal Bond with Conditional Defeasance." *Law Quarterly Review* 82 (1966): 392–422.

——."The Place of Slade's Case in the History of Contract." *Law Quarterly Review* 74 (1958): 381–97.

Slights, William W. E. "*Genera Mixta* and *Timon of Athens.*" *Studies in Philology* 74 (1977): 39–62.

Smith, Abbot Emerson. *Colonists in Bondage: White Servitude and Convict Labor in America, 1607–1776*. Chapel Hill: University of North Carolina Press, 1947.

Smyth, Thomas. *De Republica Anglorum*. London, 1583.

Sokol, B. J., and Mary Sokol. *Shakespeare, Law, and Marriage*. Cambridge: Cambridge University Press, 2003.

Spinosa, Charles. "Shylock and Debt and Contract in *The Merchant of Venice*." *Cardozo Studies in Law and Literature* 5 (1993): 65–85.

——. "The Transformation of Intentionality: Debt and Contract in *The Merchant of Venice*." *English Literary Renaissance* 24 (1994): 370–409.

Staves, Susan. *Married Women's Separate Property in England, 1660–1833*. Cambridge, Mass.: Harvard University Press, 1990.

Steinfeld, Robert J. *The Invention of Free Labor: The Employment Relation in English and American Law and Culture, 1350–1870*. Chapel Hill: University of North Carolina Press, 1991.

Stevenson, Laura C. *Praise and Paradox: Merchants and Craftsmen in Elizabethan Popular Literature*. Cambridge: Cambridge University Press, 1984.

Stewart, Alan. *Shakespeare's Letters*. Oxford: Oxford University Press, 2008.

Stretton, Tim. "Contract, Debt Litigation, and Shakespeare's *The Merchant of Venice*." *Adelaide Law Review 31* (2010): 111–25.

Stubbes, Phillip. *Anatomy of the Abuses in England*. London, 1583. Ed. Frederick J. Furnivall. London: New Shakespeare Society, 1877–79.

Sullivan, Ceri. *The Rhetoric of Credit: Merchants in Early Modern Writing*. Teaneck, N.J.: Fairleigh Dickinson University Press, 2002.

Tawney, R. H. "Historical Introduction." In *A Discourse Upon Usury* (London, 1572). New York: A. M. Kelley, 1963.

Taylor, Gary, and John Lavagnino, eds. *Thomas Middleton: The Collected Works*. Oxford: Clarendon Press, 2007.

Thompson, E. P. *Custom in Common: Studies in Traditional Popular Culture*. London: Merlin, 1991.

T.F. *Pictures of Passions, Fancies, and Affections Poetically Deciphered in Variety of Characters*. London, 1641.

The Humble Remonstrance and Complaint of Many Thousands of poore, distressed Prisoners. London, 1643.

The Prisoner's Plaint, A Petition Submitted by a Prisoner in the King's Bench for Debt. London, 1622.

Thirsk, Joan. *Economic Policy and Projects: The Development of a Consumer Society in Early Modern England*. London: Clarendon Press, 1978.

Thompson, E. P. *Custom in Common: Studies in Traditional Popular Culture*. London: Merlin, 1991.

Thompson, Patricia. "The Old Way and the New Way in Dekker and Massinger." *Modern Language Review* 51 (1956): 168–78.

Thornton, Henry. *The Prisoner's Remonstrance*. London, 1649.

To the most honourable assembly of the Commons House of Parliament . . . the humble petition of the distressed prisoners in the King's Bench and Fleete. London, 1624.

Tucker, E. F. J. "The Letter of the Law in *The Merchant of Venice*." *Shakespeare Survey* 29 (1976): 93–101.

Turley, David. *Slavery*. Oxford: Blackwell, 2000.

Valenze, Deborah. *The Social Life of Money in the English Past*. Cambridge: Cambridge University Press, 2006.

Vennar. Richard. *An Apology*. London, 1616.

Vilar, Pierre. *A History of Gold Money, 1450–1920*. Trans. Judith White. London, 1976.

Vitkus, Daniel. "'Meaner Ministers': Mastery, Bondage, and Theatrical Labor in *The Tempest*." In *A Companion to Shakespeare's Works*, vol. 4. Ed. Richard Dutton and Jean Howard. Oxford: Blackwell, 2003, 4:408–27.

——. "Turks and Jews in *The Jew of Malta*." In *Early Modern English Drama: A Critical Companion*. Ed. Andrew Hadfield et al. New York: Oxford University Press, 2006, 61–72.

Walker, Lewis. "Fortune and Friendship in *Timon of Athens*." *Texas Studies in Literature and Language* 18 (1977): 577–600.

---. "Money in *Timon of Athens*." *Philological Quarterly* 57 (1978): 269–71.

Wallis, Lawrence B. *Fletcher, Beaumont & Company, Entertainers to the Jacobean Gentry*. New York: Kings Crown, 1947.

Walsh, Lorena S. "Servitude and Opportunity in Charles County, Maryland, 1658–1705." In *Law, Society, and Politics in Early Maryland*. Ed. Aubrey C. Land et al. Baltimore: Johns Hopkins University Press, 1977.

Walvin, James. *Questioning Slavery*. New York: Routledge, 1996.

Watson, Bruce. "The Compter's Prisons of London." *The London Archaeologists* 7 (1993): 115–21.

Wennerlind, Carl. *Casualties of Credit: The English Financial Revolution, 1620–1720*. Cambridge, Mass.: Harvard University Press, 2011.

West, William. *The First Part of Simboleography*. London, 1615.

Wilkinson, Henry. *The Debt Book*. London, 1625.

Wilson, Luke. "Promissory Performances." *Renaissance Drama* 25 (1994): 59–89.

——. *Theaters of Intention: Drama and Law in Early Modern England*. Stanford, Calif.: Stanford University Press, 2000.

Wolfson, Susan, and Marshall Brown. *Reading for Form*. Seattle: University of Washington Press, 2006.

Wonderfull Strange newes from Woodstreet Counter. London, 1642.

Woodbridge, Linda. *Money and the Age of Shakespeare: Essays in New Economic Criticism*. New York: Palgrave, 2003.

Woodmansee, Martha, and Mark Osteen, eds. *The New Economic Criticism: Studies at the Intersection of Literature and Economics*. London: Routledge, 1999.

Woodward, Donald. "The Background to the Statute of Artificers: The Genesis of Labour Policy, 1558–1563." *Economic History Review*, 2nd ser., 33 (1980): 32–44.

Yachnin, Paul. "Social Competition in Middleton's *Michaelmas Term*." *Explorations in Renaissance Culture* 13 (1987): 87–99.

Yoch, James J. "The Renaissance Dramatization of Temperance: The Italian Revival of Tragicomedy and *The Faithful Shepherdess*." In *Renaissance Tragedy: Explorations in Genre and Politics*. Ed. Nancy McGuire. New York: AMS Press, 1987, 114–38.

Zucker, Adam. *The Places of Wit in Early Modern English Comedy*. Cambridge: Cambridge University Press, 2011.

Index

Acknowledgments

The red thread running throughout this book is the relationship between owing and belonging. It is with deep gratitude that I acknowledge the various affiliations, collective and personal, that bind me to worlds of intellectual exchange, emotional nurturance, and institutional support. Every idea in this book has been shaped by rich conversations with colleagues, friends, and students over the years, who have, knowingly or unknowingly, contributed to my understanding of the scope and stakes of this project. I am especially grateful to Jerry Singerman for enthusiastically embracing the manuscript and for making the process appear effortless. Thanks to Caroline Winschel and Noreen O'Connor-Abel this sense of ease persisted through to the end of the process. The unbelievably generous commitment of time and energy on the part of the readers for the press reaffirmed for me the integrity of our profession. This is a much better book because of their careful engagement and insightful inquiries.

The rigorous and innovative scholarship of Valerie Forman, Jonathan Gil Harris, Natasha Korda, Theodore Leinwand, and Luke Wilson set the bar high for writing about early modern economies. Their work lay the ground for this book and sustained and inspired me at all phases of my thinking. Being able to count these people as friends—some old, some new—only deepens my already profound admiration for them. Others, whom I have yet to meet—Ian Baucom, Stephen Best, Colin Dayan, and Mary Poovey—profoundly influenced how I formulated and developed my arguments.

I was invited to present my work at various venues that include the Group for Early Modern Cultural Studies, the Renaissance Society of America, the Shakespeare Association of America, and the Modern Language Association. I was also invited to speak at Columbia University's Early Modern Seminar and Columbia University's Shakespeare Seminar, the Graduate School at CUNY, Wesleyan University's Renaissance Studies Seminar, and the Five Colleges Renaissance Studies Colloquium. I presented portions of this project at Columbia University's "Forms of Writing" conference and was an invited speaker for the 2008 Plenary Panel for the Shakespeare Association of America, for which I thank the trustees for the opportunity to present my work. Among my interlocutors at these various venues, I am grateful to David Baker, Jean Feerick, Jean Howard, William Ingram, Heather James, Zachary Lesser, Noami Liebler, Michael Neill, Karen Newman, Tanya Pollard, Ben Robinson, Peter Stallybrass, Alan Stewart, and Daniel Vitkus.

Portions of this book have appeared in journals and edited collections and I am grateful to Joseph Black, Allison Deutermann, Michelle Dowd, Arthur Kinney, Andras Kisery, Gail Kern Paster, and David Schalkwyk for their generous feedback. Particia Akhimie was my research assistant for Columbia University's "Forms of Writing" conference and her findings proved invaluable. Jonathan Mackman of the National Archives and the University of York responded in detail to my email inquires about bonds early on in my process. The librarians at the British Library were, as always, exemplary. I am especially grateful to Georgianna Ziegler who helped me comb through the Folger Library's image collection to find the perfect cover.

I count myself lucky to encounter the warmth and encouragement at regular intervals of Rebecca Bach, Gina Bloom, Mary Bly, Pam Brown, Ann Christianson, Jane Degenhardt, Stephen Deng, Mario DiGangi, Fran Dolan, Holly Dugan, Will Fisher, Stephen Guy-Bray, Roze Hentschell, Erika Lin, Megan Matchinske, Katherine Maus, Michael McClure, Madhavi Menon, Lawrence Manley, Bella Mirabella, Stephen Mullaney, Molly Murray, Susan O'Malley, Barb Sebek, Laurie Shannon, Ayanna Thompson, Valerie Traub, Henry Turner, Will West, and Adam Zucker.

I was able to make great strides toward completing this book during a faculty fellowship at the University of Connecticut Humanities Institute. I want to thank my co-fellows for their conviviality and insights, especially Dick Brown, Stuart Liberman, Charles Mahoney, and Jeremy Pressman. I am also grateful to those who participated in the Legal Studies Research Seminar, a group that provided me with a much needed and much valued intellectual home: Nina Dayton, Margaret Higgonet, Greg Kneidel, Sean Salvant, Sarah Winter, and David Yalof. I have appreciated the encouragement of my colleagues and students at the University of Connecticut, especially Raymond Anselment, Christopher Clark, Margaret Lamb, Hap Fairbanks, and John Davis, as well as the support and enthusiasm of my new colleagues at the University of Maryland.

None of this could have been achieved without the love and support of my family, and to them I owe the most and it is to them this book is dedicated. Ross, in whom I find year in and year out the pleasures of a life companion who is my best friend and my best editor. Spencer, without whose constant affection and occasional mischief we would all be lost. And Isabel, for whom my love and gratitude will forever be without bo(u)nds.

A version of Chapter 1 appeared as "*Timon of Athens*, Forms of Payback, and the Genre of Debt," in *English Literary Renaissance* 42, no. 1, Spring 2011, pages 375–400. Copyright ©2011 Blackwell Publishing Ltd. A version of Chapter 2 first appeared as "Shylock and the Slaves: Owing and Owning in *The Merchant of Venice*," in *Shakespeare Quarterly* 62, no. 1, Spring 2011, pages 1–24. Copyright ©2011 Folger Shakespeare Library. A portion of Chapter 4 appeared as "Custom, Debt, and the Valuation of Service Within and Without Early Modern England," pages 193–208 in *Working Subjects in Early Modern English Drama*, ed. Michelle Dowd and Natasha Korda. I thank Ashgate Publishing Ltd. for permission to reprint an expanded version of it here.

www.ingramcontent.com/pod-product-compliance
Lightning Source LLC
Chambersburg PA
CBHW030825310726
48980CB00006B/633/J

* 9 7 8 0 8 1 2 2 4 5 1 6 5 *